The Need for Story

The Need for Story

Cultural Diversity in Classroom and Community

Edited by

Anne Haas Dyson
University of California, Berkeley

Celia Genishi
Teachers College, Columbia University

National Council of Teachers of English
1111 West Kenyon Road, Urbana, Illinois 61801-1096

Dedicated to our favorite storytellers—our families

Grateful acknowledgment is made for permission to reprint the following material:

Lines from "The Cleaving," copyright © 1990 by Li-Young Lee. Reprinted from *The City in Which I Love You*, by Li-Young Lee, with the permission of BOA Editions, Ltd.

"Life as Narrative," by Jerome Bruner. Reprinted with the permission of *Social Research*. Copyright © 1987 by *Social Research*.

Selections from *You Can't Say You Can't Play*, by Vivian Gussin Paley. Reprinted with the permission of Harvard University Press. Copyright © 1992 by Harvard University Press.

Staff Editors: Sheila A. Ryan and Marlo Welshons

Cover Design: Barbara Yale-Read

Interior Design: Doug Burnett

NCTE Stock Number: 33002

It is the policy of NCTE in its journals and other publications to provide a forum for the open discussion of ideas concerning the content and the teaching of English and the language arts. Publicity accorded to any particular point of view does not imply endorsement by the Executive Committee, the Board of Directors, or the membership at large, except in announcements of policy, where such endorsement is clearly specified.

Library of Congress Cataloging-in-Publication Data

The need for story : cultural diversity in classroom and community / edited by Anne Haas Dyson, Celia Genishi.
     p. cm
    "NCTE stock number: 33002"—CIP t.p. verso.
    Includes bibliographical references and index.
    ISBN 0-8141-3300-2 : $19.95
    1. Storytelling—United States. 2. Multicultural education—United States. 3. Interpersonal relations. 4. Education—Social aspects—United States. I. Dyson, Anne Haas. II. Genishi, Celia, 1944– .
LB1042.N44 1994
372.64'2—dc20
                                  94-47953
                                     CIP

Contents

Weaving Communities through Story: Who Are We?

Acknowledgments

We wish to thank:

Our contributors, fine storytellers all, who provided chapters of substance and style

Our support staff, including Urvashi Sahni, Heidi Grant, Margaret Ganahl, and Ruth Cooper, all of whom are blessed with keen eyes and gracious natures

Michael Spooner, of the National Council of Teachers of English, who was unfailingly interested and supportive

David Dillon, who, as editor of *Language Arts*, provided us with our first editorial forum, "Research Currents" in *Language Arts*. Three chapters are reprinted, with minor revisions, from that journal: Chapter 3, from 65(6), 574–583 (excerpted from *Social Research 54* [1987], 11–32); Chapter 6, from 62(2), 182–188; and Chapter 13, from 66(1), 52–57.

1 Introduction: The Need for Story

Anne Haas Dyson
University of California, Berkeley

Celia Genishi
Teachers College, Columbia University

To introduce the major theme of our edited collection, we offer this classroom scene:

Louise and her four- to seven-year-old children have been studying ocean creatures. Today Sonya has brought a basket of seashells. Anthony is very excited when he sees the shells and tells this story:

Anthony: One time um I saw a little baby starfish in the tub.

Louise: Oh my goodness! Did someone put it in there to play with you?

Anthony: No. It just came out of the drainer.

The other children begin to laugh, but Anthony is quite serious.

Louise: One thing I know about starfish is that they live in what kind of water: salt water or fresh water?

Children: Salt water!

Anthony: It was in the fresh water.

Louise: I don't think I ever heard of a freshwater starfish.

Shawnda: A starfish came up the drain! [with great amusement]

Anthony: I picked it up and showed it to my mommy and then it started moving.

. . . .

Shawnda: A STARFISH CAN'T COME UP NO DRAIN!

Louise: It's an amazing story, Anthony. [said with appreciation, and Anthony, who has been quite distressed by the laughing, smiles contentedly]

Shawnda: I TELL YOU—

> *Louise:* Shawnda, I know. I know that, and you know that, but
> Anthony needs his story.
>
> And Anthony smiles at Shawnda, quite agreeing with Louise.

We all have a basic need for story, for organizing our experiences into tales of important happenings. Stories, these ubiquitous discourse forms, are of great interest in language and literacy education, particularly in light of the increasing sociocultural diversity of students in our classrooms. Through stories, teachers learn of their children's cultures, of their diverse experiences, and of their connections to family and friends. Moreover, through sharing stories—both children's own stories and those of professional authors—teacher and children create the potential for new connections that link them together inside a new tale.

Through this book, we invite our readers to participate in the exploration of story—the basic functions it serves, its connections to the diverse sociocultural landscape of our society, and its potential power in the classroom. In the following sections, we briefly introduce these three key themes, which link the chapters of our book.

Connections between Story, Self, and Others: Why Do We Tell Stories?

Stories first arise in the context of relationships, when small children acquire the potential to verbalize experiences for themselves and others (Stern 1985). With such verbal acts, children become at one and the same time narrated selves, who can tell the story of their own lives, and narrating selves, who share interpretations with others. Children, like adults, use narrative to shape and reshape their lives, imagining what could have or should have happened, as well as what did happen.

Stories, then, have interrelated evaluative and social functions, which is the first theme of our book. For example, *as an evaluator,* a commentator on significant life experiences, Anthony told about a surprising find—a baby starfish in the tub—and about sharing that find with his mom. He cast himself as a student experienced with starfish and as a family member whose experiences are shared with his mother. In telling about this past experience, Anthony was also shaping a new event. *As a social actor,* Anthony was entering into the ongoing classroom dialogue. He expected his story to be accepted and sincerely appreciated, as shown in part by his frustration with Shawnda's laughter.

The stories Anthony told to the class as a whole, which often presented a mild-mannered and polite Anthony, were quite different from the stories he told to his close friends, which sometimes presented a tough-talking Anthony. The latter Anthony did not couch his experiences within affirming relationships with grown-ups—indeed, quite the opposite:

> *Anthony:* Oh yeah. My chest is strong! 'Member when a grown-up pushed me? I wasn't even—it wouldn't even hurt.
>
> *Lamar:* Oh yeah. When James choked me I didn't even say nothing. I didn't even say, "Stop that. Stop that." I didn't even say that, see? Come over here and cho-choke me, James.
>
> . . . .
>
> *James:* Louise is right there.
>
> *Tyler:* Scared of the teacher!
>
> *Lamar:* No way. (Dyson 1993)

The stories of Anthony the cooperative student, the mother's son, the tough kid—all reveal aspects of Anthony. Within and through stories, we fashion our relationships with others, joining with them, separating from them, expressing in ways subtle and not so subtle our feelings about the people around us. As Bakhtin (1981) argued, the stories we tell place us in the sociocultural landscape in particular ways, which leads to another important theme of this book: the connections between stories, culture, and power.

Ways with Stories: Whose Stories Are Told? Whose Stories Are Heard?

In this book, we view culture as a shared way of interpreting the world—what Geertz (1973, 13) calls a shared "imaginative universe within which [members'] acts are signs." In this sense, culture is formulated through public dialogue, as people enter into and continually negotiate "socially established structures of meaning" (12). Culture is thus not a static concept—a category for conveniently sorting people according to expected values, beliefs, and behaviors. Rather, it is a dynamic one; indeed, contemporary ethnographers have portrayed individuals as members of interrelated but distinctive "imaginative universes," including those rooted in experiences shared by those of common ethnicity or race, gender, class, and age (Clifford 1988; Rosaldo 1989). Amidst this complexity, individuals are active and, at

least potentially, reflective about their own sense of cultural membership (Ferdman 1990).

Stories are an important tool for proclaiming ourselves as cultural beings. In narratives, our voices echo those of others in the
sociocultural world—what those others think is worth commenting on
and how they judge the effectiveness of told stories. That is, we evidence cultural membership both through our ways of crafting stories
and in the very content of our tales.

Storytellers often craft the sensual and metaphoric, rather than
the literal, properties of speech, as they work to convey their feelings
about—their evaluation of—the world. Feelings, after all, are not reducible to specific words, but are often conveyed best through the
musical and image-making features of language—by rhythm and
rhyme, figures of speech, and revoiced dialogue. And ways of exploit-
ing these artful (or "performative") features vary for peoples of different sociocultural backgrounds (Bauman 1986).

Moreover, the images and rhythms of our stories—not simply
the literary equipment for forming them—are rooted in our experiences as cultural beings. The ongoing discussions—indeed, arguments—about children's textbooks and school literature are all
informed by this realization. In *The Dialectic of Freedom*, for example,
Greene (1988, 127) writes of the need for granting "audibility to numerous voices seldom heard before . . . of penetrating the so-called
'cultures of silence' in order to discover what [ordinary but culturally
diverse people] think and have thought" through historical docu-
ments, literary texts, and artful objects of varied kinds. Stories have the
potential for empowering unheard voices—but stories can also con-
strain voices.

For instance, in his story about defying pain and a grown-up,
Anthony was enacting words that echo in the culture of school-
children, who often enjoy proclaiming their own power against the
adult world. Indeed, his friends easily and eagerly told their own
such stories. However, at the same time that the children were using
the stories to proclaim their identity as boys and "tough kids," those
stories were also, in a sense, claiming them. That is, the boys were
adopting dominant cultural storylines about how tough kids talk
(Foucault 1977).

Stories, and thereby aspects of children's selves, can be silenced
if listeners (including teachers and peers) do not appreciate the diverse
ways stories are crafted and the range of experiences they tap.
Shawnda's expectation that Anthony's story fit the facts, be a proper

science story, as it were, would have eliminated his story if not for the mediation of Louise; she understood Anthony's "need for story," for some kind of social connection and feeling of mutuality. Moreover, if certain stories are never heard beyond a narrow circle—for example, if stories of toughness are never echoed or challenged in stories heard in the classroom forum—they will never be "dialogized," to use Bakhtin's term. That is, they will not be rendered a story among possible stories, other ways of being; in which case, they may not be a source of identification and power but of constraint, of limits.

With this comment on the necessity of classroom dialogue, we enter into the third theme of our collection—the ways in which teachers and students might use stories to negotiate a classroom culture.

Weaving Communities through Story: Who Are We?

The storytelling self is a social self, who declares and shapes important relationships through the mediating power of words. Thus, in sharing stories, we have the potential for forging new relationships, including local, classroom "cultures" in which individuals are interconnected and new "we's" formed. Through stories by children, teachers, and professional authors, characters—given life through word pictures and verbal rhythms—enter the classroom, and in so doing they bring new life experiences and points of view. At the same time, those very images and rhythms reverberate in the memories of audience members, who reconstruct the story with the stuff of their own thoughts and feelings. In such ways, individual lives are woven together through the stuff of stories.

Moreover, just as new language and experiences enter the classroom through children's stories, children themselves gain opportunities to try on the language and experiences of others, to infuse themselves into new ways with words. Anthony's first unofficial classroom performances were raps and rhymes, but his stories were conversational in tone; by the end of the year, though, he was trying out literary phrases learned in school:

> I was at the store.
> And suddenly, somebody came and talk to my mother.
> And she knew him.
> And one by one, she dropped some apple juice.
> And she had to clean it all up.

"And suddenly [Anthony said the phrase with dramatic urgency], somebody came and talk to my mother." And then, "one by one she dropped some apple juice." We don't ordinarily think of "some apple juice" as dropping "one by one," but Anthony has nonetheless succeeded in transforming an everyday scene in the grocery store into an artful, crafted tale; and that tale has rhythms slower than those of his rap songs, and images gentler than those of his tough-guy hyperbole.

This intermingling of voices and exploring of story possibilities can only happen in classrooms where stories themselves are allowed and, just as critically, when they exist within a larger classroom context of diverse story models, appreciative, respectful listening, reflective talking, and playful ways with words. That is, the official imaginative universe of the classroom must be a permeable one, for, in culturally diverse classrooms, students will collectively embody more ways with words, more lived worlds than their teacher.

The Need for Story

The following chapters people these key themes—the purposes, socio-cultural roots, and community-making powers of stories—with children, teachers, and parents from many backgrounds and in many present circumstances. While each section highlights one of the themes, all are interwoven throughout the book.

Through our joint efforts, we, along with all contributors to this book, hope to help teachers listen more sensitively to the stories of their students and, moreover, to exploit the power of those stories for bringing children and their diverse experiences into the classroom and for forging new connections among students and teachers. To current concerns about our increasingly diverse student population and about the school's effectiveness in serving those students, we collectively declare through vivid example the need for and the power of story.

References

Bakhtin, M. (1981). Discourse in the novel. In M. Holquist (Ed.), C. Emerson and M. Holquist (Trans.), *The dialogic imagination: Four essays by M. M. Bakhtin* (259–422). Austin: University of Texas Press. (Original work published 1934–1935)

Bauman, R. (1986). *Story, performance, and event.* Rowley, MA: Newbury House.

Clifford, J. (1988). *The predicament of culture: Twentieth century ethnography, literature, and art.* Cambridge, MA: Harvard University Press.

Dyson, A. Haas. (1993). *Social worlds of children learning to write in an urban primary school*. New York: Teachers College Press.

Ferdman, B. (1990). Literacy and cultural identity. *Harvard Educational Review, 60*, 181–204.

Foucault, M. (1977). *Language, counter-memory, practice: Selected essays and interviews*. Ithaca, NY: Cornell University Press.

Geertz, C. (1973). *The interpretation of cultures: Selected essays*. New York: Basic Books.

Greene, M. (1988). *The dialectic of freedom*. New York: Teachers College Press.

Rosaldo, R. (1989). *Culture and truth: The remaking of social analysis*. Boston: Beacon Press.

Stern, D. (1985). *The interpersonal world of the infant: A view from psychoanalysis and developmental psychology*. New York: Basic Books.

Connections between Story, Self, and Others: Why Do We Tell Stories?

2 Multiculturalism, Community, and the Arts

Maxine Greene
Teachers College, Columbia University

Maxine Greene frames this collection with an expansive vision of multi-culturalism and the role of the arts in the formation of a community—and self-within-a-community—that is open to difference and change. Using literature as her base, she offers affecting answers to our underlying question, "How do we create spaces for pluralism in our selves and our lives?"

American teachers today are being asked to confront the challenges of plurality and multiplicity in ways we have seldom considered before. We have spoken often, it is true, about individual differences; we have tried to take into account ethnic differences when they have showed themselves in our classrooms. Our end in view, however, was ordinarily to draw our students (diverse though they might appear to be) into some sort of community. We strove for what Dewey called a sharing of experience, the kind of communication in which learning might begin. Dewey did recognize the diversity of groups in our society and the fact that each group had its traditional customs, but he said it was this that

> forced the demand for an educational institution which shall provide something like a homogeneous and balanced environment for the young. Only in this way can the centrifugal forces set up by the juxtaposition of different groups within one and the same political unit be counteracted. The intermingling in the school of youth of different races, differing religion, and the unlike customs creates for all a new and broader environment. Common subject matter accustoms all to a unity of outlook upon a broader horizon than is visible to the members of any group while it is isolated. (1916, 25)

He worked, therefore, for the school's assimilative forces and "steadying and integrative office."

Wondering at this today, we still suffer the erosion of community and reach out for a connectedness we feel has been lost. At once, we recognize that we are sharing a historical and cultural predicament with people all over the world. Try as we may to make things comprehensible, we are experiencing attacks on the familiar, "the irruption of otherness," as one writer says (Clifford 1988, 13), of the unexpected. Whatever common experiences there are occur in contexts where new meanings keep germinating. We can recall Dewey struggling to chart a way from what he called the Great Society to the Great Community, saying that—when the way was open—democracy would come into its own, "for democracy is a name for a life of free and enriching communion. It had its seer in Walt Whitman" (Dewey 1954, 184). If this were so, and if Dewey also believed that "the moral prophets of humanity have always been poets even though they spoke in free verse or by parable" (1958, 348), it may be worthwhile to consult what Whitman had to say about communion. He wrote about the many shapes arising in this country, the "shapes of doors giving many exits and entrances" and "Shapes of Democracy . . . ever projecting other shapes." In "Song of Myself" (Whitman 1931, 53), he wrote:

> Through me the many long dumb voices,
> Voices of the interminable generations of prisoners and slaves,
> Voices of the diseas'd and despairing and of thieves and
>   dwarfs,
> Voices of cycles of preparation and accretion,
> And of the threads that connect the stars, and of wombs and
>   of the father-stuff,
> And of the rights of them the others are down upon. . . .
> Through me forbidden voices. . . .

We cannot but wonder whether, in those affirmations regarding assimilation and integration, there were not, even seventy-five years ago, moments of recognition that there were indeed dumb and stifled voices—voices of women, of immigrants, of the "diseas'd and despairing"—that demanded a more complex, more troubling conception of community.

Today, with the recent emergence of what is called multiculturalism, with all the attendant demands and confusions and potentialities, we realize we have moved far beyond simplistic notions of melting pots and social balance wheels. We are challenged to come to terms with conceptions of difference and heterogeneity that go beyond what Dewey seems to have had in mind. We are asked to acknowledge contingency, meaning the dependence of perspective and point of view on lived situation, on location in the world. We are only beginning to realize the significance of perspectivism, of the rejection of objectivism, of fixed authorities, of standards residing in some higher realm—standards that apply to everyone and everything, like the judgments of James Joyce's "indifferent God, paring his nails" (1947, 473). Even as I write that and feel the change in tone, I cannot but introduce something that gives rise for me to the modern or post-modern notion of contingency again, a notion with which we have to come to terms.

It involves the book called *Lucy* by Jamaica Kincaid, at a moment when Lucy (who has come from Antigua to be an *au pair* girl in New York with the liberal Mariah and her family) recalls having had to memorize and recite a poem about daffodils by a long-dead poet. She realized her two-facedness in the midst of it: "Outside, I seemed one way, inside, I was another; outside false, inside true. And so I made pleasant little noises that showed both modesty and appreciation, but inside I was making a vow to erase from my mind, line by line, every word of that poem" (1990, 18). She had forgotten it, it appears, until Mariah began talking about the daffodils pushing out of the ground in the spring, and how glad they made her feel to be alive. Shown the yellow flowers in a garden, Lucy finds herself wanting to kill them: "I wished I had an enormous scythe; I would just walk down the path, dragging it alongside me, and I would cut these flowers down" (18). Then she thinks that nothing could change the fact that, where Mariah saw beautiful flowers, she saw "sorrow and bitterness." This suggests what *contingency* may turn out to mean. Lucy had grown up aware of being a colonial (or a postcolonial) in the British Empire, compelled to read and admire traditional English poets, who came to represent all that was being imposed upon the island children in the Queen Victoria Girls' School. It is clear enough that no judgment of her "incorrectness" could be validated, simply because she saw no beauty in Wordsworth's daffodils. Are daffodils, because poems are written about them, to be considered objectively valuable, worthy of everyone's awe? Is there some fixed standard against which Lucy's response must be weighed? We are becoming increasingly aware of such questions, even as we are becoming aware that there are no frameworks in which differences of response (like Mariah's and Lucy's, like the classical music critic's and the rap singer's) can ever be finally resolved.

I believe we have to make space for a reality like Lucy's and like that of the rap singer without, if we can avoid it, making either one "other," rendering either exotic or an object of amazement or compassion. I believe as well that we have to ponder the opening of our own lived spaces as members of a teaching community, people with distinctively shared concerns. Yes, indeed, as we are repeatedly reminded, those concerns must include the kinds of pedagogies required for economic survival in the contemporary technological world and, we would hope, for the decisions people will face as they seek pathways through that world. But they must also include pedagogies that enable persons to become as persons, developing in networks or relationships, seeking their freedom, finding their voices, looking through the perspectives opened by subject matters upon a "reality" that is never quite the same. Certainly it can never be identical for everyone, no matter how "normal" particular descriptions appear to be to the majority or to those in charge.

Many have begun to discover that they can best reach students with such ends in view if they try to do so against the background of their own life stories, their own narratives. Narratives, we have come to realize, are the means by which we gradually impart meaning to the events of our own lives. There is, on all sides, a growing interest in narrative or in storytelling as a mode of sense-making (Bruner 1986, 11–43). Numerous people in education are recognizing the importance of coming in touch with the patterns of their own self-formation if they are to find connection points with other human beings whose memories may link with theirs at certain junctures and, perhaps, seem alien at others. And then there are the childhood recollections of images of being cared for and of caring, and of the diverse shapes such images can take. There are the impacts of class, color, gender, the marriage condition of parents, the setting—urban and high-rising, or rural under a big sky. It is, as many have found, not only the events, the modes of action that must be recaptured; it is the landscape—perceived and felt and imagined—against which the activities have taken place.

When I, for example, confront the challenges of multiculturalism or the demands that long-overlooked words and voices should be included in our traditions and our curricula, when I am reminded how necessary it is to revise the perspectives taken upon our history, I cannot but think back to my own introduction to what was once called the great tradition and my association of certain works in that tradition with the wider world I wanted desperately to enter. I saw the great poets and playwrights and novelists as representatives of something larger, more radiant, more complex, more revealing than the *petit bourgeois* life of my family (although I did not call it that). There was something tempting, seductive, *strange* in what I saw as possible ways of being in a world somehow across the tracks from my desperately ordinary life. It must be admitted that those possible ways of being were those contained in and suggested by what we now speak of as the "Euro-centric canon." I had no means of realizing that the canon was a constructed one, a selection from the great range of human achievements made by powerful and authoritative white men. I had no means of suspecting that even they were convinced that they were giving voice to something universal, worthy of emulation, unarguably "real."

So I read what was accessible to me; and the texts opened channels in my consciousness, roadways out of the everyday. I do not believe I actually wanted to be Lady Macbeth (although I admired her fierce ambition, her audacity), but I did daydream about those shadowed castles on the Scottish moors. I did not necessarily want to be a courtesan on the Paris streets that Baudelaire described with such bitter, exquisite clarity; nor did I want to *be* Emma Bovary. I liked thinking, though, about living on the edge of respectability (even in rain-washed Paris alleys). I certainly longed to experience passions the size and complexity of Emma Bovary's or Anna Karenina's. If I died a suicide—like Emma, Anna, and Edna Pontellier in *The Awakening*—I would (I suppose I thought) attract a kind of tragic attention. (Arsenic, railroad wheels, the sea: all seemed better than Brooklyn streets or nursing homes.) What I wanted was to plunge out of the commonplace, perhaps (if I learned enough) to transmute the commonplace into an alternative reality. So I read and collected visions, some from Emily Dickinson, some from the Brontës, a few from George Eliot (especially from *Middlemarch*), occasionally (hesitantly) from Virginia Woolf. It must be admitted that most of my pictures of the possible were composed out of the stuff of novels by males—not only Flaubert, but Hawthorne, Melville, James, Hemingway, Fitzgerald. Only later was I forced to realize the degree to which my reality was constructed by such males—by what they saw and expected of the women they wrote about. Not all of what they wrote suggested something splendid and tragic, but the very fact that they paid attention created an ambiance quite other than what I found at home.

It took quite awhile before I could even begin to come to terms with what Woolf pointed out in *A Room of One's Own*. Women, she said, "burnt like beacons" in the works of the poets; they were "heroic and mean; splendid and sordid; infinitely beautiful and hideous in the extreme; as great as a man, some think even greater. But this is woman in fiction. In fact, as Professor Trevelyan points out, she was locked up, beaten, and flung around the room" (Woolf 1957, 45). It took me a long time to realize that discrepancy, as it took me years to realize women's absence from history. I was not conscious of the fearsome silences where women's actual voices were concerned: silences like those Tillie

Olsen (1978, 6) had in mind when she wrote of literary history "dark with silences," of the "unnatural silences" of those who work too hard to express themselves, of those who do not have the word. I mention this now because the recognition of such silences played such an important role in my narrative. It was marked by the many occasions when I tried to speak in ways that pleased, in a tone like that of male colleagues— analytic colleagues, empirically oriented colleagues—not in my own existential, semiliterary style. (My colleagues said, "Soft, that is what it is. Soft cognition. That is what she has.") I was like Kincaid's Lucy in some manner—two-faced, making solemn calculative noises. I say this because I need to suggest what it was like to learn to pay heed to the silences. I say it because I realize how it made me attentive to multiplicity, to perspectivism, to the importance of having enough courage to look through my own eyes—and, yes, speak in my own faulty voice.

There were kindred experiences in museums when I was growing up. I saw Botticelli, of course, and felt no objection to that naked Venus. I saw El Greco paintings, Turner's, Cézanne's, Monet's, and I simply (silently) claimed them as my own, as I did the writers in the "great tradition." They gave me a sort of litany, in fact, as time went on. Much later, I tried to flood domains of teacher education with talk about the images and texts I loved so well. I wanted to infuse my pedagogy with talk about the great European and American poets, as well as Dostoevski and Tolstoy and Chekhov and even (when I dared) Dante and Cervantes. Only later did I take heed of the vacancies in the paintings I loved so well: the ways women were rendered, made into figures of vanity, objects to be looked at (as the Elders peered at the bathing Susannah). Berger, in his *Ways of Seeing* (1984), reminds us that even today advertising, journalism, television depict women differently than they do men. "The ideal spectator," says Berger, "is always assumed to be male and the image of the woman is designed to flatter him" (64). The woman, Berger keeps reminding us, is more often than not treated as a thing or an abstraction. The woman is frequently nude; the man, perhaps in uniform or staring from behind a hedge, perhaps dressed for a picnic on the grass, is clothed and covered and dignified. The woman may hold a mirror or an apple to confirm her narcissism or her fatal seductiveness. I could not see earlier in my life, largely because I was working so hard to join the great canonical community. I wanted those paintings to take me in, even as I wanted to internalize what they showed, because then I would belong.

I need to make this present now because it gives me some mode of understanding the obliteration of others, the silencing, the distortion. We need only recall Toni Morrison's *The Bluest Eye* (1972) and live again the fearful attacks on the psyche of the little black girl, Pecola Breedlove. She was brought up in a school that imposed the basal reader *Dick and Jane* in all its terrible irrelevance to the life of a poor and unloved child. She wanted, above all else, to have blue eyes and look like Shirley Temple, because only then, she believed, would her human reality be acknowledged. Pecola is driven mad by that as much as the rape she suffers, but there is something about the distorting pressures of the basal reader and the Shirley Temple image that remains recognizable to me, even though my life has been far, far kinder.

It is interesting to note, in Olsen's story "I Stand Here Ironing," a similar reference to Shirley Temple, this one in connection with the narrator's daughter, the child of "depression, war, and fear." Midway, the mother recalls the daughter fretting over her appearance, "thin and dark and foreign-looking at a time when every little girl was supposed to look or thought she should look like a chubby blonde replica of Shirley Temple" (Olsen 1976, 20–21). At the end, when she sums it up and finds she cannot "total" all that had happened, she thinks again that her daughter "was dark and thin and foreign-looking in a world where the prestige went to blondeness and curly hair and dimples, she was slow where glibness was prized." It takes time—it took me time—to realize the damage done by the culture's icons, especially to those who know no way of naming them and are offered no way of confirming their own identities or, as Olsen put it, to know that they are more than dresses on the ironing board, "helpless before the iron."

How do we solve the problem of inducting the young into what Dewey spoke of as a "homogenized and balanced environment"—or, better, accustom them to a "unity of outlook upon a broader horizon than is visible" to the members of isolated groups? Once we recognize that situation—"depression, war, and fear" perhaps, color perhaps, class perhaps—cannot but affect vantage point even on shared experience, we can no longer take for granted the easy achievement of a "unity of outlook." I cannot but think of Spike Lee's film *Do the Right Thing* and confront once more the racial prejudices, the conflicting lifestyles, the contesting meanings in one neighborhood in Brooklyn, New York. There is the appalling recognition of how difficult it can be to resolve the tensions that exist even among well-meaning Blacks, Italians, Koreans, Irish, not to speak of the misunderstandings among age groups. No one is wholly right or wholly wrong in that film. And we are properly left with the ambiguities, asked to choose, unable to choose between the examples of Malcolm X and Martin Luther King. Inevitably this connects with the spectacle of Los Angeles not long ago and the specters of what is to come.

West (1989) stresses the urgent importance of acknowledging the "distinctive cultural and political practices of oppressed people" without highlighting their marginality in a fashion that further marginalizes them. He writes of the need to examine all Eurocentric or patriarchal discourse in relation to the resistance of black and other long-silenced people. We have, he tells us, to look at their multiple contributions to the culture, especially where the popular arts are concerned. "Black cultural practices," he points out,

> emerge out of an acknowledgement of a reality they cannot *not know*—the ragged edges of the real, of necessity; a reality historically constructed by white supremacist practices in North America. . . . These ragged edges—of not being able to eat, not to have shelter, not to have health care—all this is infused into the strategies and styles of black cultural practices. Of course, all people have undergone some form of social misery, yet people of African descent in the United States have done so in the midst of the most prosperous and wealthy country of the world. (West 1989, 93)

It is not just a matter of seeing or of breaking through the conditions of our minds that imposes invisibility on so many. It is a matter of helping change the practices, doing something to mend the ragged edges. E. L. Doctorow's *Ragtime* (1975) comes back to me, along with the landscape of denial and manipulation it painted, one on which (I must admit) I lived many years of my early life. I am not sure if it was the 1954 Supreme Court decision and what I read about the so-called dolls experiment conducted over the years by Kenneth Clark that demonstrated the damage done to black children's identity by separation and exclusion over the years. (Who can forget those children selecting out the white dolls as more beautiful, more acceptable?) There was Coles's wonderful *Children of Crisis* (1967) as well, making so many readers comprehend for the first time how Ruby and other brave black southern youngsters actually felt about themselves in a bland, white-dominated world.

Doctorow wrote at the beginning of his book, referring to New Rochelle in 1906 (much before my time but profoundly relevant, even so):

Theodore Roosevelt was President. The population customarily gathered in great numbers either out of doors for parades, public concerts, fish fries, political picnics, social outings, or indoors in meeting halls, vaudeville theatres, operas, ballrooms. There seemed to be no entertainment that did not involve great swarms of people. Trains and steamers and trolleys moved them from one place to another. That was the style, that was the way people lived. Women were stouter then. They visited the fleet carrying white parasols. Everyone wore white in summer. Tennis racquets were hefty and the racquet faces elliptical. There was alot of sexual fainting. There were no Negroes. There were no immigrants. (1975, 3–4)

The story, of course, has focally to do with a decent, intelligent black man named Coalhouse Walker, who is cheated, never acknowledged, never understood, never *seen*. He launches upon his own fated strategy of vengeance, which ends when promises are broken and he is shot down in cold blood.

Because of my own blindnesses, my own incapacities to see and hear, I need (as some others do) to reflect back on my own landscape as a teacher. I need to create and re-create my own project in these days of pluralism and multiplicity. I realize that I am doing this not solely as a separate individual, autonomous, with my own unique vision of the world. I have begun to agree with those who say that the very notion of a unique individual was an eighteenth century construct, developed when laissez-faire theories and free enterprise systems were developing. In these different times, I have to perceive my subjectivity as open to the common, involved in intersubjectivity on all sides, entangled in languages that have come down to me in great skeins of intertextuality and patterns of thought and contexts that make my self-reflectiveness part of a whole. In any event, it has become very important to me to fill the voids, the holes in my own experience when it comes to being with others and being in the world.

All this appears at least as necessary as taking more and more books on diverse cultures out of the library, although that is essential too. When I face the astonishing gaps in my past readings, I remain incredulous. There are, for example, those Maxine Hong Kingston (1989) calls "China Men," who chopped trees and laid railroad tracks in the dust of the Sandalwood and Sierra Nevada mountains. I knew about the Chinese Exclusion Acts, I am sure, but I did not really understand what they entailed. And even today, I cannot understand why I was not even curious about the men who built the railroads and were responsible, after all, for that moment in Utah, that moment of the Golden Spike, when the tracks met coming from east and west. I never knew about such a person as Ah Goong, described by Hong Kingston, whose papers were burned in the San Francisco fire, whose

> existence was outlawed by the Chinese Exclusion Acts. The family called him Fleaman. They did not understand his accomplishments as an American ancestor, a holding, homing ancestor of this place. He'd gotten the legal or illegal papers burned in the San Francisco earthquake and fire; he appeared in America in time to be a citizen and to father citizens. He had also been seen carrying a child out of the fire, a child of his own in spite of the laws against marrying. He had built a railroad out of sweat, why not have an American child out of longing? (Kingston 1989, 151)

Do we not as teachers have at least to take that into account, as we do the experiences of the mothers and daughters described by Amy Tan, of the Latin and Central American, the Mexican dreams and memories and endless journeys recounted by Octavio Paz, by Jorge Luis Borges, by Gabriela Mistral, by Gabriel García Márquez, by Clarice Lispector, whose visions, whose realities, whose ideas of time and death and history were so lacking in the things I learned? And what of those bodies, those faces in the murals done by Diego Rivera, and of Frida Kahló's images, and of the Chicano syncretic uses of mainstream styles, their pop sculptures, their domestic altars? What of all these? I am not saying that one tradition should replace another; I am not attempting to invent new hierarchies and absolutes. It is only a mode of seeking out ways of paying heed, connecting in some manner with the lived lives of diverse children, wanting to enter in and at once to remain themselves.

There are more, so many more. There are the grandchildren of the Holocaust survivors. Ought we not to know some of what Cynthia Ozick (1989) has had to tell in *The Shawl* or in *The Cannibal Galaxy?* The same Cynthia Ozick, writing about metaphor and memory, reminds us of how metaphor can translate memory into a principle of continuity, when she writes about the transforming effects of memory. She speaks of dead writers who seem to contain our experience when we turn to them; and here, she writes,

> we have an exact counterpart of biblical memory: because you were strangers in Egypt. Through metaphor, the past has the capacity to imagine us, and we it. . . . Those at the center can imagine what it is to be outside. The strong can imagine the weak. Illuminated lives can imagine the dark. . . . We strangers can imagine the familiar heart of strangers. (Ozick 1989, 283)

Many of the same ideas occur to me when I ponder theories of teaching and education. And, certainly, if we are to become attuned to those places, become aware of those places where our selves and the selves of others are to be intertwined, we must be open to our own horizons, to the patterns and, yes, the vacancies in the landscapes against which our stories are told.

When I speak of Ozick's work, or Morrison's, when I reach out to Kingston's work, or to Mary Crow Dog's autobiographical *Lakota Woman*, or when I try to summon up the sounds of mambo by referring to Oscar Hijuelos's *The Mambo Kings Sing Songs of Love*, I am not suggesting that our students have read or should have read the works relevant to their own ethnic or religious or class identities; nor am I suggesting that they ought to if they want to know who they are. I do so because I want to suggest that teachers break out of the confinements of monologism, open themselves to pluralism, become aware of more possible ways of being and of attending to the world.

There is little question, it seems to me, that Lucy will respond quite differently to the component parts of what is called "cultural literacy" by those insistent on defending the canon, the Word. "All significant human achievements 'are' many things," says Booth (1988, 420), "and they are many things that their makers were unaware of and would deplore." He says as well that we all ought to become pluralist "because pluralism serves ends that are even more important than any conceivable comprehensive and coherent theory about our discourse." That is why we have to allow Lucy's readings to enter in, open the way to the Chinese child's memories of her grandfather's stories, presume that the Lakota adolescent's perspective is in some way shaped by the stories she had heard.

Fischer (1986) tells us that ethnicity is reinvented and reinterpreted in each generation by each individual and that it is often something quite puzzling to the individual. It is, in fact, an emotional component of identity "transmitted less through cognitive language or learning . . . than through processes analogous to the dreaming and transference of psychoanalytic encounters" (231). Each person— Chinese American, Hispanic American, Jewish American, African American—has to find a voice or style that does not violate the several components of her or his identity. Each one, Fischer suggests, must undertake a search for coherence grounded in a connection to the past, and the meaning abstracted from the past can become an ethic workable for the future. Surely, any teacher interested in doing more than leveling students into conformity ought to pay heed to this. The vision

Fischer speaks of, the grounds people discover, the ethical traditions they feel a part of: all this has much to do with their choosing themselves as part of the American community—or members of the community-in-the-making, which may (or may not) become democracy. Fischer also makes the point that our new approaches to reading, which encourage the participation of readers in the production of meanings, may eventually activate in readers the desire for *communitas* with others, "while preserving rather than effacing differences" (Fischer 1986, 232–233).

There are many, inside and outside literary criticism and the "whole language" movement in teaching, that are taken with the idea that there are no preexisting, predefined meanings hidden in works of literary art. Rather, the reader who chooses to engage with *The Bluest Eye* or with Isabel Allende's *Eva Luna* or Lawrence Thompson's *Imagining Argentina* or Don DeLillo's *Mao II* must be willing to work to achieve the work as meaningful against the background of a lived, often contradictory world. Moreover, assuming the text to be an open text, susceptible to a range of interpretations, the reader is or may be provoked to look through multiple perspectives while the reading is progressing—and not solely, say, the perspective provided by the narrator (by the child Claudia, say, in *The Bluest Eye,* by the storyteller Eva Luna) or by the other characters in the book, each of whom will provide a different vantage point on what is happening. There are the perspectives of the book's author, of available critics—those who focus on the work itself, those who see the work in a live context, those who see the work as making a demand on attentive readers, appealing to their freedom and even their indignation. Booth (1988) has written that every student ought to come to respect the powers of at least two contrasting ways of looking at or grasping whatever work is being studied. He knows that only when alternative possibilities come alive "are we driven beyond imitation into thought" (337).

Seeking *communitas* with others while preserving differences, we would like students to realize the sense in which the readers present to a given work have to lend Pecola Breedlove or Eva Luna or DeLillo's J. B. Salinger character, Bill Gates, their lives. That means that the tragic aunt's suicide in Hong Kingston's *The Woman Warrior* is in some sense the readers' suicide, as the way she fixes her hair is the readers', and the childbirth. After all, it is the readers who bring those words, those letters printed on a neutral page, alive. It means that the Cuban musicians in *The Mambo Kings Sing Songs of Love* are given their melancholy and heated lives by readers whose consciousness is pierced by Hijuelos's words. The scarred storyteller in Vargas Llosa's *The Storyteller* is given his "reality" as a Jew who transforms himself into a member of an Andean Indian tribe, as is Fermina Daza, who is loved and waited for for fifty years in *Love in the Time of Cholera*, by the amazing Gabriel García Márquez. The materials of the readers' experience, in consequence, cannot but be ordered on each occasion in unfamiliar ways. When that happens, readers see dimensions of that experience that are ordinarily invisible, hear aspects of it ordinarily lost in silence. Not only may there be a pull towards *communitas*; the readers may be moved to new modes of self-definition in their very awareness of difference—difference between a familiar reader self and the self of Pecola or the Mambo player or Ozick's Rosa clinging to the shawl that hid a baby in a concentration camp. To obviate or deny such difference even in the name of universalism is to homogenize, to refuse the distinctiveness of the diverse persons surrounding us in this world. Also, it is oddly to insist that we coincide with our ordinary selves each day that we live, refusing difference by petrifying ourselves.

Of course we have the most difficult choices to make, especially if we are committed to pluralism and, at once, to a recognition that something in common must be achieved, something life affirming and shared as it is kept alive. Some are fortunate to be working in magnet schools or other small schools that have already begun to shape communities in their rooms and corridors. Others are fortunate to work in schools where mingling already takes place, even among relative strangers.

There will always be difficulty in affirming plurality and difference while working to build a community. More than a century ago, men like de Tocqueville saw the dilemma in a culture whose coherence seemed endangered by individualism in conflict with overwhelming social conformity. Multiculturalism sharpens the dilemma in many ways, once the distinctiveness and passion of multiple voices are attended to, and once the need for conformity or, at least, common agreements becomes urgent. The community I hope we are seeking, however, ought not to be identified with conformity. As in Whitman's ways of saying, it is a community welcoming of difference and sensitive to need. Something life affirming in diversity must be discovered, even as something shared emerges out of the diversity, something that can be deeply—if only provisionally—recognized as constituent of a common world.

Yes, the choices are difficult. There are, most of us realize, many bridges still to build—enabling the children of newcomers to develop the capabilities needed for coping with the society they are entering without threatening identification with their own. There are demands as well to enable young persons to understand and resist their own prejudices and stereotypes without making them regard them as purely private, idiosyncratic deficiencies. Multicultural approaches to teaching and curriculum must allow for the continuing expansion of the culture's conversation. They have to allow for a variety of ways to initiate different strangers into that conversation, even as they have to empower all kinds of persons to imagine what Ozick calls "the familiar hearts of strangers." It is with such urgencies in mind that I am moved to argue for including the several arts in the new curricula. Not only do engagements with the arts move persons to be present to inner and outer conditions; they provide occasions, as I have tried to say, for a reaching out towards alternative ways of being human, of being in the world. Also, informed engagements with literature, painting, film, drama, music, and the rest depend upon and provoke the release of imagination. Releasing imagination, they free persons to break with the taken-for-granted, with what appears to be "normal" and unchangeable; they arouse persons to reach towards the possible, to look at things as if they could be otherwise.

Freire, whose pedagogy and view of heightened consciousness have moved countless learners to look beyond the given, surely has been concerned to challenge people to look at things that way. He has continually made the point, in calling for critical reflectiveness, that a person's culture ought always to be cherished and cultivated, but never absolutized. He has said that "if it were not for that, you would even find it hard to learn new things which, placed alongside your own personal history, can be meaningful" (Freire and Macedo 1987, 126). Not only ought teachers to be seeking connection points (through art experiences and storytelling) between dimensions of their own personal histories and the personal histories of those they teach; students ought to be offered more and more time for telling their stories, sharing them with all of those around. Given an expanding consciousness of diversity and the importance of social justice and equality, their telling ought to be informed (at least now and then) with outrage at injustices and violations. Not only do teachers and learners together need to tell and choose; they ought to look towards untapped possibility, explore what it signifies to transform.

Realizing how entangled racial conflicts are with class inequities and the "ragged edges" of things, we can no longer remain in good faith if we ignore the social ills that erode mutuality of relationship, that promote envy and greed. Not only are communities eroding, along with families; there is also an eerie sense of hopelessness all around, an awareness of incoherence accompanying a loss of confidence in shared guidelines and norms. On the one hand, there are those who try to deal with the advent of strangers by receiving newcomers into their home and school places as generously as they can. On the other hand, there are those who fear destruction of the tradition or who fear that the shocks of popular culture (incivilities, addictions) will increase with the continuing arrival of strangers. They fear that old faiths will be shredded, with nothing to replace them. They envisage flags blowing in tatters in an unfamiliar wind. It is there that attacks on multiculturalism begin.

We cannot predict the common world that may be in the making; nor can we finally justify one kind of community more than another. We can bring warmth into the places where persons come together, however. We can bring in the kinds of laughter that threaten monologism and rigidity. And surely we can affirm and reaffirm the value of principles like justice and equality and freedom and commitment to human rights, because without these we cannot even call for the decency of welcoming and inclusion. Only if more and more persons, in their coming together, incarnate such principles and choose to live by them and engage in dialogues in accord with them are we likely to bring about democratic pluralism and not fly apart in chaos and cacophony. All we can do is to speak with others as passionately and eloquently as we can about justice and caring and love and trust; all we can do is to look into each other's eyes and squeeze each other's hands. We want our classrooms to be reflective and just; we want them to pulsate with a plurality of conceptions of what it is to be human and to be fully alive. We want them to be full of the sounds of articulate young people, with ongoing dialogues involving as many as possible, opening to each other, opening to the world. And we want them to care for one another, as we learn more and more about caring for them. We want them to achieve friendships, as each one stirs to wide-awakeness, to renewed consciousness of possibility.

With nothing resolved, I would end with a section from Li-Young Lee's "The Cleaving" (1990, 86–87), which deals with the two meanings of the term—and with the world:

What then may I do
but cleave to what cleaves me.
I kiss the blade and eat my meat.
I thank the wielder and receive,
while terror spirits
my change, sorrow also.
The terror the butcher
scripts in the unhealed
air, the sorrow of his Shang
dynasty face,
African face with slit eyes. He is
my sister, this
beautiful Bedouin, this Shulamite,
keeper of sabbaths, diviner
of holy texts, this dark
dancer, this Jew, this Asian, this one
with the Cambodian face, Vietnamese face,
   this Chinese
I daily face,
this immigrant,
this man with my own face.

Or this woman. Or this child. We can only open ourselves, imagine, try
to heal and try to see.

References

Berger, J. (1984). *Ways of seeing.* New York: Penguin.

Booth, W. C. (1988). *The company we keep: An ethics of fiction.* Berkeley: University of California Press.

Bruner, J. (1986). *Actual minds, possible worlds.* Cambridge, MA: Harvard University Press.

Clifford, J. (1988). *The predicament of culture.* Cambridge, MA: Harvard University Press.

Coles, R. (1967). *Children of crisis* (Vol. 1). Boston: Little, Brown.

Dewey, J. (1916). *Democracy and education.* New York: Macmillan.

———. (1954). *The public and its problems.* Athens, OH: Swallow Press.

———. (1958). *Art as experience.* New York: Capricorn Press.

Doctorow, E. L. (1975). *Ragtime.* New York: Random House.

Fischer, M. M. J. (1986). Ethnicity and the post-modern arts of memory. In J. Clifford and G. E. Marcus (Eds.), *Writing culture* (194–233). Berkeley: University of California Press.

Freire, P., and Macedo, D. (1987). *Literacy: Reading the word and the world.* South Hadley, MA: Bergin & Garvey.

Joyce, J. (1947). *A portrait of the artist as a young man.* New York: Viking Press.

Kincaid, J. (1990). *Lucy.* New York: Farrar, Straus, & Giroux.

Kingston, M. H. (1989). *China men.* New York: Vintage International.

Lee, L.-Y. (1990). *The city in which I love you.* Brockport, NY: BOA Editions.

Morrison, T. (1972). *The bluest eye.* New York: Pocket Books.

Olsen, T. (1976). I stand here ironing. In *Tell me a riddle* (9–21). New York: Dell.

———. (1978). *Silences.* New York: Delacorte.

Ozick, C. (1989). *Metaphor and memory.* New York: Alfred A. Knopf.

West, C. (1989). Black culture and postmodernism. In B. Kruger and P. Mariani (Eds.), *Remaking history* (87–96) Seattle: Bay Press.

Whitman, W. (1931). *Leaves of grass.* New York: Aventine Press.

Woolf, V. (1957). *A room of one's own.* New York: Harcourt Brace.

3 Life as Narrative

Jerome Bruner
New York University

The primacy of narrative is highlighted in this chapter as Jerome Bruner practices "experimental psychology." He analyzes the life stories of four members of the Goodhertz family and in the process demonstrates how a literary look at everyday language gives us a new understanding of the phrase a well-examined life.

I would like to try out an idea that may not be quite ready, indeed may not be quite possible. But I have no doubt it is worth a try. It has to do with the nature of thought and with one of its uses. It has been traditional to treat thought, so to speak, as an instrument of reason. Good thought is right reason, and its efficacy is measured against the laws of logic or induction. Indeed, in its most recent computational form, it is a view of thought that has sped some of its enthusiasts to the belief that all thought is reducible to machine computability.

But logical thought is not the only or even the most ubiquitous mode of thought. For the last several years, I have been looking at another kind of thought (Bruner 1986), one that is quite different in form from reasoning: the form of thought that goes into the constructing not of logical or inductive arguments, but of stories or narratives. What I want to do now is to extend these ideas about narrative to the analysis of the stories we tell about our lives: "autobiographies."

Philosophically speaking, the approach I shall take to narrative is a constructivist one—a view that takes as its central premise that "world making" is the principal function of mind, whether in the sciences or in the arts. But the moment one applies a constructivist view of narrative to the self-narrative, to the autobiography, one is faced with dilemmas. Take, for example, the constructivist view that "stories" do not "happen" in the real world but, rather, are constructed in people's heads. Or as Henry James once put it, stories happen to people who know how to tell them. Does that mean our autobiographies are constructed, that they had better be viewed not as a record of what happened (which is in any case a nonexistent record), but rather as a continuing interpretation and reinterpretation of our experience? Just as the philosopher Nelson Goodman (1978) argues that physics or painting or history are "ways of worldmaking," so autobiography, formal or informal, should be viewed as a set of procedures for "life making." And just as it is worthwhile examining in minute detail how physics or history go about their world making, might we not be well advised to explore in equal detail what we do when we construct ourselves autobiographically? Even if the exercise should produce some obdurate dilemmas, it might nonetheless cast some light on what we might mean by such expressions of "a life."

Four Self-Narratives

Let me turn to the business of how a psychologist goes about studying issues of the kind that we have been discussing. Along with my colleagues Susan Weisser and Carol Staszewski, I have been engaged in a curious study. While it is far from done (whatever that may mean), I would like to tell you enough about it to make what I have been saying a little more concrete.

We were interested in how people tell the stories of their lives and, perhaps simple-mindedly, we asked them to do so—telling them to keep it to about half an hour, even if it were an impossible task. We told them that we were not interested in judging them or curing them, but that we were very interested in how people saw their lives. After they were done—and most had little trouble in sticking to the time limits or, for that matter, in filling up the time—we asked questions for another half hour or so, questions designed to get a better picture of how their stories had been put together. Had we followed a different procedure, we doubtless would have obtained different accounts. . . . Many people, ranging in age from ten to seventy, have now sat for their portraits, and their stories yield rich texts. But I want to talk of only four of them now: a family—a father, a mother, and their grown son and grown daughter, each of their accounts collected independently. There are two more grown children in the family, a son and daughter, both of whom have also told their stories, but four are enough to handle as a start.

We have chosen a family as our target because it constitutes a miniature culture and provides an opportunity to explore how life stories are made to mesh with each other. . . . . .

If you should now ask how we propose to test whether these four lives "imitated" the narratives each person told, your questions would be proper enough, though a bit impatient. The position I have avowed, indeed, leaves entirely moot what could be meant by "lives" altogether, beyond what is contained in the narrative. We shall not even be able to check, as Neisser (1987) was able to do in his studies of autobiographical memory, whether particular memories were veridical or distorted in some characteristic way. But our aim is different. We are asking, rather, whether there is in each account a set of selective narrative rules that lead the narrator to structure experience in a particular way, structure it in a manner that gives form to the content and the continuity of life. And we are interested, as well, in how the family itself formulates certain common rules for doing these things. I hope this will be less abstract as we proceed.

Our family is headed by George Goodhertz, a hard-working heating contractor in his early sixties, a self-made man of moral principles, converted to Catholicism in childhood and mindful of his obligations, though not devout. Though plainly intelligent and well informed, he never finished high school: "had to go to work." His father was, by Mr. Goodhertz's sparse characterization, "a drinker" and a poor provider. Mr. Goodhertz is neither. Mrs. Goodhertz, Rose, is a housewife of immediate Italian descent: family oriented, embedded in the urban neighborhood where she has lived for nearly thirty years, connected with old friends who still live nearby. Her father was, in her words, "of the old school"—arrogant, a drinker, a poor provider, and unfaithful to her mother. In the opening paragraph of her autobiography she says, "I would have preferred a better childhood, a happier one, but with God's influence, I prayed hard enough for a good husband, and she [sic] answered me."

Daughter Debby, in her mid-twenties, is (in her own words) "still unmarried." She graduated a few years ago from a local college that she never liked much and now studies acting. Outgoing, she enjoys friends, old and new, but is determined not to get "stuck" in the old neighborhood with the old friends of her past and their old attitudes. Yet she is not ambitious, but caught, rather, between ideals of local kindliness and of broader adventure, the latter more in the existential form of a desire for experience than by any wish to achieve. She lives at home—in Brooklyn with her parents in the old neighborhood. Her thirty-year-old brother, Carl, is about to finish his doctorate in neurophysiology at one of the solid if not distinguished Boston-area universities. He is aware of how far beyond family expectations his studies have taken him, but is neither deferential nor aggressive about his leap in status. Like his sister Debby, he remains attached to and in easy contact with his parents, though he lives on his own even when he is in New York working at a local university laboratory. At school,

Carl always felt "special" and different—both in the Catholic high school and then in the Catholic college he attended. The graduate school he chose is secular and a complete break with his past. He is ambitious to get ahead, but he is not one to take the conventional "up" stairway. Both in his own eyes and, indeed, by conventional standards, he is a bit eccentric and a risk taker. Where Debby (and his mother) welcome intimacy and closeness, Carl (like his father) keeps people more at arm's length. Experience for its own sake is not his thing. He is as concerned as his sister about not being "tied down."

And that, I now want to assure you, is the end of the omniscient auctorial voice. For our task now is to sample the texts, the narratives of these four lives—father's, mother's, son's, and daughter's—to see not what they are *about*, but how the narrators *construct* themselves. Their texts are all we have—although we may seem to have, so to speak, the hermeneutical advantage of four narratives that spring from a common landscape. But as you will see, the advantage that it yields is in narrative power and possibility, not in the ontology of verification. For one view of the world cannot confirm another, though, in Clifford Geertz's evocative phrase, it can "thicken" it.

Let me begin the analysis with Burke's pentad (1945), his skeleton of dramatism, and particularly with the setting or Scene of these life stories. Most psychological theories of personality, alas, have no place for place. They would not do well with Stephen Dedalus in Joyce's *Portrait of the Artist as a Young Man*, for he is inexplicable without the Dublin that he carries in his head. In these four life narratives too, place is crucial and it shapes and constrains the stories that are told or, indeed, that could be told. Place is not simply a piece of geography, an established Italian neighborhood in Brooklyn, though it helps to know its "culture" too. It is an intricate construct, whose language dominates the thought of our four narrators. For each, its central axis is "home," which is placed in sharp contrast to what they all refer to as "the real world." They were, by all their own accounts, a "close" family, and their language seals that closeness.

Consider the psychic geography. For each of our narrators, "home" is a place that is inside, private, forgiving, intimate, predictably safe. "The real world" is outside, demanding, anonymous, open, unpredictable, and consequently dangerous. But home and real world are also contrastive in another way, explicitly for the two children, implicitly and covertly for the parents: home is to be "cooped up," restricted by duties, and bored; real world is excitement and opportunity. Early on, the mother says of the children, "We spoiled them for the real world," and the father speaks of "getting them ready for the real world." The son speaks of its hypocrisies that need to be confronted and overcome to achieve one's goals. It is a worthwhile but treacherous battlefield. The daughter idealizes it for the new experience to be harvested there. Each, in his or her way, creates a different ontological landscape out of "the real world" to give it an appropriate force as the Scene in the narratives they are constructing.

One thing that is striking about all four narratives is the extent to which the spatial distinction home-real world concentrates all four of them on spatial and locative terms in their autobiographical accounts. Take Carl. His account is laden with spatial metaphors: *in/out, here/there, coming from/going to, place/special place*. The movement forward in his story is not so much temporal as spatial: a sequential outward movement from home neighborhood to Catholic school to the library alone to college to the Catholic peace movement to graduate school and then triumphantly back to New York. In his *Bildungsroman* of a life story, the challenge is to find a place, the right place, and then a special place in each of these concentric outgoings. For Carl, you get involved *in* things, or you feel *"out* of place." You "go to" Boston or to a course or a lab, and fellow students "come from" prestigious schools. Or "I started gaining a fairly special place in the department," and later "I ended up getting a fairly privileged place in the department." The "special places" *allow, permit, make possible.* "After about six months I really started settling in and enjoying the program and enjoying the opportunities it gave me." And later, about the students who get a special place, "The faculty are committed to shielding their graduate students from negative repercussions of failure."

Two things are both surprising and revealing about Carl's language. One is the extent to which his sentences take self as object, and the other is the high frequency of the passive voice. With respect to the latter, some 11 percent of his sentences are in the passive voice, which is surprisingly high for such an action-oriented text. But they both are of a piece and tell something interesting about his world making. Recall the importance for Carl of "place" and particularly of the "special place." Whenever he recounts something connected with these places, the places "happen" and then he acts accordingly. His sentences then begin with either a passive or with self-as-object, and then move to the active voice. At a particular colloquium where he knew his stuff, "It allowed me to deal with the faculty on an equal footing." Or of his debating-team experience, "It taught me how to handle myself." Occasions in these "special places" are seen as if they had homelike privileges: allowing and permitting and teaching. It is as if Carl manages the "real world" by colonizing it with "special places" that provide some of the privileges of home.

With Debby, thirty-seven of the first one hundred sentences in her life narrative contain spatial metaphors or locatives. The principal clusters are about her place in the family (the *gap* or *span* in ages); the life layout ("the house I was brought home to is the house I live in now"; or "I traveled, my relatives are all over the country"; or "I've been coming to the city by myself ever since I was fourteen"); the coming-back theme ("everybody except me has gone out and come back at one time or another").

So much for Scene, at least for the moment. Come now to the agentive, to Burke's Actor. Rorty's typology (1976) turns out to be enormously useful, for in all four self-portraits the tale moves from Actor as figure, figure becoming person, person becoming a self, self becoming an individual. Well into her fifties, even Mrs. Goodhertz has finally taken a job for pay, albeit working as secretary for her husband's heating-contracting business, motivated by the desire for some independence and the wish not to get "stuck" raising her elder daughter's child. She remarks that it is "her" job and that she now "works." The transformation of her language as she runs through the chronology of her life is striking. When she speaks of her childhood, self is often an object ("everything was thrown at us"). But finally, by the time she takes her first job as a young woman, "I decided to take things in my own hands." Throughout her account, she "owns her own experience," to use Rorty's phrase. More than eight in ten of her sentences contain a stative verb—a verb dealing with thinking, feeling, intending, believing, praying—in contrast to five in ten for her more action-oriented husband. One is easily deceived, reading Mrs. Goodhertz's self-portrait, into thinking that she is accepting of fate, perhaps passive. Instead, she believes in fate, but she also believes that fate can be nudged by her own efforts. And we rather suspect that the style is cultivated, for a closer analysis of her language reveals a very high "subjective level" as carried in those stative verbs.

We must return again to Scene, or perhaps to what might better be called *mise-en-scène*. Both the elder Goodhertzes—unlike their children—construct their lives as if they constituted two sides of a deep divide. That divide is marked by an escape from childhood, an old life, indeed, an old *secret* life of suffering and shame as figures in unbearably capricious family settings. Personhood is on the other side of the divide. Mrs. Goodhertz gets to the other side, to personhood, by "praying for the right husband" and getting him, of which more in a moment. Mr. Goodhertz crosses the divide by work, hard work, and by the grace of "the owner [who] took me under his wing." To him, achieving mastery of your work and, as we shall see, helping others help themselves are the two dominant ideals. For her, it is somewhat more complex. The linguistic vehicle is the *"but . . ."* construction. She uses it repeatedly, and in several telltale ways, the most crucial being to distinguish what *is* from what *might have been,* as in talking about teenage drug taking: " . . . but I am blessed *my* kids didn't start in on it," or "I would have been stricter, but they turned out with less problems than others." The construction is her reminder of what *might* have been and, at the same time, a string on her finger to remind her that she is the agent who produces the better even on the other side of the . . . *but.* . . . Her courtship and marriage are a case in point. Yes, she was waiting for God to bring the right man, *but* in fact she decided the moment her eyes fell on Mr. Goodhertz that *he* was the man and knew not an instant's remorse in throwing over her then fiancé.

Their secret childhoods provide a unique source of consciousness for the elder Goodhertzes. It is a concealed secret that they share and that provides the contrast to what they have established as the organizing concept of "home." Mrs. Goodhertz's knowledge of her macho father as a bad provider, a drinker, a philanderer is secret knowledge, quickly and hintingly told in her narrative in a way that brooked no probing. It was there only to let us know why she prayed for a good husband and better life for her children. Mr. Goodhertz goes into even less detail. But note the two following quotations, both about hopes for the children, each said independently of the other. Mr. Goodhertz: "I wanted to give them all of the things I didn't get as a kid." And Mrs. Goodhertz: "To a point, I think, we try not to make our children have too much of what he had."

So Debby and Carl start on the other side of the divide. Each of them tells a tale that is animated by a contrast between a kindly but inert, entrenched, or "given" world and a "new" one that is their own. Carl is a young Werther. His tale begins with the episode when, as an aspiring young football player, he and his teammates are told by the coach to knock out the opposing team's star quarterback. He keeps his own counsel, quits football, and starts on his own road. For Debby, the tale is more like the young Stephen Hero in the discarded early version of *Portrait.* She exposes herself to experience as it may come, "trying" in the sense of "trying on" rather than striving. Her involvement in acting is in the spirit of trying on new roles. Of life she says, "I don't like doing one thing . . . the same thing all my life, . . . shoved into a house and cooped up with four kids all day." If Carl's autobiography is a *Bildungsroman*, Debby's is an existential novel. His account is linear from start to end, but it is replete with what literary linguists call *prolepsis*. That is to say, it is full of those odd flash-forwards that implicate the present for the future, as in "if I had known then what I know now" and "learning to debate would stand me in good stead later." His narrative is progressive and sequential: the story tracks "real time." It "accounts" for things, and things are mentioned because they account for things. Privileged opportunities "happen to" him, as we have seen, and he turns them into ventures.

The exception to Carl's pattern is the dilemma of moral issues—as with the coach's murderous instructions or his becoming a conscientious objector in the Vietnam war, inspired by the Berrigans. Then his language (and his thought) becomes subjunctive rather than instrumental, playing on possibilities and inwardness. In this respect, he is his father's son, for Mr. Goodhertz too is principally oriented to action (recall that half his sentences contain nonstative verbs), save when he encounters issues he defines as matters of morality. Don't condemn, he would say, "you never know the whole story." And in the same spirit, Mr. Goodhertz's self-portrait is laced with literally dozens of instances of the intransitive verb to *seem*, as if he were forever mindful of a feather edge separating appearance from reality. When Carl decided he would become a conscientious objector against the Vietnam draft, his father stood by him on grounds that Carl's convictions, honestly arrived at, were worthy of respect even though he did not agree with them. Carl unwittingly even describes his intellectual quest in the same instrumental terms that his father uses in describing his ducting work. Both emphasize skills and know-how, both reject received ways of doing things. Theirs is "instrumental" language and thought, as well suited to talking about heat ducting as to Carl's strikingly procedural approach in visual physiology. The father confesses to having missed intimacy in his life. So, probably, will Carl one day. Their instrumental language leaves little room for it in their discourse.

Debby's highly stative language is specialized for the reception of experience and for exploring the affect it creates. It is richly adjectival, and the adjectives cluster around inner states. Her own acts are almost elided from her account. The past exists in its own right rather than as a guide to the present or future. In recounting the present, she uses vivid analeptic flashbacks—as in an unbid memory of an injured chicken on the Long Island Expressway, the traffic too thick for rescue.

Like so many of her images, this one was dense with plight and affect. It evoked her tenderness for helpless animals, she told us, then veering off to that topic. And so her order of telling is dominated not by real-time sequences, but by a going back and forth between what happens and what she feels and believes, and what she felt and believed. In this, and her heavy use of stative verbs, she is her mother's daughter—and, I suspect, both are locked in the same gender language. Finally, in Debby's self-story, "themes and variations" are as recursive as her brother's is progressive, and hers is as lacking in efforts to give causes as his is replete with causative expressions.

Recipes for Structuring Experience

You will ask whether the narrative forms and the language that goes with them in our four subjects are not simply expressions of their inner states, ways of talk that are required by the nature of those internal states. Perhaps so. But I have been proposing a more radical hypothesis than that. I believe that the ways of telling and the ways of conceptualizing that go with them become so habitual that they finally become recipes for structuring experience itself, for laying down routes into memory, for not only guiding the life narrative up to the present, but for directing it into the future. I have argued that a life as led is inseparable from a life as told—or more bluntly, a life is not "how it was" but how it is interpreted and reinterpreted, told and retold: Freud's *psychic reality*. Certain basic formal properties of the life narrative do not change easily. Our excursion into experimental autobiography suggests that these formal structures may get laid down early in the discourse of family life and persist stubbornly in spite of changed conditions. Just as Gusdorf (1980) argued that a special, historically conditioned, metaphysical condition was needed to bring autobiography into existence as a literary form, so perhaps a metaphysical change is required to alter the narratives that we have settled upon as "being" our lives. The fish will, indeed, be the last to discover water—unless it gets a metaphysical assist.

My life as a student of mind has taught me one incontrovertible lesson. Mind is never free of precommitment. There is no innocent eye, nor is there one that penetrates aboriginal reality. There are instead hypotheses, versions, expected scenarios. Our precommitment about the nature of a life is that it is a story, some narrative however incoherently put together. Perhaps we can say one other thing: any story one may tell about anything is better understood by considering other possible ways in which it can be told. That must surely be as true of the life stories we tell as of any others. In that case, we have come full round to the ancient homily that the only life worth living is the well-examined one. But it puts a different meaning on the homily. If we can learn how people put their narrative together when they tell stories from life, considering as well how they *might* have proceeded, we might then have contributed something new to that great ideal. Even if, with respect to life and narrative, we discover, as in Yeats's line, that we cannot tell the dancer from the dance, that may be good enough.

References

Bruner, J. S. (1986). *Actual minds, possible worlds.* Cambridge, MA: Harvard University Press.

Burke, K. (1945). *A grammar of motives.* New York: Prentice-Hall.

Goodman, N. (1978). *Ways of worldmaking.* Indianapolis, IN: Hackett.

Gusdorf, G. (1980). Conditions and limits of autobiography. In J. Olney (Ed.), *Autobiography: Essays theoretical and critical.* Princeton, NJ: Princeton University Press.

Neisser, U. (1987). *Autobiographical memory.* Unpublished manuscript, Emory University.

Rorty, A. O. (1976). A literary postscript: Characters, persons, selves, individuals. In A. O. Rorty (Ed.), *The identity of persons.* Berkeley: University of California Press.

4 The Power of Personal Storytelling in Families and Kindergartens

Peggy J. Miller
University of Illinois at Urbana-Champaign

Robert A. Mehler
University of Illinois at Chicago

In this chapter, Peggy Miller and Robert Mehler focus on a particular kind of conversational story, the story of personal experience. They illustrate an aspect of the social construction of self through the culturally diverse routines of storytelling and at the same time raise questions about the role that personal narratives might play in classrooms.

This paper is concerned with conversational stories of personal experience—oral stories in which the narrator re-creates a remembered experience from his or her life. We will examine the role that personal storytelling plays in early childhood socialization and self-construction, focusing primarily on the home and secondarily on the kindergarten classroom. We assume that the learning that occurs at home during the preschool years is not only important in its own right, but that it is relevant to what happens later in the classroom. We take it as a given that the more we know about the understandings that young children create at home under everyday conditions, the better placed teachers will be to build upon and complement the strengths that children bring to the learning experience at school. Hence the first part of the paper will be devoted to home-based research on personal storytelling.

An earlier version of this chapter was presented by the first author in a Division C invited address at the 1991 annual meeting of the American Educational Research Association, Chicago. The research reported in this chapter was supported by grants awarded to the first author by The Spencer Foundation and The Smart Foundation. We wish to express our gratitude to the families, teachers, and children who participated in these studies.

In the second part of the paper, we will present some findings from a recent ethnographic study of how personal storytelling is—and is not—practiced in kindergarten classrooms. Personal stories are quite different from written stories both in the channel of communication and in other genre conventions. Despite these differences and the fact that the school's mission in the early grades is to introduce written language to children, many educators have believed that personal storytelling can serve as an effective bridge into schooling and early literacy (e.g., Bruner 1984; Rosen 1988). This intuition is reflected in approaches to reading and writing that build upon children's ability to articulate orally their personal experiences (e.g., Allen 1976; Calkins 1982) and in the widespread use of show-and-tell or sharing time in the early grades.

Our work on personal storytelling at home affirms these intuitions in that it contributes to the growing body of empirical evidence that personal storytelling is an area of strength for many preschoolers—including preschoolers from low-income and minority backgrounds (Eisenberg 1985; Heath 1983; Miller and Sperry 1988; Snow et al. 1991; Sperry 1991). When we say an area of strength, we mean not just that young children are surprisingly skilled narrators, but that they are interested in personal storytelling, participating frequently and avidly (Miller 1989). In addition, they use personal stories as tools for expressing and making sense of who they are.

Children's involvement in personal storytelling is also an involvement with other people, including more experienced members of the culture, who wittingly or unwittingly expose them to a complex and varied set of narrative practices (to be described below). Although it has long been recognized that myths and traditional tales, embodying the collective wisdom of a people, are powerful socializing tools, less attention has been given to the socializing potential of the less formal and more modest genre of personal storytelling. On first impression, personal stories may seem like idle tales, for they are told by ordinary people in the course of their everyday goings-on.

Yet for many people they are not idle tales. A recent compilation of American family folklore (Zeitlin, Kotlin, and Baker 1982) contains numerous adult testimonials both to the humor and the deterrent value of parental stories of personal experience. Novelist Eudora Welty (1984) traces her dramatic sense—her appreciation that everything happened in scenes—to the stories of personal experience she overheard in conversation. Norman Maclean's (1976) autobiographical fiction originated, he says, in the stories he told his children when they were young, stories that conveyed to them "what kind of people their parents are or think they are or hope they are" (ix). In *Talk That Talk,* an anthology of African American storytelling, Kathryn Morgan (1989) presents stories of her great-grandmother's experiences in slavery. Passed down orally through four generations, these stories continue to guide and inspire her: "Frankly, Caddy comes to my rescue even now when some obstacle seems insurmountable to me" (296).

To these individuals, then, personal stories were significant in a variety of ways—as moral tales, models of exemplary lives, humor, dramatic art, self-relevation. A basic thesis of this paper echoes these convictions: we shall argue that even when told informally and without didactic intent, even when not addressed directly to the young, personal stories play a powerful role in childhood socialization and are especially consequential for self-construction.

A Discourse Model of Socialization

This view of personal storytelling rests on two related assumptions about ordinary talk: (1) that it is a pervasive, orderly, and culturally organized feature of social life in every culture (e.g., Gumperz and Hymes 1972); and (2) that it is a major, if not the major, mechanism of socialization (e.g., Ochs and Schieffelin 1984). Research on language socialization (e.g., Schieffelin and Ochs 1986) and moral development (e.g., Shweder and Much 1987) has shown that the flow of social and moral messages is relentless in the myriad small encounters of everyday life. Although certain general properties of language make it an especially effective purveyor of meanings, little is known as yet about the socializing implications of particular, culturally constituted species of talk.

Yet any model of socialization that takes language seriously as a socializing medium has to grapple with this problem. The model that we favor borrows heavily from Vygotskian theory (Rogoff 1991; Vygotsky 1934/1987; Wertsch 1985) and from practice approaches to narrative (e.g., Bauman 1986; Ochs and Taylor 1992). In this model, institutions are organized in ways that bring novice and member together recurrently for activities which are mediated by particular forms of discourse, which lead to social and psychological consequences for the novice. From this perspective, stories are seen as situated communications. Like literacy, personal storytelling is not monolithic; rather, stories defined in particular ways are told for particular purposes in particular contexts of use.

Applied to the family—the institution in which early socialization occurs—the model suggests that family members socialize young children into systems of meaning by involving them, intentionally or unintentionally, in particular kinds of discourse. The meanings that children create by participating in these verbal practices are constrained by how messages are packaged in discourse, and thus the model requires that we identify and describe the types of everyday discourse that occur in families. As we shall see, one type of discourse that flourishes in families from many cultural traditions is personal storytelling.

This model suggests that the child's habitual participation in personal storytelling has several consequences. One important consequence is the acquisition of narrative skills. Another, and the one most germane to the topic at hand, is self-construction. Obviously many sorts of discourse occur in families, and there is a sense in which self-construction is implicated in each. Why single out personal storytelling? Our rationale, developed elsewhere (Miller in press; Miller et al. 1990), is that the stories people tell about remembered experiences from their own lives provide an important, indeed a privileged site for self-construction because multiple sources of narrative-self-affinity (e.g., temporal, evaluative) converge in this narrative genre.

Taking, then, personal storytelling as the type of discourse to examine as a medium of childhood socialization and self-construction, this model of socialization raises several important questions, all of which revolve around the notion of practice. Is personal storytelling routinely practiced in families from different backgrounds? How is it practiced vis-à-vis children? What are the implications of these practices for self-construction in early childhood? Before we address these questions, the first author will relate how she came to study stories of personal experience.

Personal Storytelling at Home

Stories from South Baltimore

I first got interested in personal storytelling when I was doing ethnographic research on early language socialization in South Baltimore, an urban, working-class community whose residents are descended from people of German, Polish, Irish, Italian, and Appalachian origin (Miller 1982). The children I studied were two-year-old girls of unmarried mothers. Family income was very low, educational level was very low, and the children were growing up in extended families. Although I had not gone to South Baltimore to study storytelling, it soon became clear that stories of personal experience were a major form of adult talk. I was impressed, as I listened, not only by the ubiquity of these stories, but by the vigor and skill with which they were told. Men and women alike were accomplished narrators, capable at times of inspired performances.

But as a woman studying children and child rearing, I spent more time with women and heard more stories and more intimate stories from them. I was not surprised to learn that pregnancy and childbirth were favorite narrative topics for women. The following excerpted example was told by a grandmother:

Example 1

I was in there twelve minutes . . . I made it into the hospital, I made it back, they cut my underwear off and I made it in the room, the doctor comes in and he said, "You'll be in here at least a couple more hours," 'cause the prior year I had had Agnes, and I was in there forty some hours, and he goes to walk out the door, and that was it. He said, "Well, old speedy!" I said, "Oh thank God!" [laughs] I was in the labor room, had her, and was back over in my room, and they were feeding the babies, and they come out and say, "What happened to the lady, now, where's she at?" And they said, "She already had the baby!" I was like a celebrity.

While stories of pregnancy and childbirth occurred in everyday conversation, they were obligatory at baby showers, an all-female ritual event. On these occasions, mothers and grandmothers reveled in relating experiences that had occurred years or even decades earlier to an audience who had heard the tales many times before. Apparently, assuming the mother role remained a lasting touchstone of female identity.

However, the maternal self was only one of many narrated selves that these women projected in their stories. Also prominent was the tough, angry, clever, assertive self:

Example 2

[The narrator was a factory worker who operated a machine that assembled boxes.] And my boss come by the other day and wanted me to work it. And I said, "I'm not doing it." . . . I tell you why he wanted me to work because the floor lady is going on vacation that week. The sprayer is going on vacation that week. Dorothy's going on vacation that week. She's the stacker in there. And I'm goin that week. And that's four of us out in one week and that's gonna kill him because Mildred's been missing a lot of time. . . . I'm not running it. I told him. I said, "There's no way, Al." I said, "Na-uh." I said, "You asked who wanted to take their vacation first so Mildred took hers 'cause I told her she could." I said, "but there's no way I'm gonna give up my week's vacation," I said, "because I'm gonna tell you," I said, "I really worked hard this year for that."

Example 3

I was walkin on Charles Street—and the girl happens to be my girlfriend now. She big and fat, boy. She could sit on me and flatten me out, but I stuck up to her. Her name was Janie. And she hung with the bad people too, boy. And she says, "Look at the big-nosed B-I-T-C-H." And I turned around and I says, "Uh, you talkin to me? I SAID, ARE YOU TALKIN TO ME?" I says, "Well, you fat slob you, I put you in a skillet and strip you down to normal size, if you mess with me."

In these and other similar stories, the narrator created an interpersonal drama around a self-protagonist who was bold, quick-witted, feisty, and protective of her rights and her dignity. These qualities were highly valued by women in South Baltimore and figured prominently in their theories of child rearing (Miller and Sperry 1987).

But another feature of these stories deserves comment, namely, that they are strikingly effective tellings. The last story in particular is highly "performed" in the Hymes (1975) and Bauman (1986) sense, drawing attention to the storyteller's narrative skill and to the communicative act itself. Note the strategic selection of narrative topics and the artful deployment of repetition, parallel constructions, taboo words, original metaphors, shifting rhythms, and modulation of volume. These and other artistic effects function not only to convey the point of the story, but to create in the audience an appreciation of the performance. The self as narrator—the inhabited self as distinguished from the represented self-protagonist—is thereby affirmed.

To summarize, from this initial work in South Baltimore I learned that personal storytelling was habitually and avidly practiced by adults in this community and that it was a rich source of patterned messages about who the narrator is or claims to be. These impressions led me to wonder about the developmental implications of growing up in such a dense narrative environment and about how South Baltimore compared with other, culturally different communities.

Since then we have undertaken further ethnographic research both in South Baltimore and elsewhere that speaks to these questions. We are currently engaged in a comparative study of the role that personal storytelling plays in early childhood socialization. This study includes four research sites in Chicago (low-income African American, middle-class African American, working-class white, middle-class white). A fifth group (middle-class Chinese in Taipei) permits a cross-cultural perspective on the American groups. What is emerging from this program of research is a pattern of both similarities and differences in the narrative experiences of young children from different cultural backgrounds. In the next sections we will briefly outline some of our findings.

Personal Storytelling Practices

Given the key role accorded to discourse in our model of socialization, an important goal of this research has been to develop a clearer, more adequate conception of personal storytelling itself. In keeping with the model introduced earlier, our approach has been to treat stories not as disembodied texts—as we have in working the preceding examples rhetorically into this text—but as integrated performances, embedded in their immediate contexts of use (Miller and Moore 1989). Narrative practices are situated, socially conducted narrative activities that are meaningful within a culture, occur regularly, bear a family resemblance to one another in their discourse form, and take place within the hearing of young children.

In further defining narrative practices for comparative purposes, we found it necessary to make an analytic distinction between two sets of parameters (see Miller and Moore 1989 for further details). The first set concerns the particular version of personal storytelling that prevails in a given community or culture, that is, indigenous, genre-defining properties. The genre itself varies cross-culturally along many parameters. For example, Miller, Fung, and Mintz (1991) found that everyday personal storytelling was much more likely to function in an explicitly didactic manner in middle-class Chinese families in Taipei than in middle-class white families in Chicago. Chinese narrative practices were more likely to include explicit references to moral and social codes and to evoke from the child confessions and promises not to transgress in the future.

In addition, all of the longest and most elaborate Chinese stories, but none of the American stories, were structured so as to establish the child's rule violation as the point of the story. For instance, one of the longest co-narrations in the Chinese corpus began with the caregiver directing the two-and-a-half-year-old child to tell Aunty (the researcher) why she had gotten spanked the day before. Through a series of queries from the caregiver and responses from the child, it was established that the child had interrupted a church meeting and was punished for her misdeed. The story ended with the child's explicit commitment not to disrupt church meetings. This co-constructed story was thus bounded at the beginning by the caregiver's demand that the child confess and at the end by the child's promise not to transgress in the future.

Although values pervaded the stories in the white middle-class American corpus, none forefronted the child's transgression in this way. For example, a two-and-a-half-year-old initiated a story about going to the dentist to have her tooth pulled and about the ensuing visit from the tooth fairy. A rule violation was referenced only once, as the final contribution to the co-narration: an older sibling said, "Mollie was eating bad food so she had to go to the dentist and he had to pull the tooth out." Both the placement of this contribution and the fact that no one commented or elaborated upon it, rendered the rule violation peripheral to the main action of the story.

The second set of parameters has to do with whether and how personal storytelling is made available to children. For example, censorship of story topic on behalf of children appears to differ, occurring less frequently in the poorer communities. However, there are also important similarities: personal storytelling occurred routinely as part of everyday family life not only in South Baltimore, but also in the five communities in our comparative study. In addition, children in all these communities were exposed to personal storytelling in several ways: stories were told *with* young children as co-narrators, *about* young children as ratified participants, and *around* young children as co-present others (see Miller in press for further details). By the age of two-and-a-half years, children participated verbally in these practices (Miller and Sperry 1988; Miller et al. 1990; Miller et al. 1992).

The Narrated Self as Relational Self

In addition to these findings concerning the widespread, frequent, and varied practice of personal storytelling during the preschool years, another insight gained from this work is that the narrated self is a relational self, that is, a self that is defined in relation to others. This was evident in all three types of exposure to stories. And it was evident at multiple levels of analysis. For example, we found that both younger (two-and-a-half years) and older (five years) preschoolers located the self in a social nexus when co-narrating or telling stories *with* another person (Miller et al. 1992). (Each age group in this study consisted of three children from each of the following communities: low-income African American, working-class white, and middle-class white in Chicago and middle-class Chinese in Taipei.) In other words, the child portrayed himself or herself as "being with" another person in some past event. At the same time, the child was "being with" another person in the present, that is, in the very act of co-narrating the past event.

Moreover, these levels of relatedness were connected. This was evident, for example, in the use of social comparison as a means of defining self and other: not only did the majority of social comparisons of self and other occur when a sibling or peer participated in the co-narration, but the focal child was usually compared with siblings or peers in the recounted event. A link is thereby established between the event of narration (who participated in the co-narration) and the narrated event (what was talked about). In addition, at times the narrator altered her account of her own past experience, depending on what the co-narrator said. For example, after her mother challenged her version of a fight with another child, a two-and-a-half-year-old from West Side (a low- income African American community in Chicago) reversed her claim about who hit first. Andrea: "No, she fight me. I—I hit her BACK." Mother: "Because YOU hit her first. You don't hit her back, you hit her first." Andrea: "I hit her first. . . ."

The relational nature of narrated selves was also apparent when personal stories were told *about* young children (Miller in press). In this practice, a family member addressed a story to another person in the child's presence, referring to the child in the third person. The narrator cast the child as the story protagonist and often drew him or her into the narration as a ratified participant by asking questions. When family members told stories in this way, they provided interpretations of the child's own actions, linking those actions to someone else's prior actions, to the child's subjective experiences, and to the interpersonal consequences. They personalized for the child the culture's interpretive strategies by applying them to the child's own experiences.

Even telling stories *around* the child—in which caregivers addressed stories of their own personal experience to other people in the child's presence—is plausibly relevant to children's self-construction. Through this practice, children are exposed to narrated interpersonal dramas in which the most important people in their lives communicate who they are (Miller in press). For many children, these stories constitute a steadily available and constantly updated resource about significant others. A child who has achieved a minimal ability to comprehend oral stories and who is inclined to listen can gain access to otherwise inaccessible experiences: those that are temporally inaccessible (What happened to my mother before I was born?), spatially inaccessible (How did my older brother fare in school?), and affectively-cognitively inaccessible (Why did my uncle punch my grandfather?).

Implications of Personal Storytelling at Home

In sum, our research on personal storytelling within a model of socialization that privileges discourse practices led us to see that, although children from different cultural and socioeconomic backgrounds encountered different definitions of personal storytelling and somewhat different norms of exposure, all participated in a complex, varied, and recurring network of narrative practices that mediated family-child relations on a daily basis. By the time they entered kindergarten, they had experienced several years of involvement in personal storytelling, both as listeners and narrators. It had become a mode of organizing their experiences that was second nature to them.

From these studies we also learned something about the process of self-construction. When a type of discourse—personal storytelling—is taken as the unit of analysis and when it is examined as a set of situated practices, the narrated self emerges as a relational self. This insight, in conjunction with the finding of daily recurrence, suggests that personal storytelling is an important means by which young children, together with family members, experience and reexperience self in relation to other. They suggest that a comprehensive account of self-development would have to be much more dynamic than has previously been envisioned: it would have to take into account not only the child's moment-by-moment interpersonal encounters, but his or her participation in iterative narrations of those encounters, which are themselves embedded in moment-by-moment interpersonal encounters.

Personal Storytelling in Kindergarten Classrooms

These are some of the implications we see for a theory of self-construction. What about the implications for children as they move from the family into school? If, as we have argued, selves are relational, then as children enter school, they face the new task of understanding self in relation to teacher and fellow students and of coordinating who they are at home with who they are at school. How are these tasks accomplished? Are they accomplished through the same type of narrative discourse that flourished in the child's preschool home environment? To answer these questions, we undertook an ethnographic study of kindergarten classrooms.

The classrooms we studied are located in the same white working-class community where we are studying personal storytelling at home. Daly Park (a pseudonym) is a largely Catholic community whose members are of Polish, Irish, and German descent, with a growing minority of Hispanic families. Daily contact with kin is common, and intergenerational families often occupy separate floors in the same row house. Many of the parents grew up in Daly Park and attended the same elementary school that their children now attend.

The second author made weekly observations in three of the six elementary schools in the community (one public and two parochial schools). These observations, which were audio-recorded, spanned a period of four months in one classroom and a year and a half in the other two. The rationale for this design was twofold. First, we chose to study several classrooms in order to determine whether we could make generalizations about how personal stories were used in kindergarten classrooms in this community. Second, the longitudinal design permitted us to observe the ongoing process of self-construction and of changes over the academic year.

Among the three classrooms, we found a great deal of variation in the extent to which personal experience was incorporated into classroom talk. One of the parochial classrooms did not have any regular child-oriented speech events; the children's only official oral activity took the form of responses to tutorial questions posed by the teacher. In the public school classroom, show-and-tell occurred daily, but was not defined as a narrative activity. Instead, each child took a turn describing in a few brief sentences some object that he or she had brought from home. By contrast, in the second parochial classroom, personal storytelling occurred much more frequently and across a number of different events. Not surprisingly, variation in incidence seemed to be related to class size. The classroom where personal narrative occurred most frequently had a teacher-pupil ratio of 1:14, compared with 1:22 and 1:25 in the other classrooms.

Even in the smaller class, many of the references to the children's personal experience consisted of narrative fragments or brief allusions to past events. Very few personal stories either by teacher or children were as complex as those told in homes, and almost none were as fully performed. Tizard and Hughes (1984) and Wells (1986) reported parallel findings for talk in general for both working-class and middle-class children. Thus "talk of personal experience," rather than "personal storytelling," more accurately describes what we saw in this classroom.

We identified several ways in which talk of personal experience functioned in this classroom. From the beginning of the school year, both teacher and students drew connections between the child's personal experiences with others out of school and the moral and educational lessons of the classroom. The teacher frequently made such connections during "bible-rug time," a daily event when the whole class gathered together for opening prayers and discussion. Similar to sharing-time (Michaels 1981, 1986), this was a time when the children were encouraged to report on experiences that had happened outside the classroom. Although the event was defined in terms of an individual child as speaker, it was also highly collaborative: the teacher not only held the floor for the student, but asked questions, evaluated the child's responses, and elaborated on the experience. During the process, she frequently interpreted the child's out-of-school experience with others in terms of the moral framework of the classroom, often by recasting the child's personal ("I") experience in collective ("we") terms.

For example, after Mary had recounted her experience of having her tonsils removed, the teacher recast the experience in terms of evaluative generalizations about doctors and how they make "us" well:

> *Teacher:* Were you scared of that hospital?
>
> *Child:* No.
>
> *Teacher:* Do you think hospitals are mean places?
>
> *Child:* No.
>
> *Teacher:* No, or doctors? Are doctors mean? Are they mean to people?
>
> *Child:* They make us well.
>
> *Teacher:* That's right. They give us shots to make us well.

In events like these, not only did the moral framework of the classroom get constructed through the joint participation of teacher and child, but the child's self got positioned and defined relative to the teacher as spokesperson for that framework. A link is thus made from the child's interpersonal experience with doctors outside the classroom to the moral framework inside the classroom, from the child's (past) experience of self in relation to doctors to a self who aligns herself or himself in the (present) narrating event with the teacher's perspective on that past experience.

At other times during the day, the teacher made connections in the opposite direction, that is, from a general lesson to the child's interpersonal experiences outside the classroom. For example, during a lesson about baptism, the teacher drew an analogy between the concept of God's family and the child's family, inviting each child to say who belonged to his or her family.

As the academic year progressed, we heard more talk about the children's past experiences in the classroom itself. Teacher and children recounted events that had happened to the class collectively (e.g., a field trip) or to individuals in the class. The teacher also concretized and affirmed the morals of written stories by linking them to one or another child's experience in the classroom. For example, while reading a book aloud to the whole class, the teacher contrasted the "nice" behavior of the story characters with the aggressive behavior of a student who had injured another child in the classroom two days earlier. Also, the children increasingly invoked the teacher's voice of moral authority in their commerce with one another, especially in the context of peer conflict and tattletaling. On these personally urgent occasions, they recounted a peer's misdeeds or justified their own actions by referring to the rules of the classroom. At the same time, they negotiated who they were in relation to others, aligning themselves with or distancing themselves from one another and from the teacher.

Another type of personal storytelling that increased across the school year reflected the children's growing awareness of their own history as learners in the classroom. Five months into the school year, three students were talking to one another as they sat around a table doing their worksheets. They discussed how the teacher had shown them the correct way of writing at the beginning of the year. They also compared themselves favorably with the younger, unschooled children at the local day care center. They then made a series of matching claims, accompanied by written demonstrations, about how they used to make their letters: Heidi: "I used to make a four when I was in . . . class. I used to go like that." Mary: "This is how I used to make a four." A bit later, Mary added, "I used to make my threes like that. Or like that. Now I make it like that." In this interaction, the children not only made autobiographical claims concerning the self as learner in the classroom, but established an alliance among peers through matching claims to similar autobiographical experiences as learners. Happily, in this instance the children seemed to see themselves as eager and able learners.

In sum, these observations in three kindergarten classrooms in one urban, working-class community revealed that personal narrative occurred only in the classroom with the most favorable teacher-pupil ratio. That classroom did not provide as rich a context for personal narrative as did many families in the same community. Rarely if ever was storytelling practiced for its own sake during class, although such performances may well have occurred on the playground or in sub-rosa peer talk. When students and teacher did refer to the child's past experience, it was often in the service of an instructional goal. Accounts of personal experience were used to mediate between the child's experiences outside the classroom and the moral and educational framework of the classroom. At the same time, the child got positioned in that framework in relation to teacher and fellow students. In addition, the children used narrative increasingly to organize their experiences in school and to negotiate an identity in relation to teachers and peers. Peer-produced autobiographies of the self as learner were especially interesting in this respect.

Establishing a comfortable identity in school is surely part of what it means to get off to a good start in school. Although our findings suggest that recounting personal experiences is one route by which this goal can be supported, we do not mean to imply that it is the only route. It would be difficult to overemphasize the importance of students' day-by-day experiences of achievement and failure in the classroom, quite apart from whether those experiences are replayed in narrative. Nor do we mean to imply that talk of personal experience is necessarily positive for the child. There is just as much potential for undermining as for supporting identity, both at the content level (e.g., by repeatedly recounting experiences of failure, making invidious comparisons between the child's past experiences and peers' experiences or between home and school) and at the discourse level (e.g., by using styles of discourse that interfere with those that children bring from home) (Michaels 1981, 1986).

Despite these cautions, we believe that personal storytelling deserves more attention from researchers and teachers because it is a type of discourse that many preschoolers from diverse backgrounds know and appreciate. In particular, more attention should be paid to personal storytelling as highly performed verbal art. Storytelling for its own sake, as opposed to talk of personal experience, did not occur in "official" classroom talk during any of our observations. Yet it may well be important to the process of self-construction for those children whose impulse to narrate first takes root in personal storytelling at home.

References

Allen, R. V. (1976). *Language experiences in communication.* Boston: Houghton Mifflin.

Bauman, R. (1986). *Story, performance, and event: Contextual studies of oral narrative.* New York: Cambridge University Press.

Bruner, J. (1984). Language, mind, and reading. In H. Goelman, A. A. Oberg, and F. Smith (Eds.), *Awakening to literacy* (193–200). Portsmouth, NH: Heinemann.

Calkins, L. M. (1982). *Lessons from a child: On the teaching and learning of writing.* Portsmouth, NH: Heinemann.

Eisenberg, A. (1985). Learning to describe past experiences in conversation. *Discourse Processes, 8,* 177–204.

Gumperz, J. J., and Hymes, D. (1972). *Directions in sociolinguistics: The ethnography of communication.* New York: Holt, Rinehart, & Winston.

Heath, S. B. (1983). *Ways with words: Language, life and work in communities and classrooms.* New York: Cambridge University Press.

Hymes, D. (1975). Breakthrough into performance. In D. Ben-Amos and K. S. Goldstein (Eds.), *Folklore: Performance and communication* (11–74). The Hague, Netherlands: Mouton.

Maclean, N. (1976). *A river runs through it.* Chicago: University of Chicago Press.

Michaels, S. (1981). "Sharing time": Children's narrative styles and differential access to literacy. *Language in Society, 10,* 423–442.

———. (1986). Narrative presentations: An oral preparation for literacy with first graders. In J. Cook-Gumperz (Ed.), *The social construction of literacy* (94–116). New York: Cambridge University Press.

Miller, P. J. (1982). *Amy, Wendy, and Beth: Learning language in South Baltimore.* Austin: University of Texas Press.

———. (1989, October). *Socialization through narrative.* Paper presented at the meeting of the Society for Psychological Anthropology, San Diego, CA.

———. (in press). Narrative practices: Their role in socialization and self construction. In U. Neisser and R. Fivush (Eds.), *The remembering self.* New York: Cambridge University Press.

Miller, P. J., Fung, H., and Mintz, J. (1991, October). *Creating children's selves in relational contexts: A comparison of American and Chinese narrative practices.* Paper presented at the meeting of the Society for Psychological Anthropology, Chicago.

Miller, P. J., Mintz, J., Hoogstra, L., Fung, H., and Potts, R. (1992). The narrated self: Young children's construction of self in relation to others in conversational stories of personal experience. *Merrill-Palmer Quarterly, 38,* 45–67.

Miller, P. J., and Moore, B. B. (1989). Narrative conjunctions of caregiver and child: A comparative perspective on socialization through stories. *Ethos, 17,* 428–449.

Miller, P. J., Potts, R., Fung, H., Hoogstra, L., and Mintz J. (1990). Narrative practices and the social construction of self in childhood. *American Ethnologist, 17,* 292–311.

Miller, P. J., and Sperry, L. L. (1987). The socialization of anger and aggression. *Merrill-Palmer Quarterly, 33,* 1–31.

———. (1988). Early talk about the past: The origins of conversational stories of personal experience. *Journal of Child Language, 15,* 293–315.

Morgan, K. L. (1989). Caddy buffers: Legends of a middle class black family in Philadelphia. In L. Goss and M. E. Barnes (Eds.), *Talk that talk* (295–298). New York: Simon & Schuster.

Ochs, E., and Taylor, C. (1992). Family narrative as political activity. *Discourse and Society, 3,* 301–340.

Ochs, E., and Schieffelin, B. B. (1984). Language acquisition and socialization: Three developmental stories and their implications. In R. A. Shweder and R. A. LeVine (Eds.), *Culture theory* (276–320). New York: Cambridge University Press.

Rogoff, B. (1991). The joint socialization of development by young children and adults. In M. Lewis and S. Feinman (Eds.), *Social influences and socialization in infancy,* (253–280). New York: Plenum.

Rosen, H. (1988). The irrepressible genre. In M. MacLure, T. Phillips, and A. Wilkinson (Eds.), *Oracy matters: The development of talking and listening in education* (13–23). Philadelphia: Open Press.

Schieffelin, B. B., and Ochs, E. (1986). Language socialization. In B. Siegel (Ed.), *Annual Review of Anthropology* (163–191). Palo Alto, CA: Annual Reviews.

Shweder, R. A., and Much, N. C. (1987). Determinations of meaning: Discourse and moral socialization. In W. Kurtines and J. Gewirtz (Eds.), *Moral development through social interaction* (197–244). New York: Wiley.

Snow, C. E., De Temple, J. M., Beals, D. E., Dickinson, D. K., Smith, M. W., and Tabors, P. O. (1991, April). *The social prerequisites of literacy development.* Symposium presented at the annual meeting of the American Educational Research Association, Chicago.

Sperry, L. (1991). *The emergence and development of narrative competence in African-American toddlers from a rural Alabama community.* Unpublished doctoral dissertation, University of Chicago.

Tizard, B., and Hughes, M. (1984). *Young children learning.* Cambridge, MA: Harvard University Press.

Vygotsky, L. (1934/1987). *Thinking and speech* (N. Minick, Trans.). New York: Plenum.

Wells, G. (1986). The language experience of 5-year-old children at home and at school. In J. Cook-Gumperz (Ed.), *The social construction of literacy* (69–93). Cambridge: Cambridge University Press.

Welty, E. (1984). *One writer's beginnings.* Cambridge, MA: Harvard University Press.

Wertsch, J. V. (1985). *Vygotsky and the social formation of mind.* Cambridge, MA: Harvard University Press.

Zeitlin, S., Kotlin, A., and Baker, H. (1982). *A celebration of American family folklore: Tales and traditions from the Smithsonian collection.* New York: Pantheon.

Ways with Stories:
Whose Stories Are Told?
Whose Stories Are Heard?

5 Multicultural Literature for Children: Towards a Clarification of the Concept

Mingshui Cai
University of Northern Iowa

Rudine Sims Bishop
The Ohio State University

Mingshui Cai and Rudine Sims Bishop take on the challenge of defining the concept of multicultural literature. *They acknowledge the need for a broad range of literatures representing many vantage points, and they also argue for the literature of* parallel cultures, *whose members articulate the necessary "insider's perspective."*

Multicultural literature is a concept in search of a definition. It would be difficult to pinpoint its origin, but it may be safe to assume that the term *multicultural literature* came after the advent of the multicultural education movement in the 1960s (Banks 1979). With the advance of multicultural education in the last decade, multicultural literature has begun to flourish. Many publishers of children's books, responding to this trend, have created fliers listing the "multicultural" titles they publish. Their definition of multicultural literature is implicit in the selection of books included on their lists. Typically, such lists contain a wide variety of works, including translations of popular board books for preschool children into languages other than English, stories about European immigrants to the United States, stories set in countries in all parts of the world, nonfiction about peoples and places, and literature about racial or ethnic groups within the United States. Educators and librarians have variously defined multicultural literature as works that focus on "people of color" (Kruse and Horning 1990, vii) or "books other than those of the dominant culture" (Jenkins 1973, 50). What all these definitions have in common is an agreement that multicultural literature is about some identifiable "other"—persons or groups that differ in some way (for example, racially, linguistically, ethnically, culturally) from the dominant white American cultural group. With so much variety, however, it becomes difficult, if not impossible, to discern the defining characteristics of multicultural literature.

This problem may exist because, as it is generally conceived, the definition of multicultural literature is contingent not on its literary characteristics, but on the purposes it is supposed to serve. The literature is one component of the multicultural education movement and is generally intended to further the goals of that movement. Multicultural education is essentially a reform effort intended not only to combat intolerance and foster a sense of inclusion, but to fundamentally change education and society. According to Banks (1991), the most important goal of multicultural education is "helping students to acquire the competencies and commitments to participate in effective civic action in order to create equitable national societies" (28). Even more explicitly, Nieto (1992) places multicultural education in a sociopolitical context and defines it this way:

> Multicultural education is a process of comprehensive school reform and basic education for all students. It challenges and rejects racism and other forms of discrimination in schools and society and accepts and affirms the pluralism (ethnic, racial, linguistic, religious, economic, and gender, among others) that permeates the curriculum and instructional strategies used in schools, as well as the interactions among teachers, students and parents, and the very way that schools conceptualize the nature of teaching and learning. Because it uses critical pedagogy as its underlying philosophy and focuses on knowledge, reflection, and action (praxis) as the basis for social change, multicultural education furthers the democratic principles of social justice. (208)

If multicultural literature is to serve the cause of educational reform, then clarifying the concept and identifying its characteristics is not an intellectual exercise, but a vital necessity.

It is interesting to note that, among the curricular components of multicultural education, the label "multicultural" seems to be reserved for literature and to a lesser extent the arts. Professional educational journals do not generally contain references to "multicultural social studies" or "multicultural history." This may be because literature and the arts reach beyond the intellect to appeal to the affect. Some time ago, Dorsey (1977) pointed out the importance of literature in a pluralistic society. The juxtaposition of diverse cultural groups, he argued, inevitably leads to interference in communication among groups, which can be overcome only if individuals can transcend their own cultural limitations:

> Sociology and anthropology never seek this end. Their function is to rationalize alien social structures without disturbing the student's commitment to his own. Literature seeks and attains a deeper empathy with the alien, an empathy which challenges one's own most basic presuppositions. (18)

> At present diversity is everywhere tolerated in theory, punished in practice, and nowhere justified or justifiable beyond an appeal to solipsism. But America has no choice. Only a genuinely pluralistic society can henceforth prosper here. It must be nurtured in our diverse hearts. And for that we need literature, which is the language of the heart. (19)

Literature, then, is expected to play a unique role within the context of multicultural education.

Pedagogical Definitions

Generally, educators (e.g., Norton 1987; Austin and Jenkins 1983) who are committed to using literature as a means of furthering the cause of multicultural education share Dorsey's view. They offer long lists of the values of multicultural literature. Defining the term, however, is a more complicated problem. When we conceive multicultural literature in terms of the purposes it might serve in the curriculum, we are approaching the theoretical problem of definition from an educator's perspective. We are less concerned with the nature of the literature itself than with the way it can function in school settings. In this sense, *multicultural literature* is a pedagogical term, rather than a literary one. Rather than suggesting unifying literary characteristics, the term implies a goal: challenging the existing canon by expanding the curriculum to include literature from a wide variety of cultural groups. Controversy over the classic canon exists in the academic literary community as well. Viewed in a global context, the controversy is among countries over what constitutes the world canon of classics. Within the United States or other English-speaking countries, the controversy is between the dominant and nondominant groups. The question raised is: Should the literary works of the best writers from nondominant groups such as African Americans, Hispanics, Chinese Americans, and women also be included in the canon of American literature and taught in English departments? Multicultural literature programs in precollege settings can be seen in part as a continuation or duplication of the efforts to include ethnic literatures in the curriculum in colleges. The difference is that English departments do not typically offer multicultural or multiethnic literature courses; they offer "world literatures" or ethnic or "minority"[1] literature courses.

In the strictest sense of the term, multicultural literature should include the literature of the dominant cultural group, just as world literature should also include American literature. Taken literally, both multicultural literature and world literature are identical with literature per se—the literary creation of humanity. The significance of the labels lies in their indication of the pluralistic nature of American society and of the world, and thus of the rationale for including literatures from historically underrepresented, nondominant groups and countries in the curriculum.

That this is so can be seen in a definition of multiethnic[2] literature by Carlson (1972) and accepted by Norton (1987): "Multiethnic literature is the literature about a racial or minority ethnic group that is culturally and socially different from the white Anglo-Saxon majority in the United States, whose largely middle-class values are most represented in all American literature" (503). This definition is self-contradictory. If multicultural literature is the literature about *a* "racial or minority ethnic" group, why is it called *multi*cultural? How does it differ from "minority or ethnic" (for example, Mexican American or African American) literature? In the third edition of *Through the Eyes of a Child*, Norton (1991) changes Carlson's definition to: "Multicultural literature is literature about various minority ethnic groups that are culturally and socially different from the white Anglo-Saxon majority in the United States" (530). Here, the term does not indicate the multicultural nature of any single work, but of a category of works. It is an educator's term, used to imply a challenge to the domination of one cultural group and its literature in the curriculum.

A Literary Definition

Given the great variety represented by books placed under the rubric "multicultural," it is difficult to define multicultural literature in terms of literary features such as theme, structure, language, or style. Dasenbrock (1987), however, in a piece on multicultural literature in English, offers a two-part definition that does focus on the intrinsic nature of the literature itself. He uses the term multicultural literature "to include both works that are explicitly about multicultural societies and those that are implicitly multicultural in the sense of inscribing readers from other cultures inside their [the works'] own cultural dynamics" (10).

The word "societies" in the first part of Dasenbrock's definition refers to societies in the English-speaking world, which use the same language, but have diverse cultural heritages. But what he means by "a multicultural society" is unclear. Does it refer to a whole country with multiple cultures or an ethnic group whose members, by virtue of the nature of their interactions with other groups, may assimilate more than one culture and may therefore be bicultural or even multicultural? Given the second part of Dasenbrock's definition, multicultural literature would include almost all literature that is written in English. The first type is subsumed under the second: "the explicitly multicultural is also implicitly multicultural" (10).

The linguistic medium is the defining element here. Dasenbrock states that "literature in English has become increasingly cross- or multicultural, as writing about a given culture is destined—because of its language, English, and its place of publication, usually London or New York—to have readers of many other cultures" (10). The four books he analyzes as typical examples are by writers from diverse cultures and areas: R. K. Narayan (Indian), Maxine Hong Kingston (Chinese American), Rudolfo Anaya (Mexican American), and Witi Ihimaera (Maori). Although these authors are all writing about their own cultures, presumably with both a Western or dominant majority audience and a "local" audience in mind, according to Dasenbrock's definition, multicultural literature may also include texts about Western or dominant majority cultures with references to "minority" or "Third World" societies, or with members of such groups as their intended audience.

From an educator's perspective, this kind of multicultural literature may not be in tune with the goals of multicultural education, for some literary works by writers of mainstream cultures either in the English-speaking world in general or in the United States in particular may "inscribe" readers from dominated groups "inside their own textual dynamics" for the purpose of indoctrinating them with mainstream cultural values. In fact, many literary works, including such classics as Shakespeare's *Merchant of Venice* or Mark Twain's *Huckleberry Finn*, may fit Dasenbrock's definition, but exhibit anti-Semitism or racism.

Advocates of multicultural literature are well aware that such literature may be tainted by racism and other negative attitudes, most obviously shown in the stereotyping of people of color and in the presentation of ethnocentric perspectives. The criteria they set up for selecting multicultural literature invariably include "avoiding stereotypes" and "presenting minority perspectives" (e.g., Council on Interracial Books for Children 1974; Klein 1985; Rudman 1984; Norton 1991). That well-written books may need to be examined for such nonliterary factors demonstrates the tension between pedagogical and literary approaches to defining the term multicultural literature.

At this point, it may be best to hold onto the pedagogical definition because it is already widely circulated in educational institutions and serves as a banner in multicultural education. For purposes of this paper, the pedagogical definitions—those referring to literature about underrepresented groups—will serve as an important foundation. Keeping in mind the tension between pedagogical and literary aspects of the term, however, we have attempted to move toward clarifying the concept of multicultural literature by suggesting that it is an umbrella term that includes at least three kinds of literature: world literature, cross-cultural literature, and "minority" literature or literature from parallel cultures.[3]

"World Literature"

As we pointed out earlier, the term *world literature,* logically interpreted, would include all literature, as would the term *multicultural literature.* We have also tried to make clear, however, that these terms as they are generally used today in the United States are essentially pedagogical, or even political, implying at the very least an intent to include the literatures of underrepresented peoples, American and otherwise, in the curriculum of schools in the United States. From that perspective, we would narrow our own definition of "world" literature to include folktales, fiction, and the like from non-Western countries or other underrepresented groups outside the United States, generally peoples from the Southern or Eastern Hemispheres. We would include in this category adaptations by American writers, but not necessarily the European classics such as Hans Christian Andersen's tales, because they are hardly underrepresented in the literature curriculum. Thus Snyder's retelling of the Japanese tale *The Boy of the Three-Year Nap* (1988) would be categorized as world literature, as would translations of books which originated in relevant places, such as Schami's *A Handful of Stars* (1990), an autobiographical novel set in

Damascus, Syria. In spite of the inadequacy of the label, this could be a useful category, because many educators who define multicultural literature in terms of its focus on members of nondominant cultural groups in the United States still include folklore and other literature from what might be considered the "root cultures" of those groups. Educators who write about African American literature, for example, usually include African folktales in their discussions, and those who write about Chinese American literature include Chinese folktales.

Cross-Cultural Literature

One way to circumscribe the conflict between pedagogical and literary definitions is to narrow the conceptual boundary of Dasenbrock's definition of multicultural literature to include only (1) literary works explicitly about interrelations among people of different cultures, without apparent focus on the unique experience of any one culture or cultural group, and (2) those about people from a given cultural group by a writer from another cultural group. We may term these kinds of literary works "cross-cultural" literature. This label suggests that there exist cultural gaps in the world that need to be crossed and, more importantly, that there may be gaps between the author's cultural perspective embodied in the literary work and the cultural perspective of the people his or her work portrays.

In children's literature, a large number of books fall into the first subcategory. Their intention seems to be to inculcate acceptance of cultural diversity or to foster constructive intercultural or interracial relationships. The depth and scope of their explorations vary, as does the extent to which they are successful in engendering the desired effects. An example of the most superficial is Baer's picture book entitled *This Is the Way We Go to School: A Book about Children around the World* (1990), which compares the different ways children go to school in twenty-two countries. The subject is interesting and the illustrations are appealing to young children, but although the book may be informative about cultural differences, it does not touch the heart. A more touching book of this kind is Friedman's *How My Parents Learned to Eat* (1984). It tells how a child's American father, a sailor, met her Japanese mother, a schoolgirl, in Japan and overcame the barrier of cultural difference to get married. But the difference, the center of the plot conflict, is only reflected in ways of eating—with chopsticks or with a knife and fork.

Unlike these two books, some others deal with cross-cultural issues in the United States, such as the difficulties a child from an ethnic minority group encounters in adjusting to a new cultural environment or to serious interracial conflicts. An example of the former is Surat's *Angel Child, Dragon Child* (1989), which is about a Vietnamese girl's difficulties associating with her classmates after her family moved to the United States. Many examples of the latter type are older books published during the 1960s and early 1970s when the Civil Rights Movement of that era was receiving much attention. A typical example is *The Empty Schoolhouse* (Carlson 1965), a story about school desegregation. A more recent book that deals with interracial tensions is Spinelli's 1991 Newbery Medal winner, *Maniac Magee* (1990), which features a white, larger-than-life hero who, despite becoming alienated from both the black and white communities in a small Pennsylvania city, manages to bring both communities together.

Still other books in this category seem to promote acceptance of diversity by simply visually focusing on or including characters from differing racial or cultural backgrounds or by building a story about such characters on some topic unrelated to racial prejudice or other such conflicts. Their intent seems to be to promote respect for racial and cultural diversity. Such a book is Jones's *Matthew and Tilly* (1991), which focuses on the friendship between a white boy and an African American girl. They have a spat over a broken crayon, but discover that they miss each other and that their friendship is more important than anything so trivial.

The second type of cross-cultural children's literature, for the most part, contains works by white writers about the experience of people from parallel cultures. They do not simply center around inter-relations between cultures; they attempt to depict the unique experience of characters from parallel cultural groups by reflecting the consciousness and sensibility of people who are members of those groups. One example is Levine's picture book *I Hate English* (1989), which portrays a Chinese girl's attitude towards the English language when she moved to the United States from Hong Kong with her family. Another is the popular *Knots on a Counting Rope* (Martin 1987), a story about a blind Native American boy and his grandfather. Both books are written from the perspective of the main characters and try to delineate their thoughts and feelings, as well as their experiences. The defining feature of this category is the authors' attempt to look at the experience of a member of a parallel cultural group other than their own from inside that experience. Authors do not always succeed. In *I*

Hate English, we hear a false note oversimplifying the theme of identity. In the British colony of Hong Kong, English is the instructional language in most schools, and the girl seems to have learned the language quite well. Slapin and Seale (1989) criticize *Knots on a Counting Rope* as being marred by the author's ignorance of the cultures of native peoples and its catering to romanticized mythology about Native Americans.

Banks (1979) proposed a hierarchical typology of cross-cultural competency, that is, "skills and understandings necessary to function cross-culturally" (249). We may use this typology to evaluate the cross-cultural competence of writers and see if they are able to represent a culture from its unique perspective. Banks has four levels of competence: (1) "the individual experiences superficial and brief cross-cultural interaction; (2) the individual begins to assimilate some of the symbols and characteristics of the 'outside' ethnic group; (3) the individual is thoroughly bicultural; (4) the individual is completely assimilated into the new ethnic culture" (251). The fourth level represents the ultimate cross-cultural competence. It occurs only "when the primordial individual has been almost completely resocialized" and becomes one with the "host culture in terms of behavior, attitude, and perceptions" (250). The acquisition of the cultural perspective, as we understand it, marks the attainment of this level. Banks's typology was designed to set up goals of cross-competence for students, yet we may wonder who among white writers writing about minority experience can claim to have attained that level.

The authors' level of cross-cultural competency usually is not clearly shown in picture books or shorter books. The test lies in the longer books, which cover a wider range of experiences. The authors often betray their alien perspective in small details, the representation of which requires a native's (often unconscious) sensibility more than acquired knowledge. The white authors' ethnocentric attitude is also revealed in these subtle details, in spite of their good intentions. For example, as Thompson and Woodard (1985) point out, in *The Empty Schoolhouse* the narrator's remarks about skin and hair betray "the subtle and probably unconscious perspective which presents a young black girl in terms of self-hatred and a feeling that white is preferable to dark" (43). Emma Royall says, "Her [Lullah's] skin is like coffee and cream mixed together and she has wavy hair to her shoulders. Me, I'm dark as Daddy Jobe and my hair never grew out much longer than he wears his." That this comparison implies appraisal is footnoted by her comment on her brother: "Little Jobe looks like me and Daddy Jobe, but he's a handsome boy all the same." What sounds like appreciation of her little brother's features is in fact racial self-deprecation.

The Slapin and Seale book (1989) contains a review of another novel, Wallin's *Ceremony of the Panther* (1987), which demonstrates the difficulty of attaining a high level of cross-cultural competency. Even though the reviewer recognizes that the author's sympathies are clearly with the people about whom he writes and judges the book to be well written, the reviewer still finds it not quite on the mark:

> For a Native reader, the rhythm is off; . . . there are jarring notes. For example, "The old Miccosukee world was a dangerous place [compared to what, I wonder], full of spirits and enemies and magical warfare." He tells us that Grandmother Mary "had been a great medicine woman," and refers to her "spells." Native rites are no more "spells" than are the ceremonies of the Judeo-Christian tradition. (Slapin and Seale 1989, 370)

The final judgment of the reviewer is that Wallin "has attempted to draw contrasts between modern and traditional ways of living without being able to give the spirit and feel of it" (372).

Parallel Culture Literature

The final category we propose is parallel culture literature. This is literature written by authors from parallel cultural groups to represent the experience, consciousness, and self-image developed as a result of being acculturated and socialized within those groups. Like language and art, literature is an essential part of a people's heritage. In this sense, parallel culture literature is the literature *of* a cultural group. "Outsiders" may write *about* a cultural group, may do so with great skill, and may produce a meritorious work, but their works do not belong to the group unless they have been accepted as a group member. A history of the literature of a parallel culture will not include books by these "outsiders." We distinguish national literatures in the same way. Can a successful book about American culture by an Australian be considered American literature? Of course not. The controversy around insider-outsider difference that haunts children's literature is not so prominent in adult literature. How many white writers have ever entered the annals of the adult literatures of American peoples of color?

Parallel culture literature, it should be pointed out, is not the same as the second subcategory of cross-cultural literature. This was made clear in an earlier analysis. In an examination of the representation of African American experience in 150 realistic fiction books for children, Bishop (Sims [Bishop] 1982), divided the surveyed books into three categories: social conscience books, melting-pot books, and culturally conscious books. The categories were derived from an analysis based on three factors: intended audience, presumed concept of African American culture, and the author's implied sociocultural perspective. Social conscience books, all of which were written by white writers, mainly dealt with black-white conflicts such as those centered on desegregating schools and communities. Most of those books were marred by ignorance, paternalism, or racism. The melting-pot books centered on racial and cultural integration or homogenization. Some of these were marred by paternalism, and all excluded any unique African American cultural perspective. Both types of books, in terms of the categories we propose in this chapter, would be considered cross-cultural or intercultural. The third of the Sims [Bishop] categories, the culturally conscious books, tried to capture something of the uniqueness of African American experience. Twenty-eight percent of those books were written by white authors and in the present classification would also be considered cross-cultural. This type of cross-cultural literature is distinguished from the literature of a parallel culture by the authors' alien ethnic identity and often also by varying degrees of the authors' alienation from the perspective of the native culture they write about.

A cultural group's perspective is its world outlook, shaped by its shared experience, "collective memories and frames of reference" (Blauner, cited in Sims [Bishop] 1982, 9). A literary work is inevitably informed and infused with the author's perspective, reflected in "the choice of detail to include, the descriptions of things and people, the things that are emphasized or de-emphasized" (Sims [Bishop] 1984). This perspective is not easy to define in abstract terms because it is not only registered in apparent values, beliefs, and attitudes, but is also embodied in subtle perceptions, feelings, emotions, gestures, and behaviors. A perspective in this sense cannot be learned solely from books about a cultural group; it can be acquired only from experience, from immersion in that culture. Yet in the Sims [Bishop] survey, only 47 percent of the books about African Americans were written from an "insider's perspective."

To stress the difficulty of acquiring a cultural group's perspective does not mean to deny outsiders the right to portray that cultural group. It is meant to emphasize the need for outsiders to fill in the cultural gap themselves before they can close it for others. It is also meant to point to the fact that literature from parallel cultural groups has a unique role to play in multicultural literature programs, because writers from those groups best represent their own cultures. To promote understanding of parallel cultural groups and to help students from those groups develop a sense of cultural identity and value their cultural heritage, we should first choose works from the literatures of parallel cultures. Well-intended and well-written cross-cultural books will also help, but they must be chosen with care and caution.

The 1982 analysis may have offered a guide for examining books about other groups, and it may yet be useful for those examining books about other parallel cultures in the United States. Placing the earlier analysis in the larger context of multicultural literature, however, demonstrates that many works of cross-cultural literature may not serve the purposes of multicultural education, for instead of dispelling ignorance and prejudice, as they intend, they may reinforce them.

The value of parallel culture literature in multicultural education should be clear, particularly in the social context of the United States. Multicultural education was introduced as an answer to the challenges of a culturally diverse society. From a global perspective, multicultural education may promote cultural awareness and appreciation among young people of the world, including the United States. But the more immediate concern for this country is interracial relationships. With their truthful reflection of reality and their immediate relevance to social issues, parallel culture literatures would contribute greatly to realizing the objectives of multicultural education. If as Dorsey pointed out, "literature is the language of the heart," the literature of a parallel culture opens the group's heart to the reading public, showing their joy and grief, love and hatred, hope and despair, expectations and frustrations, and perhaps most importantly, the effects of living in a racist society. Voices from the heart, once heard, can change other hearts.

Conclusion

Our purpose in this paper has been to clarify the concept of multicultural literature as it is commonly used in educational circles. If multicultural literature is to serve the cause of multicultural education, then we must be clear about the meaning and connotations of the term. We have offered what we hope is a useful classification system. Literature, because it is composed of imaginative works of art, resists any easy categorization, and our categories will inevitably leak. Our purpose, however, is not to provide exercises in classification, but to clarify, perhaps to delimit, the concept of multicultural literature. When all the books "other than those of the dominant culture" (Jenkins 1973, 50) are lumped together under the label of multicultural literature, publishers and educators alike may feel satisfied that they are helping to meet the goals of multicultural education, when in fact they may be only beginning. When "multicultural book lists" are overwhelmed with folktales, historical fiction, and cross-cultural literature, the voices of contemporary parallel cultures may be drowned out. Without those voices, it is easy to lose sight of the goals of multicultural education, and the function of multicultural literature within that context, which is, after all, to open students' (and teachers') minds and hearts so that they learn to understand and value both themselves and people, perspectives, and experiences different from their own. Building a just and equitable society requires no less.

Notes

1. The use of the term *minority* is problematic and will, where possible, be avoided. In those cases where we have used the word, we place it in quotation marks to indicate our discomfort. Nieto, in *Affirming Diversity: The Sociopolitical Context of Multicultural Education* (1992), presents her rationale for avoiding the term and articulates reasons with which we agree. She points out that the term *minority*, as it has typically been used in the United States, connotes low status. Historically the term has been used to refer only to racial minorities and not to describe white ethnic groups, such as Swedish Americans, who also constitute numerical minorities. Such usage confers lower status on the groups so labeled. She further points out that, even in situations where such groups are no longer in the numerical minority, the term *minority* is frequently still applied, thus retaining its pejorative connotation (for example, "majority minority" schools, instead of primarily black). This connection between minority and low status causes Nieto to label the term offensive (17).

2. The terms *ethnic* and *minority* are often used interchangeably in the literature on multicultural education, as are the terms *multiethnic* and *multicultural*. Here, we follow the usage of the person being cited. Banks, in "Shaping the Future of Multicultural Education" (1979), offers an important distinction. He defines an ethnic group as "an involuntary group which shares a heritage, kinship ties, a sense of identification, political and economic interests, and cultural and linguistic characteristics" (238). It is one kind of cultural group. In *Teaching Strategies for Ethnic Studies* (1991), Banks defines an "ethnic minority" group as having "unique physical and/or cultural characteristics that enable people who belong to mainstream groups to identify its members easily and thus to treat them in a discriminatory way" (14). In this

sense, the term *minority* is itself sometimes used in a discriminatory way, as Nieto points out (see Note 1).

3. The term *parallel cultures* is borrowed from Virginia Hamilton, who used it in her acceptance speech when she received the Boston Globe–Horn Book Award for *Anthony Burns: The Defeat and Triumph of a Fugitive Slave* (1988). (See *The Horn Book*, LXV(2), March/April, 1989.) Hamilton used the term this way: "If this were the life of any ordinary individual not of a parallel culture who became enormously famous . . . " (183). Although the term may not be perfectly suited as a substitute for the uncomfortable term *minority*, it has the advantage of according equal status to the cultures designated as parallel. (One concern might be that, as Hamilton used the term and as I have used it in the past, it clearly refers only to groups other than the dominant white cultural group so that, alongside its connotation of equality, there is also a sense in which it designates "otherness" in relation to the dominant culture.) The relevant definition of *parallel* is not the geometric one, referring to lines that never meet, but the one referring to likeness or similarity or to comparisons that show likeness. For example, we can speak of parallel customs in different societies or finding parallels between and among cultures.

References

Austin, M. C., and Jenkins, E. (1983). *Promoting world understanding through literature, K–8*. Littleton, CO: Libraries Unlimited.

Banks, J. A. (1979). Shaping the future of multicultural education. *Journal of Negro Education, 48*, 237–252.

———. (1991). *Teaching strategies for ethnic studies* (5th ed.). Needham Heights, MA: Allyn and Bacon.

Carlson, R. K. (1972). *Emerging humanity: Multiethnic literature for children and adolescents*. Dubuque, IA: William C. Brown.

Council on Interracial Books for Children. (1974). *10 quick ways to analyze children's books for racism and sexism*. New York: Author.

Dasenbrock, R. W. (1987). Intelligibility and meaningfulness in multicultural literature. *PMLA, 102*(1), 10–19.

Dorsey, D. (1977). Minority literature in the service of cultural pluralism. In D. Fisher (Ed.), *Minority language and literature*. New York: Modern Language Association of America.

Hamilton, V. (1988). *Anthony Burns: The defeat and triumph of a fugitive slave*. New York: Knopf.

Jenkins, E. (1973). Multiethnic literature: Promise and problems. *Elementary English, 50*, 693–699.

Klein, G. (1985). *Reading into racism: Bias in children's literature and learning materials*. London: Routledge & Kegan Paul.

Kruse, G. M., and Horning, K. T. (1990). Looking into the mirror: Considerations behind the reflections. In M. V. Lindgren (Ed.), *The multicolored mirror: Cultural substance in literature for children and young adults.* Fort Atkinson, WI: Highsmith.

Nieto, S. (1992). *Affirming diversity: The sociopolitical context of multicultural education.* New York: Longman.

Norton, D. E. (1987). *Through the eyes of a child: An introduction to children's literature* (2nd ed.). Columbus, OH: Charles Merrill.

———. (1991). *Through the eyes of a child: An introduction to children's literature* (3rd ed.). Columbus, OH: Charles Merrill.

Rudman, M. (1984). *Children's literature: An issues approach* (2nd ed.). New York: Longman.

Sims [Bishop], R. (1982). *Shadow and substance: Afro-American experience in contemporary children's fiction.* Urbana, IL: National Council of Teachers of English.

———. (1984). A question of perspective. *The Advocate, 3,* 145–146.

Slapin, B., and Seale, D. (Eds.). (1989). *Books without bias: Through Indian eyes.* Berkeley, CA: Oyate.

Thompson, J., and Woodard, G. (1985). Black perspectives in books for children. In D. MacCan and G. Woodard (Eds.), *The black American in books for children: Readings and racism.* Metuchen, NJ: Scarecrow Press.

Children's Books

Baer, E. (1990). *This is the way we go to school: A book about children around the world* (S. Björkman, Illustrator). New York: Scholastic.

Carlson, N. S. (1965). *The empty schoolhouse.* New York: Harper.

Friedman, I. R. (1984). *How my parents learned to eat* (A. Say, Illustrator). Boston: Houghton Mifflin.

Jones, R. (1991). *Matthew and Tilly* (B. Peck, Illustrator). New York: Dutton.

Levine, E. (1989). *I hate English* (S. Björkman, Illustrator). New York: Scholastic.

Martin, B., Jr. (1987). *Knots on a counting rope.* New York: Holt.

Schami, R. (1990). *A handful of stars* (R. Lesser, Trans.). U.S. edition, New York: Dutton.

Snyder, D. (1988). *The boy of the three-year nap* (A. Say, Illustrator). Boston: Houghton Mifflin.

Spinelli, J. (1990). *Maniac Magee.* Boston: Little, Brown.

Surat, M. (1989). *Angel child, dragon child.* New York: Scholastic.

Wallin, L. (1987). *Ceremony of the panther.* New York: Bradbury.

6 What Is Sharing Time For?

Courtney B. Cazden
Harvard University

Courtney Cazden highlights the critical role of teachers as responders to the stories children tell. She suggests that teachers may find themselves more receptive to children whose cultural backgrounds are similar to their own, because they share with those children cultural norms for storytelling. Thus she argues for the importance of teacher sensitivity and self-awareness. It is these qualities that yield classrooms with space for a diversity of children and stories.

Jerry: Ummm, two days ago, ummm, my father and my father's friend were doing something over the other side, and my sister wanted uhhh, my father's friend to make her a little boat out of paper, and the paper was too little. He used his dollar and, ummm, my sister undoed it and we, ahhh, bought my father and my mother Christmas presents.

Teacher: A man made a boat out of a dollar bill for you?! Wow! That's a pretty expensive paper to use!

Sharing Time, a routine event in many primary grade classrooms, is of special interest for several reasons. First, it may be the only opportunity during official classroom air time for children to create their own oral texts: to say more than a short answer to teacher questions and to speak on a self-chosen topic that does not have to meet criteria of relevance to previous discourse. Second, because one purpose of Sharing Time is to allow a sharing of personal experiences, it is often the only official classroom air time when out-of-school experiences are acceptable topics in school. Otherwise, talking to the teacher about out-of-school life may be restricted to transition moments such as before school or while waiting in line. In fact, a teacher shift from listening to not listening to such stories is a clear marker that school has officially begun: "I can't listen now, Sarah, we have to get started" (that is, we have to enter a different discourse world in which what you're talking about, no matter how important to you, is out of bounds). Third, in addition to Sharing Time's unique features in expected length and topic of children's speech, it is of interest as a context for producing narratives—perhaps the most universal kind of text.

Given these features of what might seem a routine and unimportant part of the school day, important questions can be raised. What kind of narratives do children tell? Are there differences in the stories that seem related to different home backgrounds? What is the role of the audience—teacher and other children? In a series of studies begun by Sarah Michaels in California and continued with me in the Boston area, we have tried to answer these questions. I will report here only what we have learned about the kinds of responses that teachers make.[1]

Most teachers make some response—either a comment or question—to each Sharing Time narrative. The responses we observed can be placed along a dimension of the extent to which teacher and child share a sense of appropriate topic and appropriate way to tell about it. At one end is the enthusiastic appreciation of Jerry's teacher:

> A man made a boat out of a dollar bill for you?! Wow! That's a pretty expensive paper to use!

At the opposite end is another teacher's negative reaction to Deena's day:

> *Deena:* Um, I went to the beach Sunday, and to McDonald's, and to the park. And I got this for my birthday. My mother bought it for me. And, um, I had, um, two dollars for my birthday, and I put it in here. And I went to where my friend named Gigi—I went over to my grandmother's house with her. And, um, she was on my back, and I—and we was walking around by my house, and, um, she was heavy. She was in sixth or seventh grade—
>
> *Teacher:* [interrupting] OK, I'm going to stop you. I want you to talk about things that are really, really very important. That's important to you, but tell us things that are sort of different. Can you do that?

Between these extremes are a variety of responses. I have ordered them into four categories, but readers are encouraged to consider alternate orderings and their reasons for them.

First, and closest to the appreciation end, are cases where the teacher has clearly understood the story and simply comments or asks a question for further information, as Carl's teacher did:

> *Carl:* Well, last night my father was at work. He—every Thursday night they have this thing, that everybody has this dol-

lar, and it makes up to a hundred dollars. And my—and you've gotta pick this name out . . . and my father's name got picked. So he won a thousand dollars—a hundred dollars.

Teacher: Tell us what he's gonna do with it.

Carl: He's gonna pay bills.

A second type of response leads to an extended collaboration between questioning teacher and reporting child that results in a more complete story about an object or event than the child would have produced alone. Here is an example about making candles:

Mindy: When I was in day camp, we made these candles.

Teacher: You made them?

Mindy: And, uuh, I, I tried it with different colors, with both of them, but one just came out. This one just came out blue, and I don't know what this color is.

Teacher: That's neato. Tell the kids how you do it from the very start. Pretend we don't know a thing about candles. OK, what did you do first? What did you use? Flour?

Mindy: Um, there's some hot wax, some real hot wax, that you just take a string and tie a knot in it and dip the string in the um wax.

Teacher: Oh, you shaped it with your hand, mmm.

Mindy: But you have—first you have to stick it into the wax, and then water, and then keep doing that until it gets to the size you want it.

Teacher: OK, who knows what the string is for?

When Mindy's teacher says, "Tell the kids how you do it from the very start. Pretend we don't know a thing about candles," she seems to be speaking from an implicit model of literate discourse—the way one should write to an unseen and unknown audience. In response to questions, Mindy was encouraged to be clear and precise and to put more and more information into words, rather than relying on shared background knowledge about candles or contextual cues from the candles she was holding, to communicate part of the intended message.

A third response is a question that expresses the teacher's perplexity, her inability to keep track of the thread of the story as the child tells it. In a third classroom, Leona told a long story about her puppy—about incidents at breakfast one morning and how he always tries to follow her to school, and then a more acute problem:

> *Leona:* [continuing] And we took him to the emergency and
> see what was wrong with him. And he got a shot. And
> then he was crying. And la-last yesterday—and now they
> put him asleep. And he's still in the hospital. And the—the
> doctor said that he hasta—he got a shot because he was
> nervous—about the home that I had. And he could still
> stay, but he thought he wasn't gonna be a—he thought he
> wasn't gonna be able to let him go. He—
>
> *Teacher:* [interrupting] Who's in the hospital, Leona?

Sometime later, we asked Leona's teacher about her problems in understanding Sharing Time stories. She answered from her experience as mother as well as teacher:

> It's confusing when you listen, because their timeframe is not
> the same as ours. When my son was six, he would suddenly talk
> about something from months earlier, and I could understand
> because I'd been there; I could make the connection. It's different
> in class. It's hard to make the connection with so many
> different individuals.

When we consider the problems teachers face in "making connections" in time for an on-the-spot response, story topics can make a big difference. Some stories, such as Jerry's paper boat and Carl's hundred dollars, are about widely shared experiences with publicly familiar scripts. But even Carl's explanation about lotteries has extensive problems of vague words: *this thing, this dollar, it makes up to, this name.* But adult listeners would get enough cues to some kind of lottery to clarify the vagueness on their own. The same might be true of Leona's puppy in the hospital, but she faced the difficult discourse problem of keeping straight the referents to two same-sex characters— the doctor and the puppy, and we know from other research (Bartlett and Scribner 1981) that this causes problems for young writers throughout the elementary school years. Other stories, such as Deena's special day, are about the more idiosyncratic events of family living. It is impossible for the teacher, listening to such stories, to clarify relationships on the child's word alone.

Fourth and last, and closest to the negative end, is a response by the teacher that shifts the topic to one the teacher either understands better or values more highly. After the teacher's request for information about who is in the hospital, Leona explains that her puppy is there because he is "vicious." This leads to a discussion of the meaning of *vicious* and then a retelling by Leona of the hospital episode, ending with "I'll tell you Monday what happened." The teacher, presumably still not understanding that Leona's concern for her puppy is a matter of his life or death, ends with a comment on dogs' need for house training.

Similarly, Deena's teacher follows her interruption of Deena's account of her day with a question about the scene of Deena's first sentence, the beach:

> *Teacher:* [continuing] And tell us what beach you went to over the weekend.
>
> *Deena:* I went to um-um—
>
> *Teacher:* Alameda Beach?
>
> *Deena:* Yeah.
>
> *Teacher:* That's nice there, huh?
>
> *Deena:* I went there two times.
>
> *Teacher:* That's very nice. I like it there. Thank you, Deena.

The teacher's topical shift to the beach could have two motivations that, in this case, converge. The beach is the scene mentioned in Deena's first sentence and thus might be considered by the teacher as the topic that should have been sustained throughout. Alternatively, going to the beach may represent the kind of familiar scenario that the teacher either finds more appropriate, or just more comprehensible, than activities among family or friends. Being able to pick up an older and larger child ("And, um, she was on my back . . . and, um, she was heavy"), no matter how important to the child, may seem to the teacher ordinary or even trivial.

Here is another example where the teacher's attempt to change the focus of the child's narration is due not to any lack of comprehension, but rather to a conflict between child and teacher about the highlights of a family outing:

> *Nancy:* I went to Old Ironsides at the ocean. [Led by a series of teacher questions, Nancy explains that Old Ironsides is a boat and that it's old. The teacher herself offers the real name, *The Constitution.* Then Nancy tries to shift the focus of her story.] We also spent our dollars and we went to another big shop.
>
> *Teacher:* Mm. And what did you learn about Old Ironsides?
>
> *Nancy:* [Led by teacher questions back to Old Ironsides, Nancy supplies more information about the furnishings inside and the costumes of the guides, and then tries to shift focus again.] I also went to a fancy restaurant.
>
> *Teacher:* Haha! Very good!
>
> *Nancy:* And I had a hamburger, french fries, lettuce and a—

Teacher: [interrupting] OK. All right. What's—Arthur's been
    waiting and then Paula, OK?

Narratives are a universal meaning-making strategy, but there is
no one way of transforming experience into a story. In the words of a
British educator (Rosen 1982), narratives are "first and foremost a
product of the disposition of the human mind to narratize experience
and to transform it into findings which as social beings we may share
and compare with those of others" (9). But while "the story is always
out there," Rosen says,

> the important step has still to be taken. The unremitting flow of
> events must first be selectively attended to, interpreted as hold-
> ing relationships, causes, motives, feelings, consequences—in a
> word, meanings. To give order to this otherwise unmanageable
> flux we must take another step and invent, yes, invent, begin-
> nings and ends for out there are no such things. . . . This is the
> axiomatic element of narrative: it is the outcome of a mental
> process which enables us to excise from our experience a mean-
> ingful sequence, to place it within boundaries, to set around it
> the frontiers of the story, to make it resonate in the contrived
> silences with which we may precede and end it. . . . The narra-
> tive edits ruthlessly the raw tape. (10–11)

Our potentiality and disposition to construct narratives is similar to
our potentiality and disposition to acquire language. In Rosen's words:

> If we are programmed to learn a language, we must still be
> exposed to a language in order to learn it and its socially consti-
> tuted use. In the same way, however universal our human bent
> for narratizing experience we encounter our own society's
> modes for doing this. There is no one way of telling stories; we
> learn the story grammars of our society, our culture. (11)

Differences of cultural background and differences in age between teacher and child will affect how the raw tape of experience is
edited and transformed; and sometimes a teacher's comments reveal
these differences. Deena's teacher asked Deena to talk only about
"things that are really, really very important . . . things that are sort of
different." Nancy's teacher expressed the same idea in other words to
one of Nancy's peers: "If you have something that was *special* for you,
that you would like to share with us, but we don't want to hear about
TV shows and regular things that happened." But who is to say what
is "important," "different," and "special" or just "regular" to someone
else? And don't our finest writers (see Welty 1984) often make stories
out of the most ordinary events of daily life?

How then should teachers think about their role at Sharing Time? The first question to ask is: What are the primary purposes for Sharing Time anyway? To build a community of children through the sharing of out-of-school experiences? To give children practice in speaking before a group? To serve as oral practice in the kind of compositions that children will later be expected to write? The best course of action for individual teachers will depend on their answer to this question.

If a teacher values a growing sense of community among children, then it may be better to divide the class into small groups for Sharing Time, as Moffett and Wagner (1976, 73–74) suggest. That way, there can be more informal questioning by other children, and more sharers can get a chance. If, on the other hand, the primary purpose is seen as oral preparation for writing, then the important question is whether it would be more effective to work with a child in a conference over an actual written text (as described by Graves 1983), rather than try to change patterns of oral narrative style. In conference, the child is no longer a performer to a mixed audience of teacher and peers. A long story that takes up a disproportionate amount of class time in oral rendition would be valued as a written composition, and the teacher can give a more considered response.

Teachers, like physicians and social workers, are in the business of helping others. But as a prerequisite to giving help, we have to take in and understand. A Piagetian psychologist (Duckworth 1982) speaks of the importance of teachers "understanding learners' understandings." A British sociologist (Bernstein 1972) puts the same idea in different words: "If the culture of the teacher is to become part of the consciousness of the child, then the culture of the child must first be in the consciousness of the teacher" (149). Important elements of that consciousness are our expectations about text structures and our presupposed knowledge about what texts are about. We usually think of the importance of these "contexts in the mind" (Cazden 1982) when we are teaching children to read, but they are just as important when the texts are oral instead of written and when the interpreter is not a reading child but a listening teacher.

Note

1. Michaels (1981) reports her study of a California classroom that included Deena and Mindy. Michaels and Cazden (1984) and Cazden, Michaels, and Tabors (1985) report our research in Boston-area classrooms

that included Carl and Leona. Separate from our research, Dorr-Bremme (1982) analyzes the social organization of Sharing Time as well as Worktime in another Boston-area classroom that included Jerry and Nancy.

References

Bartlett, E. J., and Scribner, S. (1981). Text and content: An investigation of referential organization in children's written narratives. In C. Frederiksen and J. F. Dominic (Eds.), *Writing: The nature, development, and teaching of written communication: Vol. 2. Writing: Process, development, and communication* (153–168). Hillsdale, NJ: Erlbaum.

Bernstein, B. (1972). A critique of the concept of compensatory education. In C. B. Cazden, D. Hymes, and V. John (Eds.), *Functions of language in the classroom*, (135–151). New York: Teachers College Press.

Cazden, C. B. (1982). Contexts for literacy: In the mind and in the classroom. *Journal of Reading Behavior, 14*, 413–427.

Cazden, C. B., Michaels, S., and Tabors, P. (1985). Self-repair in sharing time narratives: The intersection of metalinguistic awareness, speech event and narrative style. In S. Freedman (Ed.), *The acquisition of written language: Revision and response*. Norwood, NJ: Ablex.

Dorr-Bremme, D. W. (1982). Behaving and making sense: Creating social organization in the classroom. Doctoral dissertation, Harvard University. (University Microfilms No. 82–23, 203)

Duckworth, E. (1982). Understanding children's understanding. In V. Windley, M. Dorn, and L. Weber (Eds.), *Building on the strengths of children*. New York: City College.

Graves, D. H. (1983). *Writing: Teachers and children at work*. Exeter, NH: Heinemann.

Michaels, S. (1981). "Sharing Time": Children's narrative styles and differential access to literacy. *Language in Society, 10*, 423–442.

Michaels, S., and Cazden, C. B. (1984). Teacher/child collaboration as oral preparation for literacy. In B. B. Schieffelin (Ed.), *Acquisition of literacy: Ethnographic perspectives* (132–154). Norwood, NJ: Ablex.

Moffett, J., and Wagner, B. J. (1976). *Student-centered language arts and reading: A handbook for teachers* (2nd ed.). Boston: Houghton-Mifflin.

Rosen, H. (1982, April). *The nurture of narrative*. Paper presented at the annual meeting of the International Reading Association, Chicago.

Welty, E. (1984). *One writer's beginnings*. Cambridge, MA: Harvard University Press.

7 "The Blacker the Berry, the Sweeter the Juice": African American Student Writers

Geneva Smitherman
Michigan State University

Differences in cultural discourse styles *have been viewed primarily as problems, as "mismatches" with the discourse styles valued in school. Geneva Smitherman provides a powerful alternative vision. She details her careful studies of African American students' writing for the National Assessment of Educational Progress, and she demonstrates that, for teacher-raters of the 1980s, the use of an African American discourse style correlated positively with higher scores*

Written literacy among African American students continues to be of major concern to educators, policy makers, researchers, and the lay community. African American students have consistently scored lower than their European American counterparts in all rounds of the National Assessment of Educational Progress (NAEP) since its inception in 1969 (NAEP 1980; Applebee, Langer, and Mullis 1985). And even in that decade of remarkable progress for African American student writers, 1969 to 1979, where 1979 NAEP results indicated that they had improved *twice* as much as their white counterparts, African American students still were not writing on a par with white students, as the 1979 NAEP results also indicated.

The upward surge first evidenced in 1979 continued in the 1980s, though not with the same dramatic level of improvement. According to NAEP, from 1984 to 1988, "Black and Hispanic students appeared to show consistent improvements at all three grade levels, although the changes were not statistically significant" (Applebee et al. 1990, 9). Although black students' scores still do not parallel those of whites, there is some slight encouragement in NAEP's finding, particularly in light of their conclusion that generally in 1988 the nation's students "continued to perform at minimal levels on the . . .

writing assessment tasks, and relatively few performed at adequate or better levels" (Applebee et al. 1990, 6).

The topic of the African American Verbal Tradition—both its discourse modalities and its grammar—is frequently at the heart of discussion and concern about African American student writing. Of particular significance is the extent to which Black English Vernacular (BEV) patterns of syntax and discourse are reproduced in writing. A significant related issue concerns the potential correlation between a student's use of such BEV patterns and evaluation of his or her essay by writing instructors. This chapter addresses both issues by focusing on BEV *discourse* patterns.[1] An earlier publication discussed these issues with a focus on BEV *grammar* (see Smitherman 1991). Both the chapter presented here and the earlier article used essays written by NAEP's national representative sample of seventeen-year-old African American students from 1969 to 1988–89.

National Assessment of Educational Progress

NAEP is a federally funded survey of the educational attainments of youth and adults at four age levels: nine, thirteen, seventeen, and twenty-six to thirty-five. Its purpose is to measure growth or decline in educational achievement in ten subject areas: writing, reading, literature, science, mathematics, citizenship, music, art, social studies, and career and occupational development. Administered at five- and ten-year intervals since its inception in 1969, NAEP offers the advantage of a scientifically selected national representative sample, uniform scoring procedures and guidelines, a nationally administered, standardized test format, and a high degree of reliability and validity. For example, the percentage of exact agreement on the rating of the 1984 papers from seventeen-year-olds ranged from 89 percent to 92 percent, with corresponding reliability coefficients of .89 and .91 (Applebee, Langer, and Mullis 1985, 68). The writing task time is fifteen or sixteen minutes, depending on the task, and students submit first drafts. Previously administered by the Education Commission of the States, NAEP has been under the purview of the Educational Testing Service since 1984.

The students assessed reflect national, representative groups, in a random sample, stratified by race-ethnicity, social-educational class, region of country, urban-rural, gender, and other demographics. From 1969 to 1979, approximately 8,100 students were assessed. From 1984 to 1988, approximately 18,000 students were assessed.

NAEP's essay tasks represent three types of rhetorical modalities: (1) imaginative-narrative, (2) descriptive-informative, and (3) persuasive. For the *imaginative* modality, in the 1969 and 1979 NAEP, students were given a picture of a stork and told to make up a story about it. The prompt was comprised of three possible opening lines: (1) "I'm telling you, Henry, if you don't get rid of that thing, it's going to eat up the cat!"; (2) "But mother, I *am* telling the truth! It laid an egg in the Chevy"; and (3) "Last night a very odd-looking bird appeared in the neighborhood." In 1984, students were given a picture of a box with a hole in it and an eye peering out. They were told to "imagine" themselves in the picture, to describe the scene and their feelings about it, and to make their descriptions "lively and interesting." There was no imaginative task in 1988.

For the *descriptive-informative* task, the 1969 and 1979 students were asked to describe something they knew about, a familiar place or thing, in such a way that it could be recognized by someone reading the description. For 1984 and 1988, they were given the topic "Food on the Frontier" and asked to write an essay discussing reasons for the differences between food on the frontier and food today. Finally, for the *persuasive* modality, in 1984 and 1988 the students' task was to write a letter to the recreation department in their city or town, trying to convince the head of that department to buy either an abandoned railroad track or an old warehouse to create recreational opportunities. (We were unable to obtain the persuasive essays for 1969 and 1979; thus this longitudinal comparison was not possible.)

Issues in the Study

As a womanist linguist concerned about the educational plight of African American youth, I began this line of research in 1981, building on my dissertation research comparing the speech and writing of black students (Smitherman 1969). My study was one of the first to examine the "dialect interference" hypothesis, the notion that spoken language by blacks is a source of interference in their production of written Standard English. Analyzing oral and written samples from a group of African American junior high students for use of BEV syntactical patterns, the study concluded that, while both speech and writing exhibited features of BEV, the students used significantly more BEV grammar in speech than in writing. Subsequent work by researchers such as Whiteman (1976), Scott (1981), Wright (1984), Chaplin (1987), and my own earlier work on NAEP (Smitherman and Wright 1983;

Smitherman 1985) raised issues concerning comparisons of African American and European American student writers, methodological concerns about differential topics, audiences, task conditions for speech and writing, the importance of BEV discourse over BEV syntax in writing, and the relationship between the "students' right to their own language" and teacher ratings of student writing. The following crucial questions are examined in the research presented here:

1. Can black student writing be characterized by an identifiable discourse style rooted in the African American Verbal Tradition?

2. If so, does use of this discourse style correlate with use of patterns of BEV grammar?

3. What effect, if any, does use of an African American discourse style have on teacher ratings of black student writing?

4. Given writing with *both* BEV discourse and BEV grammar, does one dimension have greater effect on teacher ratings than the other?

Some responses to these questions emerged from the research of Scott (1981) and Chaplin (1987). Scott controlled for the methodological shortcomings in earlier studies (for example, unequivalent topics, modalities, and audiences) by using African American college freshmen's speeches and essays on identical topics, produced under identical conditions. The essays were edited by freshman composition instructors for BEV, mechanics, spelling, and punctuation. Scott then asked the writing instructors to evaluate edited and unedited versions of the students' essays. When she compared the ratings of edited essays with ratings of corresponding unedited essays, no significant difference was found. Scott concluded that other factors such as discourse patterns were probably influencing the ratings.

Chaplin used 1984 NAEP essays for her work. (Hers is believed to be the only other research on African American student writing in NAEP.) She compared African American and European American eighth- and ninth-grade students in NAEP and African American students in the 1986 New Jersey High School Proficiency Test in an attempt to identify discourse patterns differentiating black and white students. She focused on the construct of field dependency-independency, that is, the thinker's-writer's relationship to the event, idea, phenomenon, or "field" under discussion. The field dependent thinker's-writer's style demands involvement with and a lack of distancing from the phenomenon being studied, analyzed, or communicated about. There is a tendency to see things whole, rather than segmented. The field independent thinker's-writer's style demands distance from and a lack of involvement with the field. There is a tendency to view things in parts or segments.

African American psychologists have long theorized that African Americans employ a field dependent style and European Americans a field independent style (e.g., Wilson 1971; Williams 1972; Simpkins, Holt, and Simpkins 1976). Cooper (1979) did the pioneering research on linguistic correlates of field dependency, bringing together the insights of African American psychologists and communication scholars. While the notion of differing cognitive styles, varied along racial-cultural lines, has caused controversy, it is imperative to understand that we are not talking about cognitive style in the "genetic inferiority" sense used by Bereiter and Engleman (1966) or Jensen (1980). Rather, field dependency-independency emanates from different cultural orientations and world views, a view in concert with the theoretical frameworks of Humboldt (1841), Sapir (1929), Volosinov (1930), Whorf (1956), Vygotsky (1962), and more recently Hymes (1974). It can be argued that we may not sufficiently understand the exact nature of the field dependency-independency constructs, yet a great deal of research substantiates that these constructs are reliable indicators of differing cultural experiences and cosmologies. Critically, and futuristically as U.S. society becomes increasingly diverse, we must arrive at a genuine acceptance of the fact that difference does not mean deficiency.

Chaplin used black and white teacher raters to assess the African American and European American students' use of field dependency-independency as a discourse style in their essays. Her analysis led to the following observation: "[F]or more of the Black than White student writers, there was an identifiable field dependent style" (Chaplin 1987, 26). Without being given an imposed structure or racial identification of the student writers, Chaplin's readers identified two discourse features in the black student writing that marked field dependency: cultural vocabulary-influence and conversational tone. According to Chaplin, cultural vocabulary-influence represented culture-specific words, idioms, and phrases, the language that has "helped them to shape reality" and thus "become a part of their writing" (48). Conversational tone she defined as producing an essay that reads like "recorded oral language or a conversation" (37). Although Chaplin states that there were more similarities than differences in the black and white students' writing, she does conclude that "conversational tone, cultural vocabulary and Black Vernacular English were used more often by Black . . . students" (1990, 18).

In terms of implications for writing instruction, Chaplin advises that, since "Black students . . . seemed . . . less able to distance themselves from cultural influences," such instruction "should be conceived within the context of an understanding and appreciation of the Black experience" if we are to "maximize the potential that Black students have for writing development" (1990, 21). Chaplin's work has buttressed my own claims about a discernible African American discourse style of writing which I began to explore in analyzing the 1969 and 1979 NAEP essays. Those explorations were extended and developed, and the use of a black discourse style became the focal point in the present study.

Sample and Methods

In developing the methodology for this study, I felt it critical to compare African American student writers with one another, rather than with European American student writers. The research literature is quite definitive about the existence of an African American Verbal Tradition, with varying degrees of survival within the race (see, e.g., Herskovits 1941; Dillard 1972; Lincoln 1990; Thompson 1983; Labov 1972; Asante 1990; Smitherman 1986; Gates 1988). Our focus here was to analyze the degree to which this tradition survives in the writing of black students across a generational time span, rather than to assess the degree of borrowing from this tradition by European American students. Further, although black students are often disproportionately represented in "basic" writing courses, I felt it imperative to analyze a variety of black student writers, not just those deemed "basic" or "remedial." Because there is diversity of performance within race, writing norms can be derived from African American student performance.

In our study of 1969 and 1979 NAEP essays, we analyzed black discourse, using holistic scoring for field dependency. The discourse analysis involved only the sample of narrative-imaginative essays and employed general, impressionistic ratings of field involvement by a social psychologist, a graduate student in English, and me. We rated the essays holistically using a "field involvement score" based on the rater's assessment of the degree of distance of the writer from his or her subject matter. Some of the stylistic-linguistic features that this measurement involved were the presence of interaction between the writer and others, dialogue in the essay that clearly involved the writer, the attribution of human qualities to nonhuman things, and other signals that the writer was in the environment of the communication context he or she created.

For the present work, using 1984 and 1988–89 NAEP essays, we extended and refined that earlier methodology. Several writing instructors experienced in teaching African American students and one other sociolinguist, who specializes in Black English Vernacular studies, worked with me to construct a model of African American discourse to use in analyzing the essays. First, all became conversant with work on field dependency-independency, including Cooper's and Chaplin's studies and my 1985 NAEP study. Then each instructor independently read the same 25 essays, noting any features that struck him or her as discernibly African American. Next, the group members came together to discuss and compare our lists. We repeated this same procedure twice, thus ending up with a model based on independent assessment, discussion, and 85 percent agreement about the black discourse features in 75 essays in the NAEP sample. Each time we came together for discussion, we found ourselves coming up with similar concepts, different labels and terminology to be sure, but essentially the same characteristic conceptual features. We established the following set of criteria for African American discourse in black student writing:

1. Rhythmic, dramatic, evocative language. *Example:* "Darkness is like a cage in black around me, shutting me off from the rest of the world."

2. Reference to color-race-ethnicity (that is, when topic does not call for it). *Example:* "I dont get in trouble at school or have any problems with people picking on me   I am nice to every one no matter what color or sex."

3. Use of proverbs, aphorisms, Biblical verses. *Example:* "People might have shut me off from the world cause of a mistake, crime, or a sin. . . . Judge not others, for you to will have your day to be judge"

4. Sermonic tone reminiscent of traditional Black Church rhetoric, especially in vocabulary, imagery, metaphor. *Example:* "I feel like I'm suffering from being with world. There no lights, food, water, bed and clothes for me to put on. Im fighten, scared of what might happened if no one finds me. But I pray and pray until they do find me."

5. Direct address-conversational tone. *Example:* "I think you should use the money for the railroad track. . . . it could fall

off the tracks and kill someone on the train And that is very dangerius. Dont you think so. Please change your mind and pick the railroad tracks. For the People safety O.K." [From letter-writing, persuasive task]

6. Cultural references. *Example:* "How about slipping me some chitterlings in tonite"

7. Ethnolinguistic idioms. *Example:* "... a fight has broke loose"; "It would run me crazy...."

8. Verbal inventiveness, unique nomenclature. *Example:* "[The settlers] were pioneerific"; "[The box] has an eye look-out"

9. Cultural values-community consciousness. Expressions of concern for development of African Americans; concern for welfare of entire community, not just individuals, as for example several essays in which students expressed the view that recreational facilities would have to be for everybody, "young and old, and the homeless among Blacks"

10. Field dependency. Involvement with and immersion in events and situations; personalizing phenomena; lack of distance from topics and subjects.

The research team used holistic scoring to rank each essay in terms of the degree of African American discourse in the essay. We used a 4-point Likert-type scale, from 1 ("highly discernible African American style") to 4 ("not discernible African American style"). Each of the 1984 imaginative essays ($N = 432$) and a subsample ($N = 435$) of the 1984 and 1988 persuasive essays were coded independently by two members of our research team. In the case of a discrepancy in coding, a third member coded the essay. The total number of essays coded was 867. For 780 of the essays, or in 90 percent of the discourse sample, the two raters agreed independently on the discourse score assigned to the essay. (For sample essays from 1969 through 1988, see Appendix B.)

Each of the essays had also been given a primary trait score or a holistic score, or both by NAEP teachers—raters trained and experienced in holistic scoring and general writing assessment. A holistic score is an assessment of overall writing competency, what NAEP describes as "a global view of the ideas, language facility, organization, mechanics, and syntax of each paper taken as whole" (Applebee et al. 1990, 84). Further, with holistic scoring, papers are evaluated relative to one another, rather than against specific criteria, as is the case with primary trait scoring. In 1969 and 1979, NAEP raters used a 4-point scale for both types of scoring. In 1984 and 1988, NAEP raters used a 6-point scale for holistic and a 4-point scale for primary trait scoring.

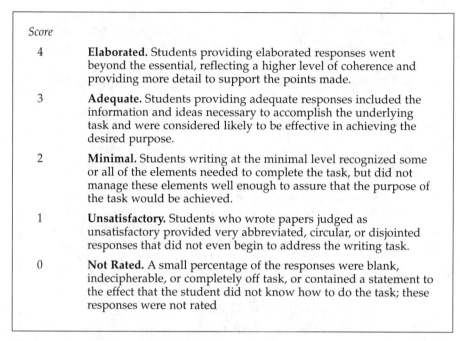

Score	
4	**Elaborated.** Students providing elaborated responses went beyond the essential, reflecting a higher level of coherence and providing more detail to support the points made.
3	**Adequate.** Students providing adequate responses included the information and ideas necessary to accomplish the underlying task and were considered likely to be effective in achieving the desired purpose.
2	**Minimal.** Students writing at the minimal level recognized some or all of the elements needed to complete the task, but did not manage these elements well enough to assure that the purpose of the task would be achieved.
1	**Unsatisfactory.** Students who wrote papers judged as unsatisfactory provided very abbreviated, circular, or disjointed responses that did not even begin to address the writing task.
0	**Not Rated.** A small percentage of the responses were blank, indecipherable, or completely off task, or contained a statement to the effect that the student did not know how to do the task; these responses were not rated

Figure 1. NAEP primary trait scale.

In primary trait assessment, papers are evaluated according to features of specific writing tasks. This score reflects the measure of student success in accomplishing the assigned purpose of the writing (Applebee et al. 1990, 6). Here, matters of mechanics, grammar, and syntax are subordinated to fluency and execution of the writing task (see Figures 1 and 2 for sample scales).

For analysis, our team's discourse scores and NAEP's rater scores were compared to ascertain the degree of correlation, if any, between use of an African American discourse style and the primary trait and holistic scores assigned to an essay by raters.

Next, the discourse scores were analyzed to examine the correlation, if any, between the production of BEV syntax and the use of a black oral discourse style. BEV syntax was measured by the percentage of realization of patterns established in the literature as BEV grammatical patterns. These variables with examples from the NAEP essays are shown in Figure 3.

The Pearson statistical procedure was used for the correlational analysis, with .05 established as the level of significance.

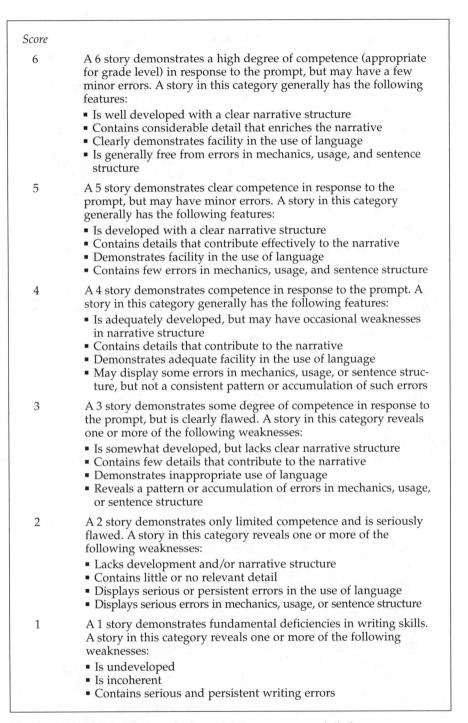

Score	
6	A 6 story demonstrates a high degree of competence (appropriate for grade level) in response to the prompt, but may have a few minor errors. A story in this category generally has the following features: • Is well developed with a clear narrative structure • Contains considerable detail that enriches the narrative • Clearly demonstrates facility in the use of language • Is generally free from errors in mechanics, usage, and sentence structure
5	A 5 story demonstrates clear competence in response to the prompt, but may have minor errors. A story in this category generally has the following features: • Is developed with a clear narrative structure • Contains details that contribute effectively to the narrative • Demonstrates facility in the use of language • Contains few errors in mechanics, usage, and sentence structure
4	A 4 story demonstrates competence in response to the prompt. A story in this category generally has the following features: • Is adequately developed, but may have occasional weaknesses in narrative structure • Contains details that contribute to the narrative • Demonstrates adequate facility in the use of language • May display some errors in mechanics, usage, or sentence structure, but not a consistent pattern or accumulation of such errors
3	A 3 story demonstrates some degree of competence in response to the prompt, but is clearly flawed. A story in this category reveals one or more of the following weaknesses: • Is somewhat developed, but lacks clear narrative structure • Contains few details that contribute to the narrative • Demonstrates inappropriate use of language • Reveals a pattern or accumulation of errors in mechanics, usage, or sentence structure
2	A 2 story demonstrates only limited competence and is seriously flawed. A story in this category reveals one or more of the following weaknesses: • Lacks development and/or narrative structure • Contains little or no relevant detail • Displays serious or persistent errors in the use of language • Displays serious errors in mechanics, usage, or sentence structure
1	A 1 story demonstrates fundamental deficiencies in writing skills. A story in this category reveals one or more of the following weaknesses: • Is undeveloped • Is incoherent • Contains serious and persistent writing errors

Figure 2. NAEP holistic scale (imaginative essay modality).

Variable	Example from NAEP Essay
ed Morpheme	
Main-verb past (MV + ∅)	Frontier *use* corn and meat for there basic food.
Main-verb-perfect (Have/Had + MV + ∅)	They have *work* hard . . . to keep the crops growing good to eat.
Verbal adjective (V + ∅)	I am writing because I am *concern* of the recreational project . . . in our town.
Passive (be + MV + ∅)	I am *lock* in an apartment with darkness looking through this little hole.
s Morpheme	
Noun-plural (N + ∅ pl)	Pioneers didn't have such *thing* . . . to keep their foods.
Noun-possessive (N + ∅ poss)	*Today* way is . . . easier.
Third-person singular (V + ∅)	But our environment of today *do* have refrigeration and things . . . can be stored.
Hypercorrection	
(N pl + s)	But today *peoples* are able to get refrigeraters and food still spoil.
Copula	
Be + main verb (∅ + MV)	I feel like someone _____ *watching* me throwing at me.
Be + noun (∅ + N)	He _____ a real good *citizen*.
Be + adjective (∅ + adj)	I think it _____ great to have some place to play.
Be + preposition (∅ + prep)	I feel really good about what _____ *around me*
Be + adverb (∅ + adj)	But it *out door*.
Subject-Verb Agreement—Present	
(Subj pl + is)	*a bird and egg is* in that car.
Subject-Verb Agreement—Past	
(Subj pl + was)	The pioneers then *was* no different than what we do today.
Perfective Done/Have	
(∅ have/has/had + MV)	. . . the food to mostley allready _____ been cooked and caned for you . . .

(continued)

(continued)

Variable	Example from NAEP Essay
Irregular Verbs	But back then they *eat* a lot of health food.
	So I *have gave* my opinions about what I think you should do.
Multiple Negation	Last night there was a straight-looking new bird in the neighborhood *no one never* seen before *nowhere*.
It Expletive	
(It + V + N)	*It* is a lot different things that would brighten up our community.
Undifferentiated Third-Person	
Plural Pronoun	... soon are later they will quiet that job because they will have alot of money in the bank for *they family* and they self.
Pronominal Apposition	
(N subj + P subj)	People in the old day *they* do not have refrigeration ...

Figure 3. Black English variables.

Results

Let us begin with a summary of the findings relative to discourse analysis and primary trait and holistic scores in NAEP 1969 and 1979. Analysis indicated the following:

1. There was no statistically significant decline in field dependency from 1969 to 1979. This finding contrasted with the significant decline in BEV syntax in the narrative mode over the decade (Smitherman and Wright 1983; see also Appendix A).

2. There was no correlation between use of BEV syntax and field dependency; that is, high users of BEV syntax do not necessarily use field dependent style, nor are those writers who use low BEV syntax predictably field independent.

3. There was no correlation between rater score and field dependency. By contrast, BEV syntax correlated significantly and negatively with rater score for both primary trait and holistic scoring. Even when all variables (sex, year, essay type, field dependency score) were factored into the equa-

tion, BEV syntax remained the most significant predictor of rater score.

Next, we turn to the 1984 and 1988 results of discourse analysis, BEV syntax, and rater scores. As detailed above, our present NAEP study used a fully developed, explicit set of criteria for identifying varying degrees of black discourse in the 1984 imaginative essays and the 1984 and 1988–89 persuasive essays. Correlations were run between (1) the discourse score and BEV syntax, and (2) the discourse score and holistic and primary trait scores.

In the case of the first relationship, results tend to support the tendency we observed in 1969 and 1979, namely, that BEV syntax and BEV discourse are *not* co-occurring variables. No correlation was found between a discernibly African American discourse style and the production of BEV syntax. In fact, of the three sets of essay data subjected to discourse analysis, *correlations were found between BEV grammar and non-African American discourse style.* Although only one of these analyses reached statistical significance, it is interesting to note that the correlations are all positive. That is, when overall BEV syntax was high, the discourse scores tended to be high also. A high discourse score on our rating scale indicated an essay that *did not have a discernibly African American discourse style,* thus suggesting that the production of BEV grammar goes up as the writing becomes less "black" rhetorically. Although we must propose this as an observed trend, not a conclusion (see Table 1), it is interesting to note that this observation coincides with that of researchers who posit that "talking black" does not have to encompass features of BEV grammar (e.g., Taylor 1992; Hoover 1978; Smitherman 1986).

In the second possible relationship—between discourse score and holistic and primary trait scores—results for 1984 and 1988–89 were highly significant, in contrast to the 1969 and 1979 findings. In

Table 1. Correlations between BEV Syntax and Discourse Style, 1984 and 1988

Essay Year and Type	R-Value	P-Value
1984 Imaginative	.0361	.45*
1984 Persuasive	.1436	.05**
1988 Persuasive	.0044	.95*

* = Not statistically significant.
** = Statistically significant at .05 or less.

the 1980s, *the more discernibly African American the discourse, the higher the primary trait and holistic scores; the less discernibly African American the discourse, the lower the primary trait and holistic scores*. This finding was statistically significant for all three data sets and for both holistic and primary trait scoring (see Table 2). What the negative correlations in Table 2 indicate is that the higher the discourse score, the lower the rater's score. As mentioned, a high discourse score indicates an essay written in a non-African American discourse style. As it turns out, these essays were assigned lower rater scores, whether assessed by using primary trait or holistic scoring criteria. This finding held regardless of the degree of BEV grammar in a given essay, at least with primary trait scoring.

As an illustration of this finding, note the opening sentences in the two essays below. The writers are responding to NAEP's 1984 imaginative essay prompt, a picture of a box with a hole in it and an eye looking out, requiring the writers to "imagine" themselves in the picture and to describe the scene and their feelings in a "lively and interesting" way. Essay 582200 begins this way (see Appendix B for entire essay):

> Well, a boy is in a box outside, may be in his or her back and looking through a square hole. He or she look like hear she is hiding from someone. Maybe he or she is 5 year old and some one is trying to find him/her to beat him or her up.

In terms of its degree of African American discourse, we rated this essay a 4, that is, distinctly non-black style. NAEP raters gave the essay a primary trait score of 1, and a holistic score of 2, both low scores. By

Table 2. Correlations between BEV Discourse and Holistic and Primary Trait Scores, 1984 and 1988

Essay Year and Type	Scoring Method	R-Value	P-Value
1984 Imaginative*	P	−.1660	.001**
	H	−.1783	.000**
1984 Persuasive	H	−.3260	.009**
1988 Persuasive	P	−.1967	.002**
	H	−.3924	.000**

P = Primary trait.
H = Holistic.
* = Imaginative task not given in 1988.
** = Statistically significant at .05 or lower.

contrast, essay 590877 begins this way (refer to Appendix B for entire essay):

> I see little kids playing around me some on the swings, and some on the sliding bord. The kids are enjoying themselfs. As for me I'm in this box because I'm afraid of all of the other kids in the park.

We gave this essay a black discourse score of 1, that is, distinctly black style. NAEP raters gave the essay a primary trait score of 3 and a holistic score of 5, both high scores.

Now, clearly both of the above essays begin with departures from Edited American English. Yet the latter essay exhibits greater fluency and power, and it is clear that this writer is on her or his way somewhere towards a product that will be rhetorically effective. In sum, what our analysis of essays by several hundred African American student writers indicates is this: given a paper with both BEV grammar and BEV discourse, the greater the degree of black discourse, irrespective of the degree-amount of BEV grammar, the higher will be the rating in primary trait scoring, that is, scoring for fluency-accomplishment of the rhetorical task.

Finally, the imaginative-narrative essay continues to be black students' strong suit. These essays were consistently assessed higher by NAEP raters than were the 1984 or 1988 persuasives. Further, the imaginatives also exhibited higher levels of African American Verbal Tradition style, as indicated by the fact that greater numbers of these essays received discourse scores of 1 or 2 by our research team than was the case with our discourse rating of persuasives.

Conclusions and Implications

The title of this chapter contains an age-old black proverb whose message speaks to the power of blackness in skin color, rhetorical fluency, and cultural affinity. For 1984 imaginative and 1984 and 1988 persuasive NAEP essays, a team of experienced writing instructors was able to identify a discernible black discourse style and establish criteria for rating the "blackness" of student essays. The team achieved a 90 percent agreement for 867 essays. Results indicated that students who employed a black expressive discourse style received higher NAEP scores than those who did not. In the case of primary trait scores, this finding held regardless of the frequency of BEV syntax (fairly low anyway, and continuing to decline over time; see Appendix A and Smitherman 1991).

There are several clear implications here for writing instructors and others concerned about African American students' written literacy. First, capitalize on the strengths of African American cultural discourse; it is a rich reservoir which students can and should tap. Second, encourage students toward the field dependency style, which enables them to produce more powerful, meaningful, and highly rated essays. Third, design strategies for incorporating the black imaginative, storytelling style into student production of other essay modalities. Fourth, deemphasize your and your students' concerns about BEV grammar; overconcentration on these forms frequently suppresses the production of African American discourse and its rich, expressive style.

As cultural norms shift focus from "book" English to "human" English, the narrativizing, dynamic quality of the African American Verbal Tradition will help students produce lively, image-filled, concrete, readable essays, regardless of rhetorical modality—persuasive, informative, comparison-contrast, and so forth. I am often asked "how far" does the teacher go with this kind of writing pedagogy. My answer: as far as you can. Once you have pushed your students to rewrite, revise; rewrite, revise; rewrite, revise; and once they have produced the most powerful essay possible, then and only then should you have them turn their attention to BEV grammar and matters of punctuation, spelling, and mechanics.

Finally, if you are worried about preparing your students for the next level ("Well, that might be okay in *my* classroom, but then what about when they pass on to Mrs. X's class. . . ."), consider the NAEP results reported here from the perspective of the teacher-raters of the 1980s and beyond. They contrast sharply with those teacher-raters in the 1969 and 1979 NAEP, where African American discourse style had no effect on rater scores. The fact that rater scores in 1984 and 1988 *positively correlated with black discourse styles* speaks favorably for the social and educational efforts of groups such as the Center for Applied Linguistics, the National Council of Teachers of English, the Conference on College Composition and Communication, and others who, over the past twenty years, have worked to sensitize teachers to the linguistic-cultural norms of the African American speech community. Many people now appear to be receptive to and subliminally aware of the rhetorical power of the African American Verbal Tradition, and in some quarters they even consciously celebrate it. Public schools and college teachers, too, now appear to understand that "the blacker the berry, the sweeter the juice."

Appendix A: Overall BEV Scores

Overall BEV Scores, 1969 to 1988–89

Essay Type	Year	BEV Mean
1969 to 1979		
Imaginative	1969	.11
Imaginative	1979	.09*
Informative	1969	.10
Informative	1979	.14**
Persuasive	Not available	Not available
1984 to 1988–89		
Imaginative	1984	.11
Imaginative	Not given in 1988	—
Informative	1984	.10
Informative	1988	.06**
Persuasive	1984	.09
Persuasive	1988	.05**

* = Not statistically significant.
** = Statistically significant at .05 or lower.

Appendix B: Sample Essays

Imaginative, 1969, #53

I am a sad sad bird. Nobody wants me because I am so wierd-looking. But some day just like the Negro they will realize that I am something. May be I do have a long beck. They shouldn't juge me that way. I might look dumb to them but Ihave some sense. They just wont give me change to show it. They just left me out here all by myself. They don't relize. that I'm blood and skin. I'm just as good as any other bird.

Field dependent essay, a discernible black style; NAEP rater score (2), low score.

Imaginative, 1979, #148

Last night a very odd-looking bird appeared in the neighborhood. Then suddenly upon seeing this odd-looking bird a kaos arose before serveral families. This was one of the biggest controversies in several years due to the fact that this town almost became a ghost town. It came to be that the appearance of this bird in the town was a runaway from the California state zoo. And their authorities had come to search for this bird and was offering a reward well over the town's income for a whole year. This incident was news making in more than thirty-eight states thoughtout the country. The reason the odd bird's valuability was that it was theonly of its kind left in existence. And it was carrying youn'g ready for a full life in a matter of two to three weeks. Nevertheless money to those authorities who were searching for this odd looking bird, was no object. Although the bird wich was last seen in the small village was not found there, the town's fame and popularity rose to everyone. The town was far away from being a ghost town.

Field independent essay, not a discernible black style; NAEP rater score (3), high score.

Imaginative, 1984, #582200

Well, a boy is in a box outside, may be in his or her back and loking through a square hole. He or she look like hear she is hiding from someone. Maybe he or she is 5 year old and some one is trying to find him/her to beat him or her up. There for a hour the person in the box stay there and it is getting dark. The person looking for the kid in the box knows where the kid is a waiting for that person to come out.

NAEP primary trait score (1), holistic score (2), both low; discourse score (4), not a discernible black style.

Imaginative, 1984, #590877

I see little kids playing around me some on the swings, and some on the sliding bord. The kids are enjoying themselfs. As for me I'm in this box because I'm afraid of all of the other kids in the park. In a distinance I see a baseball field and some men playing and over by the park is a Basketball court where other kids are playing. And in the picnic grounds theirs a family having a picnic. The kids are playing catch with their father while the mother I think is setting up the picnic area. In another section of the park theirs a crowd of people watching these two guys "break" dancing. "Break" dancing is a new form of dance combining some gymnistics with some regular dance moves. It is a real sight to see. Also I see some girls on the sidewalk jumping rope double dutch style thats when you use two ropes. The girls are very good to. It is a hot day so I see that the swimming pool is doing good today. I would be over their myself If I wasn't shy. It's a very hot in this box but I'm so afraid to come out. I see that a fight has broke loose by the swings. Two little kids are fighting over one see all the other kids have already taken all the other swings and their two kids and only one swing left. I think that the kids have settled their argument now.

Now here comes a big black man over by me now. He says that my mother is here to pick me up so I could go home By.

NAEP primary trait score (3), holistic score (5), both high; discourse score (1), a highly discernible African American style.

Persuasive, 1984, #050238

I think that If the ABandoned RailRoad track was not there. that we can use the money that we have saved could go on the things we need for the community center. So that the children can have many & more things to do. The RailRoad could Be destroyed so that they can make a play ground out of

It. And the ware house could have some toys In It Also Just in case It get cold or Rain. Therefore they could have toys Inside and outside.

NAEP holistic score (2), low score; discourse score (4), not a discernible black style.

Persuasive, 1988, #520462

> How are you doing? Fine I hope!
>
> I'm writing you this letter in reference to you making your purchase in buying the warehouse.
>
> I think that in buying the old warehouse, we could paint it and fix it up and make it out of a gym for the kids during the week and on weekends and on Fridays we could have Bingo and maybe once or twice a month on Sundays we could give a super.
>
> During the week we could have the children come here after school and do their homework and then let them play a little basketball, until about 5:30 p.m.
>
> On Fridays at about 7:00 we could set up for Bingo and sell the cards 8 for $10 and that way we could help pay for the pot and have 14 games and cherry betts.
>
> Every first or last Sunday in the month we could give a super for the community and sell each plate for $3 to $5.
>
> If you have any questions, please feel free to call me at 288-8263.
>
> > Sincerly,
> >
> > Ms. Zenitta

NAEP holistic score (4), high score; discourse score (1), a highly discernible black style.

Note

1. This chapter is a revised version of my presentation at the Columbia University Conference on African American Language and Communication, New York, October 26, 1991. The research on which this chapter is based was funded by the National Council of Teachers of English Research Foundation with grants in 1981, 1982, and 1989. Special thanks to Joshua Bagakas, Michigan State University statistician, for assistance with statistical design and analysis; to Jules Goodison, director of the National Assessment for Educational Testing Service, and his staff, without whose help this project could not even have been started, much less finished; to family members Sam and Kathy Brogdon and Bobbi White for those grueling, twelve-hour days of work at ETS in the summer of 1989; to my Michigan State University research assistants Chanille Bouldes, Tyronda Curry, Angeletta Gourdine, and Ronnie Hopkins for assistance with data entry and coding and most of all for their patience; to Schavi Ali, Denise Troutman-Robinson, and Wanda Larrier for assistance with coding and for their wisdom and sound advice; and to my former secretary, Debbi Sudduth, for persevering. Any mistakes or shortcomings are entirely my own.

References

Applebee, A., Langer, J., and Mullis, I. (1985). *Writing trends across the decade, 1974–84.* Princeton, NJ: Educational Testing Service.

Applebee, A., Langer, J., Mullis, I., and Jenkins, L. (1990). *The writing report card, 1984–88.* Princeton, NJ: Educational Testing Service.

Asante, M. (1990). African elements in African-American English. In J. Holloway (Ed.), *Africanisms in American culture* (19–33). Bloomington: Indiana University Press.

Bereiter, C., and Engelmann, S. (1966). *Teaching disadvantaged children in the preschool.* Englewood Cliffs, NJ: Prentice Hall.

Chaplin, M. (1987). *An analysis of writing features found in the essays of students in the National Assessment of Educational Progress and the New Jersey high school proficiency test.* Unpublished manuscript, Rutgers University, Department of English, Camden, NJ.

———. (1990). A closer look at black and white students' assessment essays. *Iowa English Bulletin, 38,* 15–27.

Cohen, R. A. (1969). Conceptual styles, cultural conflicts and non-verbal tests of intelligence. *American Anthropologist, 71,* 828–856.

Cooper, G. (1979). *The relationship between errors in standard usage in written compositions of college students and the students' cognitive styles.* Unpublished doctoral dissertation, Howard University, Washington, DC.

Dillard, J. (1972). *Black English.* New York: Random House.

Gates, H. L., Jr. (1988). *The signifying monkey.* New York: Oxford University Press.

Herskovits, M. (1941). *Myth of the Negro past.* New York: Harper.

Hoover, M. (1978). Community attitudes towards black English. *Language in Society, 7,* 65–87.

Humboldt, W. V. (1841). Ueber die Verschiedenheiten des Menschlichen Sprachbaues. *Gesammelte Werke, VI* [On the varieties of human linguistic structures. Collected works]. Berlin.

Hymes, D. (1974). *Foundations in sociolinguistics.* Philadelphia: University of Pennsylvania Press.

Jensen, A. R. (1980). *Bias in mental testing.* New York: Free Press.

Labov, W. (1972). *Language in the inner city.* Philadelphia: University of Pennsylvania Press.

Lincoln, C. E. (1990). *The black church in the African American experience.* Durham, NC: Duke University Press.

National Assessment of Educational Progress. (1980). *Writing achievement, 1969–79* (Report No. 10-W-01). Denver, CO: Education Commission of the States.

———. (1985). *The reading report card, progress toward excellence in our schools: Trends in reading over four national assessments, 1971–1984.* Princeton, NJ: Educational Testing Service.

Sapir, E. (1929). *Language: An introduction to the study of speech.* New York: Harcourt, Brace.

Scott, J. (1981). Mixed dialects in the composition classroom. In M. Montgomery (Ed.), *Language variety in the south: Perspectives in black and white.* Tuscaloosa, AL: University of Alabama Press.

Simpkins, G., Holt, G., and Simpkins, C. (1976). *Bridge.* Boston: Houghton Mifflin.

Smitherman, G. (1969). *A comparison of the oral and written styles of a group of inner-city black students.* Unpublished doctoral dissertation, University of Michigan, Ann Arbor.

———. (1985). *A description of structure and discourse in selected black student writing from the National Assessment of Educational Progress* (Final Research Report). Urbana, IL: National Council of Teachers of English.

———. (1986). *Talkin and testifyin* (rev. ed.). Detroit: Wayne State University Press. (Original work published by Houghton Mifflin, 1977)

———. (1991). Black English, diverging or converging: The view from the National Assessment of Educational Progress. *Language and Education, 5,* 1–15.

Smitherman, G., and Wright, S. (1983, March). *Black student writers, storks and familiar places: What can we learn from the National Assessment of Educational Progress?* Paper presented at the annual convention of the Conference on College Composition and Communication, Detroit. [Also, (1983, December). *Interim Research Report.* Urbana, IL: National Council of Teachers of English.]

Taylor, O. (1992, June). *Presentation at African American English in Schools and Society Conference.* Stanford University, Stanford, CA.

Thompson, R. F. (1983). *Flash of the spirit: African and Afro-American art and philosophy.* New York: Random House.

Volosinov, V. N. (1973). *Marxism and the philosophy of language.* New York: Seminar Press. (Original work published 1930)

Vygotsky, L. S. (1962). *Thought and language.* Cambridge, MA: M.I.T. Press.

Whiteman, M. (1976). *Dialect influence and the writing of black and white working-class Americans.* Unpublished doctoral dissertation, Georgetown University, Washington, DC.

Whorf, B. (1956). *Language, thought and reality.* Cambridge, MA: M.I.T. Press.

Williams, R. L. (1972). *The Bitch 100: A culture-specific test.* St. Louis: Washington University.

Wilson, R. (1971). *A comparison of learning styles in African tribal groups with Afro-American learning situations and the channels of cultural connection:*

An analysis of documentary material. Unpublished doctoral dissertation, Wayne State University, Detroit.

Wright, S. (1984). *A description of the variance between the oral and written language patterns of a group of black community college students.* Unpublished doctoral dissertation, Wayne State University, Detroit

8 Gender Differences and Symbolic Imagination in the Stories of Four-Year-Olds

Ageliki Nicolopoulou
Smith College

Barbara Scales
University of California, Berkeley

Jeff Weintraub
Williams College

Ageliki Nicolopoulou, Barbara Scales, and Jeff Weintraub turn our attention to another source of difference in students' stories—gender. They portray the striking differences in the narrative styles of four-year-old boys and girls. These differences in symbolic imagination *raise thought-provoking questions about the ways in which young children construct their social worlds—and the ways in which teachers might further and expand those worlds.*

Most scholars and practitioners in the field of education are, for understandable reasons, more interested in stories written *for* children, which they read or which are told to them, than in stories that children *themselves* compose and tell. But of course the two subjects are not unrelated: when children tell stories, they reveal something important about who they are and how they see the world. By grasping the forms of symbolic imagination expressed in the stories that children *tell,* we can improve our understanding of how children comprehend and respond to the stories told *to* them and what kind of impression these stories make on them. But part of what makes children's storytelling so revealing, it is important to add, is that it plays a vital role in their own efforts to make sense of the world and to find their place in it. As both Bruner (e.g., 1986, 1990) and Paley (e.g., 1981, 1984a, 1984b, 1988, 1990) have emphasized in different ways, the stories children tell are themselves cognitive tools, and children's use of fantasy is a crucial element in their attempts to master reality.

One philosopher has argued that, if we listen carefully to children, we can see the ways in which they are little philosophers: they ponder the deepest metaphysical and ontological problems in their own way in an attempt to bring cognitive order to the universe (Matthews 1980). In a parallel fashion, this chapter will urge that we take children seriously as little artists. They use stories and other forms of symbolic expression in order to represent the world—to themselves and each other—and thereby to make sense of it. Simultaneously, they use their stories as a way of expressing certain emotionally important themes that preoccupy them and of symbolically managing or resolving these underlying themes. In constructing their stories, they draw in various ways on images and conceptual resources present in their culture, but they do not just passively *absorb* them—and the messages behind them. It seems clear that, even at the age of four, they are able to *appropriate* them and to some degree to manipulate them for their own symbolic ends. But once again, to see how they do it, we have to listen to them carefully.

The Study Plan

The present discussion is based on the analysis of a set of spontaneous stories told by a group of four-year-olds. The larger concern behind this investigation is to explore the different ways in which children use symbolic constructions to represent and organize reality—and, in this case, the ways in which these differences come to be structured by gender. Our findings suggest that, even at this early age, the boys and girls involved visualize and represent the world—and especially the world of social relations—in strikingly distinctive ways. Their differing orientations are expressed in their active use and imaginative elaboration of two distinctive and gender-related narrative styles that permeate this body of stories. Underlying these narrative styles are different forms of symbolic imagination, different emerging images of social reality, and different ways of coming to grips with that reality. They represent, among other things, quite different approaches to the symbolic management of order and disorder. In addition to broadening our knowledge of narrative diversity among young children, it seems likely that grasping these differences can help us understand tendencies toward the developmental emergence of different cognitive and cultural styles in men and women.

The Children and Their Stories

The stories we have been analyzing were composed by children attending a half-day nursery school affiliated with the Child Study Center of the University of California, Berkeley. The group involved was the class of four-year-olds, of which one of the authors, Barbara Scales, is the head teacher. The class consisted of 28 children, 14 boys and 14 girls.

The family backgrounds of the children in this group were primarily middle to upper-middle class, mostly professional or academic. In most cases, both parents worked outside the home. To prepare for some of the discussion later on, we want to emphasize that the nursery school attempts strongly and deliberately to create an egalitarian and nonsexist atmosphere; and we have every reason to believe that most of the children come from families which share this orientation.

The stories were collected by using a variant of a storytelling and story-acting technique pioneered by Vivian Paley. One optional activity in which any child in the school may choose to participate every day is to dictate a story to the teacher who is supervising the inside area that day. The teacher records the story as the child tells it. At the end of each day, all the stories dictated during that day are read aloud to the entire group at "circle time" by the same teacher. While the story is being read, the child-author and other children, whom he or she chooses, act out the story. This story-acting practice is aimed at fostering communication and the development of a common culture within the group of children by having them listen to and even actively participate in each other's stories.

The analysis is based on the complete set of 582 stories collected during the entire academic year 1988–89, which included stories told by all 28 children. About 60 percent (347) of these stories were dictated by girls and about 40 percent (235) by boys. (This corpus of stories is drawn from the "Child Study Center Archives of Children's Play Narratives" at the Institute of Human Development of the University of California, Berkeley.)

Interpretive Analysis: Narrative as Symbolic Form

Material of this kind constitutes an especially rich source of data for research that explores the role of narratives in children's construction of reality and personal identity. This is true above all because of their voluntary and spontaneous composition and because the children's storytelling activity is embedded in the ongoing framework of their everyday group life—in the "real world" of their classroom mini-culture. Furthermore, because of "circle time," these are stories that children tell not only to adults, but to other children as well.

From a methodological standpoint, the question is what kind of approach can best take advantage of the possibilities offered by this material. While a considerable amount of work on children and narratives is being done now in the overlapping disciplines of psychology and linguistics, studies that deal with children's own stories are decidedly in the minority. Even in these cases, the stories are usually generated under conditions that sharply limit their spontaneous character (often for well-considered methodological reasons, to be sure). Furthermore, for several decades the great bulk of this research has tended to focus more or less exclusively on formal elements of the stories—most typically their narrative structure—and to neglect their symbolic content (for some reviews, see Mandler 1983; Romaine 1985; Slobin 1990; Stein and Glenn 1982). We are necessarily speaking in broad terms here, and there are significant exceptions, but even when attention is paid to the symbolic content, it is usually in an incidental and unsystematic way (e.g., Sutton-Smith 1981). On the other hand, some investigations deriving from a psychoanalytic perspective obviously focus quite heavily on symbolic content (e.g., Bettelheim 1977; Pitcher and Prelinger 1963), but these analyses tend to neglect the formal elements of the stories and the cognitive styles they embody.

However, a rigid divorce between form and content in the analysis of children's narratives makes it difficult to capture precisely those features which render them important and emotionally engaging for children. The child's story is fragmented into elements that, taken in isolation, do not fully capture the point of telling and listening to stories. Studies of children's narrative competence, for example, are often strangely abstracted from the uses to which children put this competence and their purposes in doing so. Overcoming this fragmentation—reassembling the phenomenon of story as a living whole—requires an approach that can integrate the formal analysis of children's narratives into a more comprehensive *interpretive* perspective. In particular, it requires that we treat narrative form as a type of *symbolic* form, whose function is to confer meaning on experience, rather than conceiving it only in terms of linguistic structure. As Bruner has cogently put it, "The central concern is not how narrative text is constructed, but rather how it operates as an instrument of mind in the construction of reality" (1992, 233).

Thus the interpretive framework we have developed to analyze these stories attempts to capture both their form and their content and to bring out the relationship between them. In working out our approach, we have drawn on a range of sources, including several of the contributors to this volume. One especially useful source of guidance has been the mode of cultural interpretation championed by Geertz, an anthropologist (e.g., 1973), and the broader "interpretive turn" in the human sciences for which he has been a particularly influential spokesman. The guiding insight of this perspective is that the interpretation of meaning is not only a key requirement for the study of human life, but is simultaneously a central condition of human thought and action itself. Accordingly, our starting point is the premise that the children's stories are meaningful texts that, if analyzed carefully, can tell us a great deal about the ways that children grasp the world and social relationships. The crucial concern of an interpretive analysis is thus to elucidate or decode the *structures of meaning* that the stories embody and express—reconstructing not only the surface meanings of the stories, but also certain deeper patterns that organize and inform them. When they are approached in this way, children's spontaneous stories, as well as other expressions of their symbolic imagination, can offer us an invaluable and privileged window into the mind of the preschooler.

Gender-related Narrative Styles in Children's Stories

When we first set out to examine these stories, we did not have gender differences in mind, nor were we searching for different narrative styles. They emerged in the course of the analysis, and indeed took us by surprise. It had been suggested that the use of this storytelling and story-acting practice seemed to generate greater cohesion and solidarity among the children, and it was this phenomenon of social cohesion we wished to study. Our original intention was to trace the ways that themes were transmitted and elaborated within the group and became part of the children's common culture.

But as we read systematically through the entire corpus of the stories, one profound complication in this picture became increasingly apparent to us: namely, that the stories divided overwhelmingly along gender lines. Despite the fact that the stories were shared with the entire group every day, boys and girls told different kinds of stories. In fact, the kinds of stories boys and girls told differed systematically and consistently not only in their characteristic subject matter, but also in the overall narrative structure and symbolic imagination they employed.

We discovered, in other words, that this body of stories is dominated by two highly distinctive narrative styles, divided to a striking extent along gender lines, that contrast sharply (and subtly) in their characteristic modes of representing experience and in their underlying images of social relationships. In fact, these narrative styles embody two distinctive types of genuine aesthetic imagination (surprising as it may seem to assert this of four-year-olds), each with its own inner logic and coherence. In particular, underlying and unifying many of the surface themes in the stories is a preoccupation with issues of order and disorder; here we are indebted to the theoretical lead provided by Douglas, another anthropologist (particularly in Douglas 1966). In general—to anticipate our overall conclusions—the girls' stories show a strain toward *order*, while the boys' stories show a strain toward *disorder*, a difference that is expressed in both the form and content of the stories.

The subsequent discussion will flesh out what we mean in speaking of a "strain toward order" and a "strain toward disorder," formulations we have arrived at through a very flexible appropriation of some ideas in Dewey's *Art as Experience* (1958). But let us caution immediately against a possible misunderstanding: both styles involve ways of bringing order to experience. As Douglas makes clear, an image of disorder always implies a background image of order against which it is conceived; and, furthermore, the disorder of the boys' stories itself represents a kind of order. The key point is that the styles of the boys' and girls' stories represent two very different approaches to the symbolic management of order and disorder.

In this chapter we can only sketch out some of the most characteristic features which define and distinguish these two narrative styles and the cognitive and symbolic modes they embody. Although the basic patterns are rather clear once they have been mapped out, the subtleties and nuances involved produce a much richer and more complex picture than we can fully present here. To complicate matters further, individual children are often able to put their own unique stamp on the styles they employ. But here is a beginning.

The Girls' Stories: A Strain toward Order

Let us first characterize the girls' stories in terms of both form and content. The girls' stories, but *not* those of the boys, tend to have a coherent plot with a stable set of characters and a continuous plot line.

One way in which the girls *give* their stories this coherence is by structuring their content around stable sets of *social relationships*, especially (though not exclusively) *family* relationships. In fact, the extent to which the girls' stories, but not those of the boys, revolve thematically around the family group is overwhelming. Not all the girls' stories contain an explicit depiction of family relationships, but most of them do. And while the girls also represent stable and harmonious relationships in other ways, the portrayal of the family group is their prototypical mode of doing so. Therefore, it can serve as a useful focus for illustrating some of the most characteristic and pervasive features of their distinctive style. Thus the prototypical girl's story introduces a cast of characters who are carefully situated in a set of kinship relationships. Here is an example:

> Once upon a time there was a cat and a dog. And they lived in a warm snug house. And there was a mommy, a daddy, a sister, and another sister that was the big sister, and there was a brother that was the big brother, and there was a baby. And all the kids played together until it was dinner time. And then they had a lovely dinner of spaghetti and meatballs. (Martha, 4–4)

This story brings together almost all the elements that are typical of the most distinctive form of girls' stories: it revolves around a *family*, it meticulously articulates their kinship relations, and it takes place in the *home*, which is both a specific physical setting for the story and also the center of order ("a warm and snug house"). Another important element that often gives the girls' stories their coherence and continuity is their depiction of the rhythmic, cyclical, and repeated patterns of everyday domestic family life, which the girls like to recount:

> Once upon a time there's a mom, a dad, and there's a baby and a brother and a sister. The mother and father go to work and the big sister and big brother take care of the baby. Then the mother came home from work and their father came home from work. They ate dinner, and went to sleep, they woke up, and then the mom came and fed them breakfast. (Polly, 4–8)

Thus we often find that the family—after all its members have been carefully enumerated—goes to the park and comes back home. Or the parents go to work (this often specifically includes the mother) and the kids go to school, but then they come back home. Or they come home and have dinner and go to bed and wake up and have breakfast—and so on. (Boys' stories, on the other hand, very rarely depict cyclical or rhythmic action, whether in a family setting or in any other context.)

In short, these examples show that girls' stories focus on *stable settings* and *stable relationships;* they contain relatively little description of action—particularly sudden or violent action. As we will see, the boys' stories are very different in these respects.

In addition, girls' stories—again, unlike the boys'—often include romantic or fairy-tale images of kings and queens, princes and princesses, and so on. But it is striking that they are assimilated to the *family* romance, since they characteristically get married and have babies. In addition, when the girls talk about animals, they often bring them into the family by making them into pets. Here is another example:

> Two queens and two princesses lived in two houses. Once they shared the house with the queens and the princesses, two princesses came and wanted to marry two princes. And two kings came and wanted to marry the queens. Five ponies came and been their pets; two rabbits were the ponies' friends, and they were the other pets; the two zebras are the princesses' pets. The end. (Dora, 3–11)

This story also illustrates a tendency toward formal symmetry (*two* queens, *two* kings, *two* princesses, *two* princes, *two* zebras, and so on—marred, in this case, only by the five ponies) that is common in the girls' stories but very rare in the boys'. And let us point out another important contrast: boys may occasionally mention families, but in their stories practically no one *ever* gets married. (There were just three exceptions in the hundreds of stories we have.) But girls are fond of marriages and babies:

> Once upon a time there was a princess named Beauty. And she had two sisters and one dad and a mom. And then she went to a castle where a beast lived, and his name was Vincent. And then they get married. Then she has a baby. (Sonia, 4–11)

Thus the ideal world of the girls' stories tends to be centered, coherent, and firmly structured. Princes and princesses, brothers and sisters, even animals and beasts can all be enfolded harmoniously within the most stable system of social relations, those of the family unit. This is an orderly world. And, in fact, whenever order is disrupted or threatened, the girls are typically quite careful to reestablish it before ending the story—most characteristically by absorbing any threatening elements within the family unit:

> Once upon a time there was a mom. The mom was playing with two babies and there was a dad. The dad went to work. And the mom went to work. And then there came a dinosaur in a boat.

> It rode into water in the house. The parents came back home. The babies were gone. The dinosaur robbed the babies. The dad came home and said, "Babies, we're home. It's your Birthday!" Then the dinosaur branged them home and they were friends. The babies blew out the candles. They were two years old. The end. (Polly, 4–3)

The crucial point is that the girls' stories are not just orderly; they show a positive *strain* toward order.

The Boys' Stories: A Strain toward Disorder

In contrast, the four-year-old boys' stories show a strain toward disorder. Their stories are far less likely than the girls' to have either a stable cast of characters or a well-articulated plot; nor do they develop their themes in the steady and methodical manner of the girls' stories. Rather than the centered stability of the girls' stories, the boys' stories are marked by movement and disruption and often by associative chains of exuberant imagery. One might say that, if the girls' stories focus on creating, maintaining, and elaborating structure, the boys' stories focus on generating action and excitement; and the restless energy of their stories often overwhelms their capacity to manage it coherently. Thus their stories are more likely than the girls' to verge on the chaotic and often seem to begin or end almost randomly. The vigorous action that dominates the content is typically linked to an explicit emphasis on violence, conflict, and the disruption of order.

Let us begin with content. The boys' favorite characters tend to be big, powerful, and often deliberately frightening; warriors of all sorts are particularly fancied, along with monsters and huge or threatening animals. Besides the monsters, their stories are full of bears, tigers, dinosaurs, and so on—all of which are rather rare in the girls' stories. The animals that girls introduce into their stories tend to be cute and nonthreatening ones such as butterflies or bunnies. Nonviolent but scary elements such as ghosts and skeletons are also common in the boys' stories. The impulse toward disorder that lies behind their preoccupation with physical violence also comes out in bursts of extravagant, deliberately startling, and even grotesque imagery.

If the explicit depiction of the family group is a prototypical feature of the girls' stories, the corresponding motif in the boys' stories is the explicit—and generally enthusiastic—depiction of active violence. For example, here is a story that no girl in the sample would have told:

> Once upon a time there was a Triceratops, and a Tyrannosaurus
> Rex came. He bit Triceratops. But an Anatosaurus duckbill was
> watching another Anatosaurus eating plants. Tyrannosaurus
> Rex came and watched them. The duckbills run away. A No-
> dosaurus came and ate plants. A Voltursaurus came and they
> fight. All of the dinosaurs fight. Tyrannosaurus fights Tricera-
> tops. All the dinosaurs are dead except two dinosaurs: Tyranno-
> saurus is not dead and Triceratops is not dead. They become
> friends and smile. (John, 4–9)

As with content, so with form. As we noted earlier, the boys'
stories, in comparison with the girls', tend to be lacking in overall
formal coherence, as well as stability and continuity of time and space.
The typical boy's story consists, rather, of a string of dramatic and
powerful images and events, often juxtaposed in loose association. The
characters, rather than being firmly linked together, are often introduced sequentially into the story for the sake of action and thrilling
effect. The story just quoted is exceptional in having a clear resolution;
in general, the boys are much less concerned than the girls to bring
their plots to resolution. Instead, what marks the boys' stories is a
consistent striving toward action, novelty, and excess. As the next story
brings out well, the boys often strive for escalating images:

> Once upon a time there was a bear that went to the forest. Then
> a big wolf opened up his mouth. Then a beam of light came into
> a bunny's heart. Then he was a *Vampire* bunny. And soon some
> monsters came. A giant alligator came. And crocodile came to
> get the alligator. A big egg was rolling around. It belonged to the
> alligator. A tiger ran and ran and ran after a bat. And he was safe
> from the tiger. (Toby, 4–3)

As these two stories illustrate, the setting is often vague or
amorphous in the boys' stories; either it is not specified, or the action
seems to shift from one unrelated setting to another. Very few stories
center on an explicitly delineated setting, especially the home. Insofar
as the boys' stories have a plot, it is very frequently dominated by
fighting and destruction. However, as we have noted, physical violence is not the only means by which disorder can be generated.
Rule-breaking is another common theme in the boys' stories; and the
story just quoted brings out their fondness for startling and disruptive
imagery.

In short, the world of these stories is a world of violence, disruption, and disorder. What they express is a positive *fascination* with
disorder.

Now let us emphasize another point. Both the boys and the girls draw images from popular culture (including material transmitted by television, videos, and children's books), but what is interesting is that they do so *selectively*. They have already developed a differential sensitivity and preference for the elements presented to them by their cultural environment; they appropriate different elements and find ways to weave them into distinctive imaginative styles. For example, whereas the girls are particularly fond of princes and princesses and other fairy-tale characters, the boys favor cartoon action heroes such as Superman, He-Man, Teenage Mutant Ninja Turtles, and so on. The next story brings together many of the characteristic elements of the boys' stories:

> Once upon a time a teenage ninja turtle with a gun shot down a rock. Leonardo cuts that rock into half pieces. Leonardo has two swords. And the guy up high shoots the gun at Leonardo. A girl comes and has a gun in her pocket and shoots. She rides something very fast, and it runs and has two legs, and it's funny. A doggy-guy comes; he is a teenage ninja turtle, but he doesn't have any shell on his back. Doggy takes out his gun and shoots the guy up high. His name is Cone-a-lest, and he shoots back at Doggy. And they fight. They hear a voice say, "Doggy guy." It was a lion. Anything happened. And it was a saber tooth tiger. It roars and it doesn't see the lion or the guys down below and it left. The end. (John, 4–8)

"Anything happened": a typical boy's touch. In short, while the girls' stories are structured so as to maintain or restore order—cognitive, symbolic, and social—the boys' stories revel in movement, unpredictability, and disorder.

This brings us to another significant point. Given what we saw in the girls' stories, what is particularly striking about the boys' is the *absence* of stable social relationships and their frequent tenuousness when they are mentioned. The boys do sometimes identify characters as *friends*. In fact, this is the relationship they mention most commonly, though still far less commonly than the girls dwell on family relationships. But at least at the age of four, they do not yet seem to have developed a very powerful image of male friendship. In their stories, friendship is often a vague or transitory relationship, and at all events it is no guarantee of stability or harmony. Here is an especially telling illustration:

> Once upon a time there was a monster and there was a pig; and the monster wanted to kill the pig but the pig ran too fast and got away. Then the pig went into the forest and saw a live

chicken and they were friends. But they were fighting because the chicken was the greatest, so the pig went to the park; but the chicken couldn't because he was roasted by the pig and ated him all up. (Paul, 4–8)

Summary

The stories told by the boys are systematically different from those told by the girls, and the opposition goes beyond surface dissimilarities in attitudes or plot elements. The stories display two distinctive forms of symbolic imagination and involve quite distinctive ways of representing society and social relationships. It is not too much to say that these four-year-olds have already developed two distinct aesthetic styles. The style informing the girls' stories tends toward what might be called "socialist realism," while the style of the boys' can usefully be termed "picaresque surrealism." What they involve, at the deepest level, are two sharply different approaches to the symbolic management of order and disorder.

Some Illustrative Statistics and Their Interpretation: Structures of Meaning and Symbolic Reworking

Now that we have sketched out the basic patterns, let us offer some figures to illustrate some of the points we have been making. Summarized below is the frequency (technically, the mean proportions) of two of the most pervasive and significant content themes that run through the stories: explicit depictions of the family group and of active violence.

	Boys	**Girls**
Family group	14%	54%
Active violence	62%	18%

This is a simple comparison, but it makes a strong point. The reader will notice that the contrast between the boys' stories and the girls' stories is so striking that it hardly seems to require much comment. Obviously, the relative frequencies support the argument we have been making.

But, in fact, in certain important ways these figures actually *under*state the contrast involved. When we explore the deeper patterns behind these statistical comparisons, the real differences stand out even more sharply.

In the first place, the specific themes captured in these figures are, in both cases, only the most conspicuous manifestations of larger symbolic orientations. These figures for depictions of the "family group," for example, are based on a coding scheme that used fairly stringent criteria. If more lenient criteria for family themes are used, then the gap between the boys' and girls' percentages increases; and this holds even more strongly if we code for "stable and harmonious social relationships," rather than for the more specific category of family situations.

For a story to be coded as depicting a "family group," for example, it required explicit mention of a family situation involving at least two forms of kinship relation—a mother, a father, and at least one child, or one parent with several children. If we add stories that mention only one kinship relationship (such as brother-sister or mother-child), the relative frequency for the boys' stories goes to 20 percent and for the girls' stories to 65 percent. Furthermore, many of the girls' stories which do not explicitly construct an entire family situation include one implicitly, and they are noticeably more likely to do so than the boys' stories. But even more important is the fact noted earlier that the explicit portrayal of the family group is only *one* of the ways that the girls emphasize stable and harmonious social relationships in their stories. Often they dwell on relationships of this sort which very much resemble a family situation, and these shade off into relationships which seem to constitute, in this respect, the functional equivalent of a family situation. Here is an example of what we mean, and we have chosen what we think is one of the *less* obvious examples:

> Once upon a time there were three bees, three butterflies, and three ponies that were playing near the ocean. They went home and ate dinner. After dinner the butterflies, the bees, and the ponies went to bed. When they woke up the bees and the butterflies flew over the ocean, and the ponies went into the ocean. The end. (Polly, 4–2)

Correspondingly, we coded for "active violence" when characters in the stories explicitly fought, hurt, killed, ate, or actively threatened each other, or when they were explicitly depicted producing physical destruction. If the criteria are relaxed in various ways—for example, if physical destruction is depicted without an explicit agent being specified—then the boys' totals go up disproportionately (69 percent versus 20 percent). But again, physical violence is only one of the means that the boys use to generate disorder in their stories. Furthermore, the figures for the girls' stories mask the fact that the ways they *use* violence in their stories and the *attitude* displayed toward it tend to be very different from the boys' approach. For example, girls mention violence quickly rather than describing it in detail—often using the passive voice—and their accounts tend to lack the enthusiasm characteristic of the boys' stories.

This last point brings out the really crucial consideration, both methodologically and theoretically: the coding of specific themes or elements, though necessary, will always be inadequate by itself in this kind of research because an interpretive analysis is indispensable even to code intelligently. In many ways, in fact, the boys' and the girls' stories are so different in structure and intent that it is no simple matter to design uniform coding schemes which fully capture what is going on in both of them. In particular, even if the same element appears or is mentioned in a girl's story and a boy's story, its *significance* is often different in the two cases because it is *used* differently and fits into a different *structure of meaning*. Let us give an example. The following boy's story is one of the 14 percent which we coded as depicting a family group:

> There was a dad and a mom and two babies. They went to the park and there was a monster and he ate the family up. After he ate the family the monster died because there was too much family and he was fat. (Andrew, 4–4)

It is obvious that, in this story, the family imagery is not used to establish order and security, but rather to express the typical boy's fascination with violence and disorder (and it is hard not to suspect some ironic intent). Here is a milder, but equally instructive example from the same 14 percent; the family is associated with order and rules, but precisely in order to reject them:

> Once upon a time there was a bumblebee, then a yellow jacket came. They played. Then their mother came and said "clean up your room, brush your teeth, put on your pajamas, and go to bed, turn off the light, and pull up the covers." They didn't do that because they didn't want to. They wanted to play some more. Then a ghost came and took them on a ride. (Tom, 4–4)

The methodological point is that thematic elements cannot be taken in isolation and simply aggregated; each element can be understood only in the context of the larger structure of meaning within which it is embedded. In other words, as we have just indicated, what is required is an interpretive analysis that can elucidate these structures of meaning and grasp how they give significance to the particular elements. And when we undertake such an interpretive analysis, the systematic differences between the boys' and the girls' stories are even more striking than the figures themselves reveal.

These contrasting structures of meaning are brought out especially vividly if we analyze what happens when a girl introduces a typical "boy's" element or theme into her story, or vice versa. In each case, these elements are modified to conform to the characteristic model of the gender-specific narrative style.

We have already seen examples of how this is done. When a potentially threatening or disruptive animal enters one of the girls' stories, it is characteristically rendered nonthreatening. This is frequently done by identifying the animal as small or a "baby." Even the occasional monster can be neutralized with the cautionary comment that it is "a nice monster" or "a baby monster." Significantly, animals can be rendered nonthreatening by making them into "pets"—that is, by bringing them into the family and its framework of stable social relationships. In boys' stories we also see this kind of symbolic reworking, but in the opposite direction. The classic boy's counterpart to the "nice monster" is probably the "Vampire bunny," which appeared in a story quoted earlier.

This process of symbolic reworking provides one of the most convincing indications that we are dealing with a genuine contrast between two styles of aesthetic imagination—each constructing the world in accord with a distinctive symbolic *intention*—rather than a mere distribution of story traits. (Along similar lines, special insights can be gained from the analysis of "marginal stories"—that is, stories by both boys and girls that fit less sharply than most into one of the two gender-related narrative styles, and even incorporate some tension between them. Space limitations preclude further discussion here, but it is worth noting that, once the main outlines of important narrative styles are identified, "marginal stories" should not be viewed as an embarrassment, but instead merit special attention as a key to refining the analysis.)

Convergence and Divergence in the Symbolic Management of Order and Disorder

Before closing, we would like to emphasize one additional point, which in the space available can only be asserted rather than demonstrated. In this discussion, we have stressed the contrast, in both themes and formal structure, between the narrative styles informing the boys' and the girls' stories. But this is *not* to suggest that the preoccupations expressed in these stories, and the underlying issues they address, have nothing in common. On the contrary, what a close analysis of the stories reveals is that *both* boys and girls are preoccupied with issues of danger and disorder. What is different is the way they deal with them. The girls deal with threatening or disruptive elements by muffling or suppressing them: burying them under a structure of order, alluding to them indirectly, or, as we have indicated, incorporating any disturbing or potentially unpredictable figures into the structure of the family unit. In contrast, the boys deal with these elements by dwelling on them explicitly, elaborating them, and intensifying their dangerous and thrilling aura. As we put it earlier, the boys' and girls' stories represent two very different *approaches* to the symbolic management of order and disorder.

The girls' approach is exemplified by the crucial (and especially revealing) fact that they are usually careful not to end their stories until all potentially disruptive elements have been neutralized or resolved—in particular, until the family has come back home or has otherwise reestablished its grip on order. The fundamental divergence in this respect between the symbolic imagination underlying the girls' stories and the boys' could not be illustrated more sharply than by the contrast between the last two stories we will quote. Here is a girl's story:

> Once upon a time there was an old, old house. A family was living in it. There was a baby, a mother, a father, and a sister. And all the kids played Candyland. And one day when the family was out shopping, there was a fire on the street to their house. When they came back home and saw that their house wasn't there, they went to find another one. (Martha, 4–5)

The home is the locus of order, so having it burn down is disturbing. The girl is not going to end her story until she has the family find another one. On the other hand, here is a boy's story about the home:

> Once upon a time there was a moose. His name was Moose-moose. And he lived in a person's house. And he knocked a telephone off the wall. And he broke the house. And he ripped up the skeleton and he knocked the table out. And he broke the windows. Then he knocked down the house again. And then he drew on his face. And he turned the lamp on, and he let the birds out of the cage. *The end.* (Bobby, 4–7)

The story ends with chaos triumphant: a classic boy's story. But it is interesting to note that the house is always around to be destroyed a second time.

Some Lessons and Implications

This analysis has, we hope, vindicated our suggestion that we can learn a good deal by taking children seriously as little artists and by recognizing the genuinely aesthetic impulse behind their storytelling activity. The expressive imagination that animates their stories is a resource they employ for making experience intelligible and rendering it emotionally manageable and satisfying. Furthermore, underlying the different narrative styles that they use and elaborate are distinctive ways of visualizing reality, distinctive modes of ordering and interpreting the world. Exploring and elucidating these distinctive visions can deepen our understanding of the active role of children's symbolic imagination in their construction of reality and in the formation of identity, including gender identity. While the line of research on which this chapter is based needs to be further extended and refined, it is already clear that the findings reported here have implications for a wide range of issues in development and education.

The most striking implication of these findings is simply the extent to which systematic gender differences in social and symbolic imagination have begun to crystallize even at the young age of four years. A range of work in a number of fields lends support to our judgment that the contrasting narrative styles we have identified are not peculiar to our data and that they do, indeed, point to deeper differences in symbolic imagination and in cognitive and sociocultural styles. While surprisingly little systematic study of gender differences in children's spontaneous stories has been undertaken (the major exception being the work of Paley), the distinctive gender-related patterns delineated in this study appear to be broadly consistent with a number of other findings from research on gender differences in children's play (e.g., Black 1989; Paley 1984a, 1984b; Sachs 1987) and in the narrative and conversational styles of children and adults (e.g., Goodwin 1990; Goodwin and Goodwin 1987; Sheldon 1990; Tannen 1990a, 1990b). More tentatively, our findings would seem to have some bearing on the recent line of discussion, associated above all with the work of Gilligan (e.g., 1982; Gilligan and Attanucci, 1988), which has argued that men and women follow somewhat different paths of moral development and that women's moral imagination and moral reasoning are much more likely to be anchored in a concern with stable patterns of social ties and obligations. Our results also appear to resonate, in suggestive ways, with certain patterns identified in Chodorow's analysis of the social formation of gender differences in emotional and personality development (e.g., 1978, 1989).

Because the subject of gender differences in development is so complex and contentious, a cautionary note is in order. The fact that the four-year-old boys and girls in this study already display such distinctive styles of representing and grasping reality, and that they spontaneously reproduce and elaborate these differences in a classroom setting devoted to building up a common culture among them, is a significant phenomenon that demands further consideration. By themselves, however, these findings do not tell us where these differences come from, nor do they necessarily suggest that such differences are immutable. But they do bring out both how far and how deeply the processes of gender differentiation have already developed in the first four years of life, and they underscore the complexity of the dynamics involved in the formation of gender identity.

At the same time, these findings highlight the need to approach the social formation of mind and personality in a way that does not treat the child as a passive bystander in this process. In constructing their stories, both the boys and the girls draw on images and other elements that are presented to them by their cultural environment and that shape their imagination and sensibility in profound and subtle ways. But we also find that, when given the opportunity, they are able (and eager) to use these elements to put the world together in quite distinctive ways.

One larger implication of this striking fact is to remind us that the formative effect of culture is neither simple, unmediated, nor one-way. Quite practically, this means that the impact on children of the various cultural materials to which they are exposed—from TV shows to children's books to classroom curricula—will never be direct or uniform because, even at a very young age, the children bring to these materials their own distinctive interpretive frameworks, underlying concerns, and modes of appropriation. Thus the projects of adults who try to shape and advance children's development—from parents to teachers—encounter the multiple projects (themselves culturally shaped) that the children themselves are trying to pursue. The results of these encounters are neither simple nor easily predictable. Without having some sense of the inner logic of the children's own projects, adults cannot take for granted what the effects of their interventions will be.

The situation on which our research is based may provide an instructive example. The patterns we have identified seem to emerge from the complex and mutually reinforcing interaction of two ongoing processes. First, the children's distinctive narrative styles express underlying differences in their emerging cognitive modes and symbolic imagination. Second, at the same time, the use of these different styles is probably part of an effort by the boys and girls to mark themselves off from each other symbolically into different groups and to build up a sense of cohesion and shared identity within each subgroup. Therefore, the use of the storytelling and story-acting practice to build up a common culture within the classroom may also, ironically, have provided the children with a framework for the articulation of differences within this common culture. There is some indication—though at present this can only be tentatively suggested—that the narrative styles of the children's stories, rather than becoming more similar, actually polarized in certain ways during the year, precisely as the boys and girls became more familiar with each other's styles. (A dialectic of this kind would be consistent with the pattern suggested by Davies [1989] in her stimulating analysis of the dynamics of preschool children's symbolic construction of gender identities. The lesson, once again, is the need for studies to take seriously the complexity of the relationship between culture and individual development.

All these considerations lead back to the recognition, which is a unifying theme of this volume, that understanding narrative diversity is a matter of considerable practical significance for education. This is especially true because children's narrative styles involve not only different ways of representing reality, but—simultaneously—different modes of grasping and understanding it. The cognitive and symbolic modes for which these narrative styles serve as vehicles constitute important resources for children in learning and development. But at the same time, these different tools for mastering reality carry with them different emphases and sensitivities, different strengths and weaknesses.

This diversity can emerge along a number of axes. For example, studies such as those inspired by the work of Heath (e.g., 1983) and Michaels (e.g., 1981) have analyzed the different narrative styles brought to school by children from culturally distinct communities and have showed the impact of these narrative styles on the children's different routes to literacy and to broader educational success (or lack thereof). The outcomes are crucially affected by the extent to which educational practice can recognize, develop, and build on their distinctive strengths (and also recognize and address their distinctive gaps and weaknesses). But community of origin is certainly not the only source of narrative diversity within and between classrooms—as attested by the boys and girls discussed in this chapter, whose notable differences emerged within a context of very similar family and socio-economic backgrounds. The results of our study underline the need to address the dimension of gender in understanding the sources, forms, and implications of narrative diversity.

Here again, it is important to add a note of complexity. Not only does narrative diversity emerge along a number of axes, but understanding it is not simply a matter of dividing children into sharply demarcated subgroups. Children—like adults—need not be restricted to a single narrative mode, but are likely to have a range available to them for various purposes. One of the aims of education ought to be to help develop the range and richness of the narrative styles they can master and effectively employ. But if we are to foster and encourage this development in effective and educationally rewarding ways, it is important to recognize and appreciate the distinctive kinds of foundations on which it can build.

In the long run, of course, mapping out the emergence of gender differences unavoidably raises an even deeper question: Why do they occur? This is a big and difficult subject, which we can be excused for not attempting to address here. But we will venture to say that, in order to formulate intelligent questions about what causes gender differences in development, it is important to understand these differences and their developmental emergence in depth. The type of analysis presented in this chapter can contribute to that goal. It may be that appreciating and understanding the imaginative gulf between boys and girls suggested by this research can help us think about ways of starting to bridge it.

References

Bettelheim, B. (1977). *The uses of enchantment: The meaning and importance of fairy tales*. New York: Vintage.

Black, B. (1989). Interactive pretense: Social and symbolic skills in preschool play groups. *Merrill-Palmer Quarterly, 35*, 379–397.

Bruner, J. S. (1986). *Actual minds, possible worlds*. Cambridge, MA: Harvard University Press.

———. (1990). *Acts of meaning*. Cambridge, MA: Harvard University Press.

———. (1992). The narrative construction of reality. In H. Beilin and P. Pufall (Eds.), *Piaget's theory: Prospects and possibilities* (229–248). Hillsdale, NJ: Lawrence Erlbaum.

Chodorow, N. (1978). *The reproduction of mothering: Psychoanalysis and the sociology of gender*. Berkeley: University of California Press.

————. (1989). Being and doing: A cross-cultural examination of the socialization of males and females. In *Feminism and psychoanalytic theory*. New Haven, CT: Yale University Press.

Davies, B. (1989). *Frogs and snails and feminist tales: Preschool children and gender.* North Sydney, New South Wales: Allen & Unwin.

Dewey, J. (1958). *Art as experience.* New York: Capricorn.

Douglas, M. (1966). *Purity and danger.* London: Routledge & Kegan Paul.

Geertz, C. (1973). *The interpretation of cultures.* New York: Basic Books.

Gilligan, C. (1982). *In a different voice: Psychological theory and women's development.* Cambridge, MA: Harvard University Press.

Gilligan, C., and Attanucci, J. (1988). Two moral orientations: Gender differences and similarities. *Merrill-Palmer Quarterly, 34,* 223–237.

Goodwin, M. H. (1990). Tactical uses of stories: Participation frameworks within girls' and boys' disputes. *Discourse Processes, 13,* 33–71.

Goodwin, M. H., and Goodwin, C. (1987). Children's arguing. In S. U. Philips, S. Steele, and C. Tanz (Eds.), *Language, gender, and sex in comparative perspective.* Cambridge: Cambridge University Press.

Heath, S. B. (1983). *Ways with words: Language, life, and work in communities and classrooms.* Cambridge: Cambridge University Press.

Mandler, J. (1983). Representation. In J. H. Flavell and E. M. Markman (Eds.), *Cognitive development.* Vol. 3 of P. Mussen (Ed.), *Handbook of child psychology* (4th ed.). New York: Wiley.

Matthews, G. (1980). *Philosophy and the young child.* Cambridge, MA: Harvard University Press.

Michaels, S. (1981). Sharing time: Children's narrative styles and differential access to literacy. *Language in Society, 10,* 423–442.

Paley, V. (1981). *Wally's stories.* Cambridge, MA: Harvard University Press.

————. (1984a). *Mollie is three: Growing up in school.* Chicago: University of Chicago Press.

————. (1984b). *Boys and girls: Superheroes in the doll corner.* Chicago: University of Chicago Press.

————. (1988). *Bad guys don't have birthdays.* Chicago: University of Chicago Press.

————. (1990). *The boy who would be a helicopter: The uses of storytelling in the classroom.* Cambridge, MA: Harvard University Press.

Pitcher, E. G., and Prelinger, E. (1963). *Children tell stories: An analysis of fantasy.* New York: International Universities Press.

Romaine, S. (1985). Children's narratives. *Linguistics, 23,* 83–104.

Sachs, J. (1987). Preschool boys' and girls' language use in pretend play. In S. U. Philips, S. Steele, and C. Tanz (Eds.), *Language, gender, and sex in comparative perspective* (178–188). Cambridge: Cambridge University Press.

Sheldon, A. (1990). Pickle fights: Gendered talk in preschool disputes. *Discourse Processes, 13,* 5–31.

Slobin, D. I. (1990). The development from child speaker to native speaker. In J. W. Stigler, R. A. Shweder, and G. Herdt (Eds.), *Cultural psychology: Essays on comparative human development* (233–256). Cambridge: Cambridge University Press.

Stein, N. L., and Glenn, C. G. (1982). An analysis of story comprehension in elementary school children. In R. O. Freedle (Ed.), *New directions in discourse processing* (Vol. 2). Norwood, NJ: Ablex.

Sutton-Smith, B. (1981). *The folkstories of children.* Philadelphia: University of Pennsylvania Press.

Tannen, D. (1990a). *You just don't understand: Women and men in conversation.* New York: William Morrow.

———. (1990b). Gender differences in topical coherence: Creating involvement in best friends' talk. *Discourse Processes, 13,* 73–90.

9 "And They Lived Happily Ever After": Cultural Storylines and the Construction of Gender

Pam Gilbert
James Cook University of North Queensland

Pam Gilbert extends and expands the theme of gender differences in students' stories. She argues that dominant ways of reading and writing stories help to construct and maintain the hierarchical dualism *between femininity and masculinity. Through critical discourse in the classroom, teachers and students can work toward reconstructing this polarization and expanding the cultural possibilities, as well as the symbolic imagination, of girls and boys.*

One day there was a little girl called Kathleen. She found a gold pot. It was a useful pot. She rubbed it. A genie came out of it. The genie said "You have three wishes."
"I wish I had the prettiest dress in the whole world."
"But now it's your second wish."
"I wish I had long blonde hair."
"I wish I was a princess in a castle."
Then she got her three wishes. Then she was happy. In the castle the next day she got married with a handsome prince and they lived happily ever after.
THE END

Eight-year-old girl (in Dwyer 1992)

Ace is going for a walk in the forest. Suddenly the Cobra planes start firing. Ace runs for shelter. He tells the Boss. He said, "Go to bed."

I wish to thank Leanne Dalley and Bronwyn Dwyer for making the texts from their research available for this paper.

Deep goes diving. He blew up the Cobras' underwater base. Ace calls Complex. He says, "I'm on my way." They go into the Cobra's house. Ace and Complex go to the Cobra's base and get into a plane. They find a Cobra plane. They shot it down. They shoot the Cobra base. Metalhead touched metal. He blew it up.

Eight-year-old boy (in Dwyer 1992)

Whether we are reading or writing, talking or listening, it is difficult to ignore gender: to not notice how language practices are used differently by women and men, to not notice the different ways in which women and men are described, to not notice that girls' and boys' stories in classrooms can sometimes be very different.

For educators, the gendered nature of classroom language practices has been of concern for some time (see Sheridan 1983; Gilbert 1989). Over the past twenty years, issues of language access, particularly access to teacher talk, to classroom linguistic space, and to socially powerful discourse forms, have been a particular focus of research (Swann and Graddol 1988; Poynton 1985; White 1986). However, more recently the language system for which access has been sought has come under increasing scrutiny, and with this scrutiny has come an interest in the way in which language practices are involved in the social construction of gender.

The opportunity to learn to talk and write and read in the dominant practices of a society, and the access to be able to do such talking and writing and reading, are both valuable. But such opportunities need also to be accompanied by social understandings of how these practices have become dominant, how their dominance has been maintained, and whose voices and lives have consequently been marginalized or silenced. The language system is not a gender-free zone, and access to social language practice needs also to be accompanied by a critical reflexivity which allows for the possibility of dialogue and debate with dominant and entrenched meanings.

This chapter will argue that a positive approach to classroom storying must not only take account of the different ways in which groups of children access certain text types and topics—and how gender is implicated in this difference—but that it must also take account of the meanings that text types and topics allow if they are used. If our goal in the classroom is towards a greater expansion of human potential, then the entrenched polarization of much popular thinking about women and men needs to be reread. A closer consideration of the role that storying plays in the construction and regulation of this polarization may, this chapter would argue, be helpful.

School Storying

Storying is one of the most important and popular of school language practices; yet for many educators, the space and privilege allocated to story reading and story writing in classrooms raise an interesting dilemma in terms of gender equity. On the one hand, young women are often very competent with stories, becoming noticeably more fluent readers and writers in the early years of schooling than their male counterparts (Sheridan 1982; Dwyer 1992). But on the other hand, this competence (perhaps compliance) with early school literacy tasks can be questioned in terms of the social value it provides.

For example, girls generally take up a very narrow range of writing positions from which to write school stories, and these are commonly positions that rely upon a hierarchical construction of male-female relationships. Poynton (1985) claims that the stories that girls write at school are remarkably stereotypical in topic choice and character construction; that they draw predominantly upon a narrow range of topic areas such as home activities, dress and appearance, romance, and fantasy worlds; and that they are often inhabited by such characters as fairies, witches, literary figures from children's stories, talking animals, and commercial toys. By detailing some of the differences between girls' texts and those written by boys, studies by Tuck, Bayliss, and Bell (1985), Romatowski and Trepanier-Street (1987), Kamler (1992), as well as earlier work of mine (Gilbert 1989), produce similar findings about the gendered features of girls' writing.

However, the significance of this gender difference in children's story writing has not often been explored. While research studies constantly report evidence of sex difference in children's writing competence and styles, only relatively recently have educators begun to question the effect of this difference upon young women. For instance, in her discussion of the job prospects that might be related to the writing competence of high school girls, White (1986) details the superior achievement of girl writers and then suggests that such school literacy competence does not appear to lead to social power and success beyond school walls:

> Considering the disparity between women's early achievements in literacy and their subsequent paid employment, we

need to ask why it is that thousands of able girl writers leave
school and go into secretarial jobs, in the course of which they
will patiently revise and type the semi-literate manuscripts of
their male bosses, or else return in droves to the primary classroom, there to supervise the production of another generation
of pen-wise girls. (562)

Poynton (1985) goes further than this when she argues that the
competence girls demonstrate with particular styles—notably storytelling and narrative genres—is almost irrelevant in the world beyond
the school. Girls' genre competence is, she suggests, "positively dis-
abling":

> Telling fairy stories, even telling good fairy stories very well . . .
> simply doesn't count. The positions of real power and influence
> in our society necessitate command of genres for which boys'
> educational experience provides an appropriate preparation
> and girls' doesn't . . . girls' genre competence at primary school
> is not merely irrelevant but positively disabling. (36)

What social value is placed upon the literary competence young
women develop through writing fictions? Or, if we ask the question
rather differently, what has been the effect of maintaining a gendered
distinction between who is "good" at story writing and who is good
at, say, exposition? Between who will be the writers of "fictions" and
the writers of "facts"? Are fiction and narrative, as Threadgold (1992)
suggests, "the technologies which make . . . [girls] compliant subjects
of patriarchy" by keeping them away from the realms of mathematics
and science, and the "academic language of theory" (17)? Is story
writing a social practice that helps to regulate a hierarchical, gendered
order where girls will be pen-pushers for the (male) thinkers and
builders?

This is an important and disturbing question, and a related
aspect of it is to ask critical questions about how competence with
story writing is itself questionable in terms of the value it offers to
women. If we accept that language practices are social practices—that
learning to read, to write, to talk are about learning how to operate
within our culture—then story writing, as a language practice, is a
social activity. What, however, are students learning about "the social"
when they read and write stories? My argument in this chapter is that,
amongst other things, they learn to construct femininity and masculinity within a hierarchical dualism. By entering into story worlds, and
by being inserted into the storylines of their culture, students come to
know what counts as being a woman, or being a man, in the culture to

which the stories belong. They come to know the range of cultural possibilities available for femininity and masculinity—and the limits to that range. Storying becomes increasingly a cultural, rather than a personal, practice.

When they construct stories, young writers enter into familiar and well-known sets of systematically organized relationships of sequence, ordering, and signification which carry the social values of their culture. Inevitably an understanding of gender becomes an important aspect of these social values, although it is not immediately obvious as a constructed set of social relationships. Through constant repetition and layering, story patterns and logic become almost "naturalized" as truths and common sense, and this, according to Walkerdine (1990), is one of the powerful ways in which constructions of gender are authorized and regulated. Walkerdine suggests that "femininity" and "masculinity" are but fictions—but fictions which come to be regarded as real and true because of the way they are legitimated and endorsed in social practice:

> It is not that we are filled with roles and stereotypes of passive femininity so that we become what society has set out for us. Rather, I am suggesting that femininity and masculinity are fictions linked to fantasies deeply embedded in the social world which can take on the status of fact when inscribed in the powerful practices like schooling, through which we are regulated. (xiii)

It is through fictions or stories that our understanding of gender is constantly made and remade and acquires this factual status. Stories play a powerful role in the construction of femininity and masculinity and are firmly implicated in the construction of social meaning.

Storying and Social Meaning

A study of the stories that dominate in a culture at any particular time provides rich evidence of the values and social practices of that culture. Stories can show us whose histories have been authorized and whose have been silenced; whose lives have been acclaimed and whose have been devalued; whose names we will remember and whose we will never know. Stories can also show us how cultures have "read," and thus given meaning to, human relationships: how they have made sense of such diverse activities as reproduction, aggression, love, and anger; how they have sorted the flux of human experience into orders and sequences; how they have made decisions about what counts as "living happily ever after"—and what counts as "living unhappily ever after."

This is most obviously demonstrated through any historical or cross-cultural study of storying, as in, for instance, Zipes's study of the social history of selected folk tales (1983), or Dixon's analysis of British children's literature (1978a; 1978b), or the classroom workbook called *Changing Stories,* prepared by the Inner London Education Authority English Centre (Mellor, Hemming, and Leggett 1984). Research and materials such as theirs demonstrate how stories have been appropriated by dominant political ideologies of class, race, and gender, and how aspects of characterization and narrative logic have been adapted accordingly.

Stories can be changed, but they can be changed only within certain cultural and historical parameters of acceptability if they are to be authorized and legitimated. The narrative "logic" that will allow story tellings and readings to be made so that sequences of events can be read as connected and credible is a cultural and historically specific "logic." We learn this logic as part of learning the story worlds of our culture. However, as any study of the rewritings of traditional tales for contemporary children demonstrates, a selection is made as to which contemporary social meanings will be included, and this selection can indicate which social values dominate and are assumed to be cultural "truths."

For instance, in Dahl's very popular and commercially successful retelling of a number of traditional tales—*Revolting Rhymes* (1984)—he humorously and parodically plays with several of the female character constructions. His "Little Red Riding Hood" becomes almost a "Sloane Ranger" figure: an upper-class trendy who will kill, without scruple, for a fur:

> But what a change! No cloak of red,
> No silly hood upon her head.
> She said, "Hello, and do please note
> "My lovely furry WOLFSKIN COAT." (40)

And to repeat the message, this "Miss Hood" makes another appearance in Dahl's version of "The Three Little Pigs." In this one, she is phoned (while in the middle of drying her hair) by pig number three, who begs her to help him in his struggle with the wolf. Miss Hood is delighted to be of assistance. "'My darling Pig,' she said, 'my sweet, / that's something really up my street'" (46). However, the help she provides means that she acquires a brand new pigskin traveling case.

Dahl's female character for Red Riding Hood has been drawn from a rather different set of discourses than the earlier oral tales (with their gutsy peasant heroine who escapes from the wolf), or the gentri-fied bourgeois retellings by Perrault and Grimm (with their pretty, empty-headed little girl character who is completely fooled by the wolf). But Dahl's selection is obviously culturally gendered. "Miss Hood" in his stories is treacherous and vain; she is pampered, spoilt, and self-indulgent; and luxury clothing items are her particular fetish. We recognize and can make sense of the transformations or closures in Dahl's stories because we have the appropriate cultural knowledge to recognize the narrative logic he relies upon. The changes that Dahl makes to his stories come from a particular set of cultural values about women and can be read by us because those cultural values are com-monly espoused and often repeated.

But there are ways of constructing stories about women that we seldom see. These are stories that are difficult to write and difficult to understand. The conventions are unfamiliar, the narrative transforma-tions or closures not so comfortable. We do not know how to "tell" some stories—nor, sometimes, do we know how to "hear" others—as many marginalized groups have discovered throughout history. We have no well-worn patterns to follow. How, for instance, were women to tell the stories of their lives as women, when so few stories existed for them to read? When so little narrative space existed within which such storytellers and such stories could be heard? Ways in which we might organize and transform a series of events into "a story" are dependent upon the cultural paradigms of possibility available to us; they are dependent upon the social understandings accessible at spe-cific historical moments.

Storying and the Construction of Gender

Within cultures which divide people into groups dependent upon their biological sex, issues of gender are inevitably involved in story-ing. What comes to count as appropriate social practice for a "girl" or a "boy," a "woman" or a "man," becomes part of a culture's stories—bedtime stories, TV stories, movie stories, or advertisement stories; stories that are written, spoken, enacted, or constructed with visual images; stories that soothe, disturb, delight, or terrify. Consider these lines from a poem called "Sacrifices" (Haley 1979):

> A tale in a school reading book:
> a bell that could not be cast
> unless a virgin's blood tempered the metal:
> the bell-caster's beautiful daughter
> threw herself into the mould
> thus saving her father from the wrath of the emperor.

We learn how to "be" women or men, girls or boys, mothers or fathers, wives or husbands, sisters or brothers, aunts or uncles, grandmas or grandpas partly in response to the stories that we hear and participate in. Through the continual layering of such stories, we learn how to participate in our culture. We learn appropriate ways to read and make sense of experience and discover the ways in which we are "read" ourselves as gendered subjects. And we learn appropriate ways to talk and to write, although the "appropriate" ways may not always be satisfying. An Australian author, in her semiautobiographical novel *Kewpie Doll* (Hanrahan 1984), relates the female protagonist's unease with the forms of language available to her. The woman senses their inadequacy and grasps at the recognition that the language practices around her do not let her say the things she might want to say:

> Bobby Henderson talks to the taxi driver as if they are friends. How can he be a man so easily? He knows the right language, they are men together, blistered lips smiling—Yeah, they say and Too bad, mate. I've stopped being me. I am a person pretending, every word I say is wrong. (68)

However, the story patterns that surround us are often seductive in their appeal because, as Walkerdine (1990) suggests, they connect with fantasies: with deeply held desires we have to be loved, to be wanted, to be cherished. Davies (1992) sees desire as firmly implicated in storyline and suggests that centrally involved in learning to become a male or a female is the learning of "the appropriate patterns of desire":

> Because story provides a substantial and detailed manifestation of the culture, it is through story that children can learn the patterns of desire appropriate for their gender. They discover what positions are available to members of their sex and how to live the detail of those positionings and they come to understand and take up as their own the particular patterns of desire relevant to their gender. (1)

For contemporary Western women and girls, many of the stories that dominate in the popular and commercial sphere are stories that support, and construct desire for, a dualistic construction of gender. Within such a framework, femininity is linked with qualities like self-lessness, heterosexuality, beauty, modesty, gentleness, and love—qualities of femininity which we learn to desire and seek.

Stories from magazines, newspapers, TV quiz shows, soap operas, popular films, jokes, gossip, pulp fiction, and radio talk-back programs become the "fictions" of daily life that construct the "facts" of femininity:

> How to stay alluring through summer heat . . .
>
> Rape Victim's Horror Story
>
> Will Rachel keep her man?
>
> Mandy's heartbreak . . .
>
> Those telltale signs of age. Check yours out.
>
> How to find Mr. Right. Twenty tips and suggestions.
>
> Every mother's worst nightmare. Lesley breaks her silence.
>
> Secrets of a 70-year-old marriage . . .
>
> Shape-up secrets for summer
>
> ARE YOU A FOOL TO FORGIVE A CHEAT?
>
> Three amazing plastic surgery stories . . .
>
> Di's beauty secrets

Story promotions such as these support a construction of femininity which is clearly centered on heterosexuality, along with the characteristics that will make a woman heterosexually desirable. "Femininity" in stories like these becomes equated with heterosexual attractiveness, an obvious precursor to romance. The feminine woman is desired because she is desirable to men, and the characteristics that will make her desirable are "knowable" through the stories of her culture: through the constructions of women offered on MTV clips, billboards, magazines, films, and novels.

Not surprisingly, these "stories" occur in different but related form in student texts. One of the stories that Dalley (1991) collected from a teenage schoolgirl writer demonstrates the girl writer's internalization of the male gaze and the concomitant construction of desirable "femininity":

> . . . Taran began to think about his quest. He had been ordered by the king to rescue his daughter—a fat, selfish and extremely

> spoilt girl around 18 years old. The thought of going on a dangerous mission for someone such as Mirian, made Taran wince, especially seeing as it was almost time for her to marry some poor unfortunate man—likely to be Taran. (165)

The story then becomes an account of the transformation of the "fat," "spoilt," and "selfish" girl into a shapely romantic woman whom Taran will then desire: whom he will be able to fall in love with. This is the final frame of the story:

> He gazed at her as the light flickered across her pretty face. Her blue gown fitted her beautifully, highlighting Mirian's womanly figure. . . .
> "[Y]ou must of wondered why I look like I do now, when I was so fat," [Mirian replied] getting straight to the point.
> "Well, the thought had crossed my mind, once or twice," he shrugged.
> "Well, if we could move to the lounge room, I shall tell you all about my 'adventures,' and you can tell me about yours."
> "Lead on," Taran answered, feeling strangely happy to be with her, as he followed Mirian through another door. "What a wonderful night this is turning out to be," thought Taran to himself. "Especially with such a wonderful woman." (168)

This young woman writer has located her school story very comfortably within traditional romantic storylines and the narrative logic and appropriate "feminine" characteristics that accompany such a storyline. Like the story from the eight-year-old girl at the beginning of this paper—where a girl's three most precious wishes are seen to be for a pretty dress, long golden hair, and the title of Princess— this story, too, accepts the cultural importance of signifiers like material clothing and body inscription. And just as the transformation for the eight-year-old girl brought heterosexual fulfillment ("In the castle the next day she got married with a handsome prince and they lived happily ever after"), so too does it for this fifteen-year-old girl writer. Her female character has become a "wonderful woman" desired by the hero. Another feminine fantasy is fulfilled.

Resisting the Romantic Storyline

The romantic storyline is a powerful one for narrative construction, and it dominates as a "logic" in stories that involve female and male relationships. Consequently, as I have argued in earlier work (1988), young women have difficulty constructing narrative action and sequences that do not return to this line for final resolution and transformation. It is important for us to remember, however, that young writers learn the conventions of this storyline as they become increasingly immersed in children's fiction, TV stories, film texts, advertisement stories, and social life. A study of the writing of early writers is often a salutory reminder that it is possible and common for young female writers to construct texts that do not turn upon male intervention for success, or safety, or happiness—that do not slot characters and action into a familiar preromantic storyline.

Stories like the following from young girls as beginning writers are not at all unusual. For instance, in these stories from a seven-year-old,[1] girls can be adventurous—even violent:

The Spirit of Anadore

Once upon a time there was a land called Anadore. Now I will tell you a secret of Anadore.
THERE WAS A MONSTER IN THAT LAND!
And one day a little girl was walking. Her name was Shirley and she saw this great big shadow, and she was so scared she couldn't move.
And she knew it was the monster.
So she forced her body to move, and she ran home and got a knife.
Then she killed the monster. THE END

They can be brave and receive help from supernatural forces (at this stage ungendered forces!):

The Crystal Cave

I was walking down to my grandma's and on the way I saw a cave. I went in. I went deeper into the cave. I saw a witch. She was bad! I saw a horse in the cave. It let me get on its back. It was a magic horse. It killed the witch and I rode away on the horse.

And they can write about "gendered" beings in "ungendered" ways:

The Magic Rainbow

Once upon a time there lived a little boy. He stayed up late at night till 11:30. One day it was raining and he saw a rainbow. It sucked him up and he saw lots of scary monsters and he screamed and his mum on earth heard him and she came to the rescue. She was just in time because one of the monsters was there. When they were home the little boy went to bed. THE END

Very young girl writers may have no "storied" sense of transformation or narrative closure, and even though their stories may have story world characters, the narratives do not necessarily insert their characters into a cultural storyline for narrative logic.[2]

The Rabbit

Once a rabbit was walking along in a deep dark forest, until it started raining.
It rained and rained.
Then he came to a sunny place and he met a little girl playing with a ball.

However, this changes as students become increasingly familiar with cultural stories. If, as Cohan and Shires (1988) suggest, stories structure the meanings by which a culture lives, then we could expect that the stories that students construct will themselves typify the cultural meanings they encounter. An analysis of teenage girls' storying can then become an interesting indication of the way in which girls have "read" the storylines of their culture and taken up positions within such cultural storylines. It seems to be difficult for young women writers to conceive of a narrative logic which will not ultimately have their female characters move along a romantic storyline and be read from within the cluster of traits associated with romantic femininity, even when their initial story frame would have made it possible to make other "readings" and to follow other storylines.

For instance, consider these first six paragraphs of an adventure story written for a school English assignment by a fifteen-year-old Australian girl. The story is typical of many from the class, as Dalley (1991) found in her work on adolescent storying:

Aqua-Kingdom

On an early Saturday afternoon Sky decided to go for a walk up to Eagles' Hill. Nobody had been up there for years because there was a rumour that there was a room full of eagles on the top. Sky wanted to prove this rumour wrong, so she packed a picnic lunch and set off. As she got further and further up the hill she began to get a bit scared. It was getting darker and darker by the minute. She had been walking for a while until she saw a small black room on top of the hill. She looked behind her and thought of turning back but she couldn't see more than two feet in front of her face, so she decided against it.

She walked up to the door and peered into the keyhole but could see only darkness. She circled the room, but couldn't see any windows or doors.

She went back around the front and hesitantly opened the door. Nothing happened. She looked inside and all she saw was four black, blank walls and a red door opposite her.

> She walked in and closed the door behind her. She went up to
> the red door and stopped. "How could there be another door
> when I checked outside and there weren't any?" she thought to
> herself. Only one way to find out, and with that she opened the
> door.
>
> When she looked out the door, she saw the most breathtaking
> sight she had ever seen. Before she had time to take a good look
> she was sucked out of the doorway into a long dark tunnel. She
> practically floated down the tunnel and could see a bright light
> at the end. She closed her eyes as the light was getting too bright
> and seconds later flew out and landed on a pile of junk. Her
> eyelids felt very heavy so she closed them and fell into a very
> deep sleep. . . .

So far so good. These opening paragraphs could be read as an
attempt to construct the female heroine of the story as brave, independent, and strong. We could read her as careful and practical, but
still fearless and courageous, and we could read these opening paragraphs as setting a scene for a lone adventurer on a journey of discov-
ery. But because the protagonist is a woman, the reading is overlaid
with a narrative expectation that this independence and adventurous-
ness are almost "unfeminine" traits within the conventional story
paradigm and that they will be transformed into more "appropriate"
(desirable?) feminine traits through the movement of the story. The
gender of the main character almost predisposes us to expect the
imminent intervention of a male character. Unlike the lone male adventurer, the lone female heroine is a rare event in our cultural stories.
By changing the name of the character to, say, "Ged," and then all the
subsequent pronouns to "he" or "him," I would argue that we change
the frames through which those six paragraphs might be read.

In the paragraphs that follow in "Aqua-Kingdom," Sky wakes
from her "very deep sleep" and is met by a "striking young girl" who
tells her where she is and directs her to a cottage wherein waits—"the
Prince"!

> The door was opened by a handsome young man. "Hello," he
> said, "May I help you?"

Sky is advised by Shotsi (the handsome young man) that she will have
to stay for some time with him (in his cottage!) before transport back
to earth can be arranged. And, as might be guessed, during the en-
forced stay the two "grow very fond of each other":

> Sky was regretting the day she had to go. The night before Sky
> was due to go Shotsi admitted to being in love with her and he

wanted her to stay and marry him. Sky was ecstatic with happiness and joy and eagerly accepted. They were married one
week later and Sky was an official Aqua-ite. She could even
grow a tail now. Shotsi fixed it up so that Sky's parents wouldn't
notice she was missing so Sky's life was now perfect. THE END

The young adventurer has now been transformed into the romantic,
feminine woman (a "little mermaid" figure?). The male character "ad-
mits" to being in love with her—at which admission she becomes
"ecstatic with happiness and joy." He also takes charge of her life
("Shotsi fixed it up so that Sky's parents wouldn't notice she was
missing").

The romantic storyline provides a familiar and comfortable logic
for this young woman's story, and within many young women's narratives, readers can similarly trace the transformation of interesting
and often independent young people into characters who are physically weak, vulnerable, and dependent upon masculine strength and
aggression—in other words, into female characters who are heterosexually desirable and can take up places within the romantic paradigm. This should not be surprising to us. The preparation of young
girls for their insertion into the romantic storyline through comics and
early reading has been well documented (Davies 1989; Walkerdine
1990), as has the gendered narrowness of teen romance fiction and
television stories for young women readers and viewers (Christian-
Smith 1990; Gilbert 1993). Locating a space from which to write stories
that challenge dominant cultural meanings— that try to construct
other versions of "happy ever after" endings, and other versions of
"being a woman"—is not an easy task.

Towards the Telling of Other Stories

Young women will continue to find it comfortable and easy to read
and write stories that we might regard as "sexist" (that follow romantic storylines and are narrowly constructed in terms of topic selection,
character construction, choice of text type) as long as the dominant
cultural stories from television, popular print, movies, advertising,
and contemporary social practice construct femininity and masculinity in this way and legitimate and authorize such "fictions" as "facts."

One of the subject positions that is very familiar to us all is the
stereotypically gendered one. Most of us have had considerable experience of being positioned as gendered subjects, and we are able to
read, write, talk, move, and dress in ways that invite us to be "read"

as a stereotypical woman, or as a stereotypical man. But this is obviously not the only subject position available to us, nor is it necessarily a preferred one. As Weedon (1987) suggests:

> Many women acknowledge the feeling of being a different person in different social situations which call for different qualities and modes of femininity. The range of ways of being a woman open to each of us at a particular time is extremely wide but we know or feel we ought to know what is expected of us in particular situations—in romantic encounters, when we are pandering to the boss, when we are dealing with children or posing for fashion photographers. We may embrace these ways of being, these subject positions whole-heartedly, we may reject them outright or we may offer resistance while complying to the letter with what is expected of us. (86)

And this must apply to our female students. The women students who "read" cultural stories are not a seamless, coherent, or single group. They come from diverse cultural and material backgrounds, and they live and experience "femininity" differently. They can take up many different positions as young women. Nor is there a seamless, coherent, or single construction of femininity available to them. There are many ways to read "femininity" and many different women as readers and meaning makers. It is within this diversity of sign and image, of reader and readings, that there lies space for alternative constructions to be made of being a "woman," alternative stories to be told, and alternative forms of female "desire" to be constructed.

But a space must be fought for and constantly protected, given the sheer weight and dominance of so many stories that would not acknowledge that "difference," that construct femininity narrowly within a dualistic ordering of gender, that position women within a romantic storyline of possibility. As this chapter has argued, some readings of cultural stories become dominant and authorized because they are constantly repeated. These dominant readings form the major storying paradigms and are often "naturalized" as the common-sense lore of our culture. The other "quieter" stories are more difficult to hear: more difficult to find. In classrooms, we need deliberate strategies which will open out the constructedness of stories: the sets of social conventions upon which they have drawn and the cultural set of meanings through which they are read.

Comparison and juxtaposition can make it possible to read the historical specificity of many common and familiar stories; contemporary retellings of traditional tales, fables, or fairy tales are valuable source texts here (see Mellor, Hemming, and Leggett 1984). Similarly, the paradigms of possibility that exist in different story construc- tions—say, the construction of a "quality" children's literary text, or a teen romance novel, or an early graded reader, or a "60 Minutes" story, or a *Woman's Day* feature—can be explored. What is likely to be in- cluded in each of these stories, and what is not? And why? How culturally and historically specific are decisions like these (see Gilbert 1992)?

A focus on the way in which different social readings of stories can be made can also help to undermine their naturalized "common- sense" qualities: their "factual" and authorized status. What might it mean to make a "feminist" reading of a story, and how can that be done? Or how can we make a reading that could produce class inequalities? What meanings might we produce if we read stories as a language teacher? as a person of color? as a literary scholar? as a psychoanalyst? as a parent? The possibility of multiple "readings" is a powerful challenge to a text's authority, particularly if the conditions of possibility that can produce those readings become also an object of attention (see Mellor and Patterson 1991; Mellor 1992).

The challenge is to find classroom structures that will support such endeavors, and Dwyer's work (1992) with year three story writ- ers is valuable here. She found that female writers drew upon different story paradigms, depending upon whether they were in all-female writing groups or in mixed writing groups, and suggests that the range of subject positions available to young readers and writers is influenced by their peer groupings. Her argument is that the discur- sive networks brought into play by particular social groupings influ- ence story production.

The same argument might well be made for reading. My work with teenage girl readers (in Gilbert and Taylor 1991) indicated that girl readers who had access to broadly based literary textuality (and the readings that are often learnt with such access) could make read- ings of teen romance novels which foregrounded and challenged the narrow parameters of such texts. They were positioned differently by their discursive histories and so had access to a range of reading frames.

We need access to other stories for our students—and to other ways of working with narrative in the classroom. We need to fore- ground the paradoxical value of girls' competence with storying; the way in which storying works to regulate acceptable social construc- tions of gender; the richness of being able to make multiple readings of stories. And we need to foreground how stories feed into and play upon deeply held desires—and to question what purposes those desires serve. A positive pedagogy for classroom storying must include ways to encourage and support young women as they make explorations with narrative form and to help them gain access to other stories—to other ways to read themselves as gendered subjects, to other ways in which female desire might be constructed.

The storylines which dominate as authorized and common sets of social meanings in Western culture do not support women (or men) in a full and varied development of their potential as social subjects. They obscure the richness of human diversity and the plurality of social subjectivity. They deny us dignity and value.

As one storyteller claims, after an incident in which a "sturdy" peasant girl has outwitted a rich and lecherous squire and a foolish and frightened father, there are other ways for us to live "happily ever after" than to insert ourselves into dominant cultural storylines.

> As for the girl, some say she married, some say not. It matters little. What is certain is that she lived happily ever after.[3]

Notes

1. With thanks to Rebecca Gilbert for these three stories.

2. With thanks to Lara Jane Phillips for this story.

3. From "The Squire's Bride" in Riordan's collection entitled *The Woman in the Moon and Other Tales of Forgotten Heroines* (1985).

References

Christian-Smith, L. (1990). *Becoming a woman through romance.* New York: Routledge.

Cohan, S., and Shires, L. (1988). *Telling stories: A theoretical analysis of narrative fiction.* London: Methuen.

Dahl, R. (1984). *Revolting rhymes.* London: Puffin Books.

Dalley, L. (1991). *Regulating gender through genre: A study of the construction of gender in school narrative writing tasks at the year ten level.* Unpublished bachelor of education honors thesis, School of Education, James Cook University of North Queensland, Townsville.

Davies, B. (1989). *Frogs and snails and feminist tales: Preschool children and gender.* Sydney, New South Wales: Allen and Unwin.

————. (1992). Beyond dualism and towards multiple subjectivities. In L. Christian-Smith (Ed.), *Texts of desire*. London: Falmer Press.

Dixon, B. (1978a). *Catching them young 1: Sex, race and class in children's fiction*. London: Pluto Press.

————. (1978b). *Catching them young 2: Political ideas in children's fiction*. London: Pluto Press.

Dwyer, B. (1992). *The construction of narrative within one year three classroom*. Unpublished master of education thesis, School of Education, James Cook University of North Queensland, Townsville.

Gilbert, P. (1988). Stoning the romance: Girls as resistant readers and writers. *Curriculum Perspectives, 8*(2), 13–18.

———— (with Rowe, K.). (1989). *Gender, literacy and the classroom*. Carlton, Victoria: Australian Reading Association.

————. (1992). On place, parameter, and play: Exploring the cultural possibilities of genre work. *English in Australia, 99*, 19–26.

————. (1993). Dolly fictions: Teen romance down under. In L. Christian-Smith (Ed.), *Texts of desire: Fiction, fantasy, and femininity*. London: Falmer Press.

Gilbert, P., and Taylor, S. (1991). *Fashioning the feminine: Girls, popular culture and schooling*. Sydney, New South Wales: Allen and Unwin.

Haley, E. (1979). Sacrifices. In C. Ferrier (Ed.), *Hecate's daughters*. St. Lucia, Queensland: University of Queensland.

Hanrahan, B. (1984). *Kewpie doll*. London: Chatto and Windus.

Kamler, B. (1992). Constructing gender in the process writing classroom. In P. Gilbert (Ed.), *Gender, stories and the language classroom*. Geelong, Victoria: Deakin University Press.

Mellor, B. (1992). *English and reading practices*. Unpublished doctoral dissertation, University of Western Australia, Perth.

Mellor, B., Hemming, J., and Leggett, J. (1984). *Changing stories*. London: Inner London Education Authority English Centre; Scarborough, Western Australia: Chalkface Press.

Mellor, B., and Patterson, A. (1991). *Reading fictions*. Perth, Western Australia: Chalkface Press.

Poynton, C. (1985). *Language and gender: Making the difference*. Geelong, Victoria: Deakin University Press.

Riordan, J. (Ed.). (1985). *The woman in the moon and other tales of forgotten heroines*. New York: Dial Books for Young Readers.

Romatowski, J., and Trepanier-Street, M. (1987). Gender perceptions: An analysis of children's creative writing. *Contemporary Education, 59*(1), 17–19.

Sheridan, E. M. (Ed.). (1982). *Sex stereotypes and reading*. Newark, DE: IRA.

Swann, J., and Graddol, D. (1988). Gender inequalities in classroom talk. *English in Education, 2*(1), 49–65.

Threadgold, T. (1992, May). *Poststructuralist theory and the teaching of English.* Plenary paper presented at the annual conference of the English Teachers' Association of New South Wales.

Tuck, D. , Bayliss, V., and Bell, M. (1985). Analysis of sex stereotyping in characters created by young authors. *Journal of Educational Research, 78*(4), 248–252.

Walkerdine, V. (1990). *Schoolgirl fictions.* London: Verso.

Weedon, C. (1987). *Feminist practice and poststructuralist theory.* Oxford: Basil Blackwell.

White, J. (1986). The writing on the wall: Beginning or end of a girl's career? *Women's Studies International Forum, 9*(5), 561–574.

Zipes, J. (1983). *The trials and tribulations of Little Red Riding Hood.* London: Heinemann.

Weaving Communities through Story:
Who Are We?

10 Princess Annabella and the Black Girls

Vivian Gussin Paley
University of Chicago Laboratory Schools

Vivian Paley embeds a tale within a tale as she shows how stories not only enchant the listener, but also affect the way stories of everyday classroom life evolve. Artfully crafted story, too, weaves a continuous thread between the teacher's remembered self and the developing selves of her African American kindergartners.

My life in the classroom has come full circle. I entered Miss Evelyn's kindergarten class when I was five and stayed resolutely outside her inner circle, losing myself in a dark and silent forest. Now, more than half a century later, I sit with my own circle of kindergarten children, telling them of a magical bird called Magpie, who finds himself in just such a forest about to rescue just such a child as I might have been.

Something is very strange down there, thought Magpie. He swooped through the tree tops and circled the ancient castle walls. "I don't hear any birds!" he said. "Is it possible?"

Magpie was right. There were absolutely no birds in the forest below; not even the tap-tap-tap of a woodpecker could be heard. A forest without birds? This greatly disturbed the large black and white bird. It is like a lake without fish or a child without a friend. (Paley 1992)[1]

The manner in which I imagined myself lost must have varied in each fantasy but, always, at the point of greatest despair, a beautiful princess appeared to take my hand. She looked exactly like a girl in the class named Dorothy, whose blue eyes and long blond hair blurred my vision with longing. Dorothy, in turn, bore a startling resemblance to the teacher's doll that stared down at us from atop the bookcase.

Miss Evelyn treasured both the doll and Dorothy, but apparently not me; she advised my mother to keep me at home until first grade because I was too shy to join the group. When I later caught up with Dorothy, she was surrounded by adoring friends and, except in my fantasies, I still felt myself to be outside the circle.

Poor Miss Evelyn, with her untouchable doll and preference for certain kinds of pretty little girls. She did not know that those of us watching from the outside had the same feelings and fantasies as our more popular classmates. Nor did I fully understand these matters myself until I learned to see the children as they saw themselves, forever inside the unfolding scenes of a story.

I am no longer lost in the woods, though it took me awhile to find my way out. Recently, I have even regained the habit of making up stories, a practice that preserved my peace of mind when I was young. The characters have changed, but the themes of loneliness and rescue are recognizable.

Going to my desk early each morning, I prepare my new Magpie chapter much as the children may lie in bed upon awakening, trying to hold on to another dream, one they can use to begin the school day. My narratives are not so fleeting but they serve the same purpose: to smooth the passage into the magic circle.

When I read my chapter to the children, it joins all the other stories being told and played in every corner of the room. Together the children and I create an ongoing mythology that connects us to one another and establishes the continuity of our days.

Magpie hovered over the castle tower watching for signs of life. Suddenly a child's sad voice drifted through an open window. The bird landed on the sill and peered into a small room lit by a single candle. Seated on a stone floor was a young girl slowly brushing her doll's hair.

"Pretend I'm your mother, little Maruska," the girl said, "and you thought I was dead. But then I came alive again and it's your birthday." A large tear traced a shiny path down the girl's cheek and splashed onto the doll's face. "Poor baby," sighed the girl. "Father will think you are crying too."

I haven't yet decided what the doll in my story looks like, but I have brought a new doll with brown skin and curly black hair to school. There are several girls in our classroom who could be her sisters, but no one dresses the doll in lacy things and carries her about. Nor is she ever rocked, undressed, and put to bed. Our new black doll has found her way into no child's heart.

The rejection of the black doll worries me. It is one of two dolls I have recently purchased for the doll corner. The other is white and not nearly as beautiful; I wanted the black doll to be even prettier than Miss Evelyn's doll. The new white doll is an instant success and the black doll is lost in a silent forest.

Still, it is only a doll, I tell myself. If it were a child, there would be tangible ways to bring her into the circle of play. The problem is that I remember how Miss Evelyn's doll dominated my dreams; I cannot pretend the black doll is unimportant. The pictures of happy black children on our walls do not make up for the exclusion of the black doll in the doll corner. I want the black girls to like the black doll, but they don't care to accommodate me.

Kendra, Mary Ann, and Julie are the three black girls in our class. Their coloring is in the range of butterscotch to mahogany, but it is the new white doll they prize. Suddenly, I know that the little princess that Magpie is about to meet must be the color of a young robin's back.

Magpie watched the child a moment longer. Her skin reminded him of the soft brown of a young robin and her hair the black of a raven's tail. Where he came from the children were more the color of the pale peaches that grew in Princess Alexandra's courtyard.

He gave a low whistle. "Excuse me, but are you in trouble? May I come in?"

"What?" The startled child hugged her doll in alarm and turned to the window. "Oh, a pretty bird!"

"My name is Magpie. Can I help you?"

"I don't think anyone can help me, Magpie. Since no one can bring my mother back to life, there is nothing to be done." The girl wrapped her doll in a large lacy shawl that trailed along the floor and then she stood up. "But you are welcome to come in. My father and I are very fond of birds."

The children's attention has been easily captured, not because the princess is brown as a robin, but because her mother is dead and she is lonely in a silent forest. Her black identity has made no impression, I am certain, for Kendra has not asked, "Is she black?"

This is something Kendra always questions when a black person passes us in the hallway or looks out at us from the pages of a book. "Is she black?" Even when the person is as dark as a robin's back, which Kendra herself is, the question must be asked. Clearly, my princess will need a stronger racial identity.

These are matters of increasing concern to me for there are fewer black children in our school than in the past. I am not sure why this is so: some point to economic factors and population shifts, others to nearby magnet schools. But I think also that many black parents have begun to question the benefits for their children of a mostly white classroom during the early school years.

Lacking black children, I put up more black faces on the walls: Martin Luther King, Jr., Harriet Tubman, Rosa Parks, and others. I invite Kendra's mother to help us celebrate Kwanzaa, but Kendra, Mary Ann, and Julie look away. They are not eager to tell us what they know. Kendra does remember to inform us, however, that her name comes from an African storybook, and I enter the idea into my next Magpie chapter.

"Is this your castle?" Magpie asked.

The girl nodded. "I am Annabella and my father is Prince Kareem. That's an African name. We're descended from African kings and queens. Would you like to meet father? He spends a great amount of time studying birds."

Kendra still does not ask if Annabella is black. She listens to my story and smiles at the white doll in her lap. For Kendra, I think, my Princess Annabella is not black at all. She is blond and blue-eyed, for this is the way Kendra, Mary Ann, and Julie draw all their princesses, and these are the images that enter their play.

"You be Snow White and I'm Cinderella," is the way they often begin. "And this is our baby that's lost in the woods under a spider web and then we bring her home to live with us." The baby is always the white doll.

Would these three draw yellow-haired princesses if they went to an all black school? Perhaps. But that doll corner would be full of black children and black dolls, and Kendra would not have to ask if someone is black.

Nonetheless, Kendra, Mary Ann, and Julie must make use of what they have: a classroom of nineteen white children, three black girls, one Indian girl, a Japanese boy, and two white teachers. Luckily, we know something Miss Evelyn hadn't discovered: how to fill the day with stories, the children's, and now my own as well.

In my new role as storyteller, I can create image and identity to suit my teaching and private purposes. Thus, when Princess Annabella arrives in Magpie's Kingdom of Tall Pines and finds her white counterpart, Princess Alexandra, they will be represented as I tell the story by our new dolls. Henceforth, the black doll is to be called Princess Annabella and the white doll, Princess Alexandra. They shall be seated on my lap as their story unfolds.

Every day after school, Alexandra walked home with Annabella. One day, as they strolled along, hand in hand, Alexandra said, "I wish we were sisters." Annabella smiled and replied, "It's even nicer to be friends. But we can pretend to be sisters. Let's pretend we're walking in the forest and . . ."

"And pretend we have no mother or father," Alexandra continued, "and then we find a baby bear who is lost and we take him home. Maruska can be the bear." Annabella bent down to take up a handful of moss. "And we pick blueberries for supper," she said. She had never actually picked blueberries but when she played with Alexandra it often seemed the nicest thing they could pretend to do. "Pretend this is the blueberries," she told her friend, giving her the moss.

I hold up Princess Annabella, the doll, and speak to her. "Would you and your new friend, Princess Alexandra, be too worried if a witch named Beatrix tried to trap you?"

"Is it a bad witch?" several children ask.

"Only when she's jealous," I reply. "Actually Beatrix is the one who saved Magpie when he was still in his shell and lost in the forest. I'll tell you that story another time." The children look at the black and white dolls on my lap and are not worried. I am about to give these dolls an identity. Their real story is going to be revealed. There is no more important event, to each child, than the uncovering of someone's unique story.

Beatrix heard the girls from behind her tree and she was jealous. "I hate those girls," she told Magpie and he was troubled. "But, Beatrix, they've done nothing bad to you."

"Yes, they have," she snapped angrily. "They love each other and pretend things together and I have no friend but you, Magpie, which isn't the same. Those girls make me mad. I just know I'm going to do something mean." Magpie flew around Beatrix's face. "Tell me what," he urged, but the young witch shook her head. "Never mind, I haven't decided," she replied. "Go away now. I want to be alone."

However, Beatrix had already begun her mischief. As soon as Magpie was gone, she uncovered the hole she'd been digging next to the path the girls took through the forest. The hole would soon reach her underground tunnel. "Now, what would make Annabella leave the path?" Beatrix asked herself as she dug. One more jab with the shovel and she suddenly knew: a blueberry bush! Annabella was always pretending to pick blueberries.

Now, as she piled more branches over the hole, Beatrix was sorry her mother wasn't there to see the trick she was about to play on the princesses. She blinked three times and a bush filled with ripe blueberries appeared. That was easy, she thought. The problem was how to make only Annabella fall into the trap.

As it happened, however, both girls tumbled into the hole; actually, one fell and the other jumped. Annabella had spied the blueberries first. "Oh, look! I didn't know there were . . . oh, help, I'm falling!" Alexandra watched with horror as her friend disappeared through the branches. "Wait for me!" she called. "I'm coming too!" The girls dropped onto a pile of leaves and got up quickly. "This trap must have been meant for an animal," Alexandra said.

"No!" screamed Beatrix, leaping out in front of them. "I made it for Annabella. And you spoiled everything, you naughty Alexandra. I don't know why Magpie likes you!"

The princesses, of course, will become Beatrix's friends. This is expected, since they are all within Magpie's circle of love. However, what I have not anticipated is the effect my story has upon the black girls. It is as if they have been waiting for a sign from me. The Kwanzaa celebration was not the sign, nor was the Martin Luther King, Jr., observance. For these five-year-old girls, a black doll had to come alive and invite them into the magic circle.

The next morning Kendra draws her first school picture of a black girl. "This is Princess Annabella," she tells me as she embellishes the figure with dangling earrings and purple shoes. "I'm making her dark like me and Mama. My brother he isn't dark like this. Grandma Kelsey says he's our white baby but she's just joking 'cause he's really not. He's just light colored like my daddy, is all."

Here is a different Kendra than I have known, speaking casually of dark and light and telling family jokes. Soon her stories, the ones she dictates for us to act out, will take a new direction as well. A few days earlier Kendra had told this story:

> Once upon a time there was a little baby and it lived alone and it crawled into the woods. And it never come back. And it found a castle. And it never came back home. And it was lost. And it was sad.

Kendra's pre-Annabella story had a profound effect upon my own storytelling. Her lost baby, crawling through the woods, was soon followed by my own lost child, Princess Annabella. I had been telling other Magpie stories, mainly involving a tiny creature named Prince Orange Flower, who lived inside the cactus flowers of the Great Desert. But after Kendra told her sad story, Magpie flew over the silent forest.

My instincts were not mistaken. Kendra integrated my new theme into her next story:

> Once upon a time there lived a princess. And she went in the woods. And she went far away. And she found a castle. And she went inside. And she went upstairs and it was her own room. And then she heard something.

It is at this point in *my* story that Princess Annabella meets Princess Alexandra, and their story personae blend into the reality of the new dolls. All three black girls begin to play with Annabella the doll, and the princess enters their stories. Mary Ann comes closest to retelling my original story:

> Once upon a time there was a princess named Annabella. And there was Magpie. And Beatrix. Magpie told the daddy you should come quickly. Your child has fallen into a trap. Then Magpie didn't even wait 'cause he flied down and he caught Princess Annabella and said you're a naughty girl to Beatrix.

Julie's stories are never elaborate, and they will change in only one respect. There is always a little girl who meets a number of small animals and plays with them. But now her little girl is a black princess. Her story ends with "So that little girl was Princess Annabella."

It is Kendra, however, who seems most affected by the black princess, and she is compelled to give us the gift of hair. Yes, hair. The way her hair looks is important to Kendra, to her sisters and her mother, to her grandmother and her aunts. Kendra's hairstyle changes every week, and she often examines herself in the doll-corner mirror.

But she never speaks about her hair, not even to Julie and Mary Ann, as far as I have heard. Hair is part of her home life, not connected to this classroom. Perhaps it is in the same category as Kwanzaa.

Now, Kendra allows the subject of hair to enter her story:

> Once there was a girl. She went to the hairdresser. And the usual hairdresser wasn't there. And she wanted new hair because hers was short. And they curled her new hair and her little sister danced around. But the hairdresser was really a jealous Beatrix. Princess Alexandra was waiting outside and they ran home to Magpie.

When we act out Kendra's story, as we do all the stories the children tell, I ask if she is to be Annabella, the big sister. "No," she replies, "'cause I'm too young to get new hair until I'm older like my sister is."

But in her other stories, Kendra is Princess Annabella and she carries with her the black doll wrapped in a pink blanket. She has also begun to draw many figures with brown faces and black hair. Sometimes they stand beside a large bird with black and white wings. Julie and Mary Ann watch Kendra and begin their own forms of self-expression. They trace their hands and color them carefully with brown crayon, circling each finger with a sparkling ring. Our walls fill with brown hands and brown faces.

What is my own story in all of this? Is the subject racial identity or is it high drama in the Kingdom of Tall Pines? Both, I suppose, and anything else I wish to explore as I search for a new classroom voice. I am learning to savor small events and familiar characters, but I stand ready to carry along any new concept on the wings of fantasy, just as the children do in their play.

My Magpie stories have taken their characters on many unexpected paths since the dolls were given new life. We are long past our Kwanzaa celebration, and it is nearly time for Abraham Lincoln's birthday. Martin Luther King, Jr., has been returned to the picture file and a bearded Mr. Lincoln replaces him on the bulletin board. His deep-set eyes look out at us from under a stovepipe hat, and we know he is worried about slavery. What does it mean to be told that some black people were slaves? Is there a connection to Kendra, Mary Ann, and Julie?

———

Magpie flew down to the pirate ship. He found the little prince below deck in a cage with a tall dark man. "This is Kwanzaa," whispered Prince

Orange Flower. "*He's a runaway slave, from a place called America. He escaped on a ship going to Africa but these pirates stopped the ship and took him prisoner along with all the money.*"

Kwanzaa shook his head sadly. "My life is full of bad luck," he said. "The pirates had never seen a brown-skinned person before and thought I'd be a fine looking pirate. But I refused. They look meaner than the man who owned me when I was a slave."

Magpie began to pick at the lock. "How did you become a slave, Kwanzaa?" he asked.

"My brothers and sisters and I were digging for clams one day on the beach of our little village when we were stolen away by a slave ship and brought to a New Orleans slave market." Kwanzaa's eyes filled with tears. "I never saw my family again."

In due course, Magpie rescues Kwanzaa and the little prince, and the former slave has many opportunities to continue his story while I keep the Magpie narrative going at a comfortable pace. My mistake in the beginning was in covering too much territory too quickly. The children like a great deal of dialogue and enjoy staying inside a given story for a longer time than I had realized.

"I knew that if I was going to escape I had to learn to read and write," Kwanzaa told the girls as they helped build the ship in which he would return to Africa. "Another slave taught me to read the same way Abraham Lincoln's mother taught him to read, using the only book we had—the Bible."

"Who is Abraham Lincoln?" asked Princess Annabella.

"He is the American president, a good man, I can tell you, and he hates slavery."

Alexandra was surprised. "Then why does he allow it? My father would never permit slavery in the Kingdom of Tall Pines."

And so our story continues. There is much to explain, but it must make sense within the continuing story. Perhaps I can, at some point, incorporate the idea of George Washington refusing to be made a king. Alexandra's father would be astonished to hear this. Why would someone refuse to be a king?

We are making paper-strip log cabins on Lincoln's birthday. Suddenly Kendra begins to sing:

Kwanzaa is the time to celebrate
The fruits of our labor, ain't it great
Ain't it great, celebrate
Celebrate Kwanzaa, Kwanzaa
Celebrate Kwanzaa, Kwanzaa.

Kendra did not sing her song for us on the day her mother came to school, but two months later she is ready to teach us her secret. Soon a dozen or more children are singing with her as they all paste down brown strips in the shape of a log cabin.

As I walk past her table I see that she is drawing Abraham Lincoln in his tall hat next to the log cabin. And Mr. Lincoln has brown skin.

Note

1. Excerpts from the story included here appear, sometimes slightly modified, in Vivian Gussin Paley, *You Can't Say You Can't Play* (Cambridge, MA: Harvard University Press, 1992).

11 "I'm Gonna Express Myself": The Politics of Story in the Children's Worlds

Anne Haas Dyson
University of California, Berkeley

In the complex social worlds of an urban classroom, children play multiple roles: they are students in the official world, and peers and neighborhood friends in unofficial ones. Here Anne Haas Dyson focuses on how story composing helps children negotiate a place amidst this complexity. She illustrates that, at their most powerful, children's stories function as a kind of textual crossroad, *allowing children to bring worlds together in intellectually, socially, and emotionally satisfying ways.*

Louise has asked her third-grade students to compose "About the Author" pages for their new classroom-published books. The class will present these books at the upcoming publisher's party. William, Ayesha, and Rashanda, all friends, are meeting with Louise to discuss what kinds of information might be in such a section. None of them wants to write about information that is, in Rashanda's words, "personal business." William proposes to write, "I love to get in fights." Louise is a bit taken aback and asks him to think about his audience—parents, teachers, and other classroom visitors who will be coming to the party. William does not relent. "That's too bad they don't like it," he says, "I'm gonna *express* myself."

William and Louise are here enacting a familiar theme in adult-child relationships—an adult worrying about what a child will say in front of visiting relatives, curious neighbors, or strangers in public places. Language is a tool for the presentation of a social self, and part of growing up is learning how to deal with the expectations of diverse others for that self. Or so Louise was trying to tell William.

William worked awhile at his desk. Then he solemnly handed his "About the Author" page to Louise . . . and they both started to laugh. William had written that when somebody tries to "mess" with him, he "just walks away." William had turned his tough guy pose into one perfectly attuned to the audience—a rhetorical twist that both child and adult found clever.

In language arts education, we do value, as William seemed to know, child "voice" or "self-expression" and child "ownership" of text. But individuals, including children, do not have but one voice, nor do they, as solitary selves, "own" their texts.

As Bakhtin (1981) discusses, when authors compose a text, be it in speech or in writing, they also compose a *social* self. In story composing especially, they transform the everyday world, using its very voices as raw material to create an arranged, a crafted world that reaches out to others, their audience, in particular ways. While there are differences in the folk traditions of storytelling and the newer traditions of story writing, in both, composers use the performative or artful tools of repetition and rhyme, figures of speech, expressive sounds, and dialogue itself to capture their feelings and attitudes toward other people and the world (Tannen 1989). That affective quality—revealed in the details of setting, character, and action and in the sound and rhythm of the words themselves—entices the other, the audience (Bruner 1986).

This social interaction between composer and audience takes place against a landscape of social and power relations. Interactional partners reach out to each other as members of certain social groups with particular values, authority structures, and language norms. William, for example, threatened to "express" himself in a way that might alienate an audience of visiting adults and impress an audience of peers, who sometimes admire such boldness.

As William's actions suggest, in the classroom the social act of composing, be it in oral or written words, exists within a complex classroom community. There is the official classroom world governed by the teacher, but there is also the unofficial world of peers and that of the children's respective home communities, which may re-form in the classroom amidst networks of peers. Each social world has intersecting but nonetheless distinctive traditions or valued ways of using language. Thus children's language repertoires include stories, songs, jokes, and other language genres that reflect the folk traditions of their community, the popular media that pervade their lives, and also the written literature they have experienced at school and at home.

In this chapter, I focus on how stories help children negotiate their place in the complex social worlds of the classroom. As Louise, the children's teacher, noted, "The richness of children's language life is in story." This richness, though, is not in *any* story. Particularly powerful stories may come about when children's stories function as a kind of crossroad: when they bring feelings, experiences, and language from the unofficial classroom worlds of peers and neighborhoods into the official classroom community *and* when those stories are themselves ways for children to make use of artistic tools and reflective processes valued in the official world.

To illustrate the social and political complexity of stories, I draw on data collected during an ethnographic project in William's K–3 school, an urban school serving a socially and culturally diverse population (Dyson 1993). Demographically the school served mainly two neighborhoods: 52 percent of the children came from an African American neighborhood and the others from an integrated but primarily European American neighborhood; about 27 percent of the children were Anglo, but there were also small percentages of children from many different heritages. Louise had taught a K–1 during the first year of my project and expected to do so in the second year as well. But after a fall leave for a family trip, she returned to find the school in the midst of staffing problems, especially in the third grade. So Louise, who had never before taught that grade, found herself in charge of William and his peers. In the next section, I introduce readers to Louise's class. I then rely on her children, especially William, to reveal the potential power of classroom story composing.

Louise's Third Grade

Louise had a small class of twenty children, thirteen girls and seven boys (a boy-girl ratio that bothered William). Twelve of the children were African American, five were European American, one was Chinese American, one Korean American, and one biracial (African American and European American).

Upon her entry into the class, Louise initiated a writing program, as she had in the K–1 class. The children had a regular writing period; often they chose their own topics, but sometimes Louise assigned topics related to ongoing social studies or science themes. The children wrote drafts, conferred with her and peer partners, and regularly shared their work. Louise taught lessons about all aspects of composing, among them, brainstorming, paragraphing, revising and editing, and the organization of varied genres.

As a teacher, Louise stressed child reflection and decision making across the curriculum; she wanted the children, as composers, to make choices about what and how to write and to reflect on those choices. She was also open to child talk and reflection on topics they initiated. Her children were interested in the social and political world outside the classroom. Among the topics they discussed were AIDS, drugs, war, racism, apartheid, consumer boycotts, rap, varied popular movies and popular songs.

Relative to the K–1 children, the third graders were more fluent as writers. While the younger children told and drew much more than they wrote, the older ones could easily and happily write for thirty minutes or more; and they were often rather quiet as they did so—no loud sound effects and dramatic, audible dialogue as stories unfolded.

At the same time, the third graders were also warier not only about school, but also about the world in general, and with good reason, as the list of topics above suggests. Too, a number had been retained, and the children worried about "flunking" and being older and larger than everyone else, not to mention disappointing their parents. The little children all automatically signed thank-you letters to school personnel and visitors with "Love" and their name; the third graders dispensed a written "Love" much more carefully.

Moreover, peer group symbols of the "in" and the "not in" were much stronger in the third grade—kinds of music, ways of talking and dressing, even certain products could have social and symbolic meaning. ("Coke," for example, "was [for William and his friends] a white man's drink," because its sponsors "don't support South Africa.") During class music study, the younger children had taken to symphony music as if it were an adventure in raw emotion—eyes widening with crescendos, anticipating something grand, and then crinkling with their giggles when the musical climax arrived. The third graders of varied sociocultural backgrounds made clear that such music was "boring"; they preferred rap and soul.

Such efforts on the part of children to define their own social worlds as peers are common in our society and, indeed, may be inherent to the institution of schooling, where the imposition of authority seems to give rise to a counterforce, some kind of resistance, visible or not, on the part of children (D'Amato 1987; Roberts 1970). Tensions between adults and children, however, may be more visible when adults and children differ in cultural and social circumstance, when children have experienced school failure, and, moreover, when children are members of a minority group that has experienced racism in its historical, social, and economic forms (Ogbu 1987).

In Louise's classroom, both the challenges and the satisfaction, for teachers and children, of negotiating boundaries between the official world managed by teachers and the unofficial worlds managed by children were visible in the children's actions and reactions during the daily writing time. After all, this was the time when children, in William's words, were supposed to "express themselves." In the following sections, I illustrate how children could use stories to take over and resist, as well as to connect with, the official school curriculum. I want especially to demonstrate the potential of *artful* story and verse performed on classroom stages for bringing at least some children's official and unofficial worlds together in satisfying and powerful ways.

William: The Discovery of a Literary Comedian

> Charles, Crystal, and Bianca are sitting around a table writing. Charles has written about his best friends, with a bit of help from his friends at the table.
>
> *Crystal:* Dag! That's your best friends? That's all your best friends?
>
> *Charles:* No, not—ain't all my best friends. I got lotsa more best friends. They just all my best best, especially William. You should know, William is my best, best, best friend.
>
> *Crystal:* I like William. William used to make me scared at first grade.
>
> *Bianca:* He was *big!*
>
> *Crystal:* He was like—he came up to me and I was like, "MO:::MY:::!"

A handsome child, William was tall and large-boned. He was older than the average third grader, having been retained in first grade, which embarrassed him. Once he advertently let slip his age (almost ten) to his friend Darren, and when Darren expressed surprise, William immediately said "I'm turning nine. I *wish* I was turning ten." In the K–1, I had heard children discussing "big William," and perhaps this notoriety for his physique contributed to his tendency to slump in his chair—and his utter dislike for sitting on the rug, where he never did seem to get quite comfortable.

William was socially sensitive in the peer world. His large size and his vocal resistance to unappealing directions (like sitting on the rug) could be misleading. He paid attention to his friends, which included boys, like Charles, Darren, and Patrick, and girls, like Crystal and Ayesha; he knew their favorite rap groups and games, their parents and cousins, their after-school schedules and weekend plans.

He himself was into cars, going hunting, rap music, and drawing. He usually had a picture he was working on just inside his desk, ready for any available free moment. William was aware of the boundary symbolized by what's hidden just inside the desk and what's placed for display on the desk—the boundary between the official and unofficial classroom worlds. He sometimes deliberately played with that boundary, as the opening anecdote suggested. If he were in a playful, peer-oriented mood, he might repeat Louise's Standard English phrases in nonstandard English underneath his breath or, when writing a polite social thank-you to a visitor, he might recite a quite rude one. Like children the world over (Opie and Opie 1959), he very much enjoyed turning the adult world on its head.

William and his classmates, especially Ayesha, Crystal, and Darren, were also politically and culturally conscious. They were especially interested in African American historical and popular heroes. Relevant books in the school library, though, were limited in number and generally quite old. The children passed the same library books among themselves repeatedly. (One day Darren told Ayesha, who claimed that she was going to keep reading a book about Martin Luther King, Jr., until she died, "You ain't gonna go to this school that long. You gotta send your kids here and let them bring it home. And then their kids. . . .")

William and his classmates seemed to enjoy the daily writing time, although William in particular was not interested initially in its procedures of editing and revising. Eventually, with prodding, he would circle potential misspelled words, consult with an adult or a dictionary, and enter his work on the computer for final drafts. Sometimes he shared his writing during class meetings after writing time; sometimes he did not. In the next sections, I examine the social purposes of William's composing, which initially did not involve stories at all.

Curricular Coexistence and Potential Takeovers

Although William had difficulty spelling—his texts were sometimes hard to decipher—he regularly wrote texts of seventy-five words or so about his "best friends," his liking football, sports cars, and drawing, his supposed disliking of girls (a public show), his enjoyment of humor:

> I like jokes. Do you know why? Because they are fun to do and
> you can make girls and boys and women and men laugh and a
> lots of kids.

Most of his energy and his crafting went into detailed drawings of vehicles, sports heroes, and friends. In his texts, he was one of the guys, so to speak, who teased girls, told jokes, and played sports. He wrote in a conversational style, collegially addressing the *you's* of his peers.

The dominant social purpose of William's writing, and of many children in the class, seemed initially to be to declare himself as a competent kid who was a member of important social groups (like "the guys"). Such writing was not only appealing to the children, but it was also useful for Louise. Beyond getting her children writing, such texts allowed her a means for learning about her children's social lives and personal interests.

And yet the children's social agenda could coexist with the official curriculum, without necessarily wholeheartedly engaging them in it. Consider, for example, the following essay about girls:

> We have too much girls in our class, and I don't like girls at all.
> Just my mom. Do you know why I hate girls? Because they hate
> football. So I hate girls. Now do you see? I'm sorry, but I do. I
> wish girls liked football. (Spelling and punctuation corrected
> for ease of reading; William added last sentence after talking
> with Louise.)

William's piece might seem like an ideal text for critical reflection, particularly about images of girls. And, indeed, Louise did talk to William about his text. Was the point that he really didn't like *girls?* Some girls, she pointed out, like football. The point, William agreed, was that he really liked football and that he wished girls in their class did. While William did add the last sentence, his piece was not written for clear communication (or for artful performance, for that matter). It evolved in the midst of ongoing teasing between William and Crystal, who in fact liked each other. Crystal, sitting across from William as he wrote, giggled at his texts and wrote her own:

> Sometimes I wish that my Dad did not like football because
> they always watch football, baseball, and basketball. Because
> me and my mom never get to watch any T.V. with my brother.
> My brother is only 7 months and he is very cute to me. All boys

are bad because it's just a nerve in their head. I don't know [why] every boy has the same thing in their mind.

Indeed, for Crystal, such unofficial social purposes—as teasing others—could overtake the curriculum and threaten peace in the classroom community. She sometimes couched her teases in fictional stories; she then used the daily sharing time for classroom manipulation on a grand and, from my point of view, rather bold scale. Breaking the classroom rule about checking with children before writing about them, she would read stories naming certain classmates as her friends or sisters, designating certain others as their "boyfriends" and, once, still others as "wimps." (Crystal's "wimps" were April and Manrisa, two children whose social backgrounds and sense of humor were different from Crystal's. April in particular complained, and complained loudly, about the insulting designation.)

While William wrote no such stories, his texts and Crystal's were, in social purpose, similar. They used their texts to declare and manipulate their social relationships in peer worlds. While using friends as characters is a potentially helpful strategy for text development, both children—indeed, many children in the class—sometimes literally stuffed as many peers' names as possible into their pieces. The goal was direct manipulation, not subtle exploration. William's texts in particular did not seem to capture the humor and the social insight (the play with social boundaries) that was so visible just under the surface of the official curriculum.

And, in fact, it was drawing upon that language life just under the surface of the official curriculum that seemed to transform his writing. Before looking at that transformation, I introduce William's literary potential through presenting a text written as a piece of resistance (and is, I think, something of a pièce de résistance).

Curricular Resistance

Right before writing time one day, a child came into Louise's room, hand in hand with the day's playground teacher. The little girl accused William and a classmate of calling her a racially charged name. William immediately denied the charge. The playground teacher could not talk now; she had a class full of children waiting for her. The accusing child and the two boys would have to confer with her during the lunch period so that they could all have their say. Louise assured William that she understood that he felt the charge was unfair and that she (Louise) was not angry, nor was she accusing anybody of anything;

the problem would have to be talked out later. Right now, the children were to write a piece—in any genre they so chose—about rain, a kind of class celebration of the recent deluge in the midst of the California drought.

William was not consoled. He was angry. Tears streaming down his face, he took his paper and wrote a personal essay. He resisted the assignment, but he did so in a poignant way. Following are extended excerpts from his long (237 words) text:

> I don't like rain because I don't like water and I hate salt water because it tastes too salty and with salt you could die. Sometime I like Rain. Like I said I hate when people accuses me for nothing because then I get in trouble and I will be grounded for nothing all I will be (cleaning?) water not salt water. Just water. But don't let me change the subject. But I don't like to get in trouble [for] something that I didn't do. Now ain't that dumb, the dumbest thing I heard in my whole life. I know you don't want to get in trouble. . . . Rain make me mad because I hate it. It just put a curse on me and it's like I have a chocolate head with no brains and no blood. It makes me cry. And when I go home do you know what happen? *I get a whipping from my mom if I get in trouble and I cry so the bed gets wet like rain.* (emphasis added)

William's piece, a private one, was different from his usual expressive texts about sports, friends, vehicles. The difference was not simply the emotionally charged nature of the content, but also the presence of performative tools for giving shape to a feeling. One such tool was the intermingling of "voices" speaking, as it were, on different subjects. As William "changed the subject" (an organizational flaw Louise often discussed), he captured the tension between the dutiful student writing about rain and the worried child feeling wronged and wanting to make clear to his teacher the fate awaiting him. Another such tool is the use of figures of speech, as in the closing analogy, where the two voices meet: "I cry so the bed gets wet like rain."

Form, content, function are inseparable in William's piece. He expresses his feelings, but he also represents them in the very form of his writing. Still, this was not a piece for the public arena, nor was it one that Louise did or, in my view, should have discussed for its literary tools. She dealt with his feelings and the incident, and yet those tools are there. It is not that William deliberately used such performance techniques; rather, as Bakhtin (1981) might suggest, it is that William seemed to find himself in a certain place with a certain stance toward the world, and that stance made available to him tools he controlled. That stance and those tools—those of the performer taking control of an unruly world through language (Bauman 1986)—first emerged in humorous, not poignant ways. The critical text, unlike the crying piece, was not a piece of curricular resistance, but a kind of "crossroad" that engaged William wholeheartedly in both official and unofficial worlds, as I explain in the next section.

Textual Crossroads

William's performative powers emerged on the public stage clearly—and suddenly—when he wrote the first of three interconnected stories about his uncle and his pets. The first piece, written in March, was motivated by the arrival in the classroom of two pet birds. The birds reminded William, he had said, of his uncle's "cussing bird," a phrase that got the whole class laughing, as Louise recalled. Perhaps it was that laughing, that appreciation from the classroom community as a whole, that led William to write the first of his stories about his uncle's pets. His decision also could have been influenced by Louise's use of diverse sorts of stories in the curriculum, including a particularly popular anthology, *Talk that Talk: An Anthology of African-American Storytelling* (Goss and Barnes 1989); there were, she was saying implicitly and explicitly, all kinds of stories. Or, maybe, it was the accumulation of days of writing, bringing with it comfort with pencil and paper and an assurance of a public forum for presentation of work.

Whatever the reasons, William began writing what he first called "true stories," the kind "my mom likes." "True stories" was a phrase used by the observed K–1 children too—"This is a true story," a child might say, and then tell a story that could not be true, an exaggerated, humorous, and performative tale that often revealed the cleverness of the teller. (For an extended discussion of such stories in the African American oral tradition, see Smitherman 1986 and also Heath 1983.)

William, however, did not tell his true "cussing bird" story; he wrote it—a long story for him, 210 words (although subsequent ones would be longer). In doing so, he drew upon the performative skills suggested by his "cry rain" piece, which actually was written after the cussing bird. He seemed to anticipate his peers' giggles, as he quickly and with great concentration wrote about his uncle (whom he displays as not too bright) and himself (a disparaged but eventually respected character in his own tale).

William spent quite a bit of time with his uncle, who cared for him when his mother's work schedule kept her away long hours. His uncle, he felt, could be awfully bossy, and William took no small delight in a story of the teasing uncle who, in the end, was put in his place:

My Uncle and the Cussing Bird

OK this how it started. My uncle wanted a bird so bad, he tried to get one out of the sky. Now that's dumb. So one day he was hoping that he can get a bird free. And I said to my Uncle Glen, "How are you going to do that?" And he said, "I don't know." So two months later a box came, and it said bird. And my uncle started screaming and teasing me. He was saying, "Oh yes. I have a bird. Ha, ha, ha ha, ha. I have a bird. Ha, ha, ha ha, ha. And he opened it, and the bird was dead. And he started to cry. The whole couch was wet with tears. I tried onions but he started to cry more. Then, he started to cry more. The next week, more and more boxes, and he kept saying, "Ha, ha, ha ha, ha." And one day a box came—Yes yes yes! The bird said "I'm polly-want-a cracker." [And] he said, "F___ you big mouth." And my uncle never wanted a bird again. Do you know what he wanted? A fish. (Piece given conventional spelling and punctuation for ease of reading)

Through this story, William aimed to perform, to artfully entertain others, or so suggested both his performative language, rooted in storytelling traditions, and his eagerness to take the classroom stage with his work.

To elaborate, William's story was more crafted than any of his earlier pieces. There was an opening orientation to his uncle and the situation ("My uncle wanted a bird so bad, he tried to get one out of the sky"). William not only carefully sequenced a series of events, he captured the affective quality of the experience. He used evaluative comments ("Now that's dumb"), extended, expressive dialogue, and even a well-placed interruption of the story's rhythm ("Yes yes yes!").

Moreover, the two stories that followed were carefully scripted to match the initial story of the cussing bird. After that bird came the biting fish, just as had been predicted in the last line of the initial tale ("Do you know what he wanted? A fish."):

In the last story, the cursing bird liked to cuss. Let's see what happens in this story. It was 1990 and my uncle wanted a fish. So one day me and my uncle went fishing and my uncle caught a fish.

In the biting fish story, the tension between William and his uncle assumes a more dominant role. Moreover, the new performative features that were evident served to highlight this tension. For example, William shifted verb tenses, which contrasted the reported teasing of his uncle and the characteristic it typified:

> He took it [the fish] home. He started to tease me. But that was nothing big. He does it all the time.

He also incorporated voices from popular media and folk sayings, which enlivened his tale in expressive ways. When William taunts his teasing uncle, the uncle chases after him. His uncle catches him when he falls over a big rock. William yells out:

> "Well people all over the world. I'm going to die. If you want to see me before I die come see me at 2829 or call me at 754-9295." I got out and said, "I'm not going to die." And I started to say, "I'm a free man oh yeah." Then I broke out saying and started to sing, "If it wasn't for bad luck I wouldn't have no luck at all."

The "biting fish" also introduced a slapstick sort of humor, which may be why William started calling them "comedy stories." This sort of humor increased in the last of the stories, set up in the concluding lines of the "biting fish." Since a package came with a fish—which jumped up and bit his hand—his uncle decided he didn't want a fish anymore: "And do you know what he wanted? He wanted a dog."

In the last story, "The Bad Dog," William plays numerous tricks on his uncle at a party—a party to which his uncle had, in no uncertain terms, not invited him. William then reveals, in true, "true story" fashion, that he himself has been the clever person behind the obnoxious pets. It is William's turn to laugh:

> "Remember when you was laughing at me? Now ha ha ha. And remember all those pets? Here they are."

The fish jumps up and bites his uncle, the bird curses at him, and then a box arrives for his uncle. Yes. It is a dog who comes out and bites him. William gloats:

> "Do you want a dog now? Do you know why all that stuff happened to you? Why? Because I set you up that's why." Do you know what he wanted? Nothing. The end.

All three stories were huge classroom hits. Indeed, William anticipated that they would be. He finished his "cussing bird" piece right as the class was leaving for its weekly library period. William was enormously disappointed:

> *William:* That's why I want to read it on the rug, so everybody can hear it. But she said we have to go the library. Maybe she'll let us read them when we come back.

He did read the piece after the class came back from the library—and many times after that, at his classmates' own request. This anticipation—and desire for—success on the official classroom stage may have supported a change in the quality of William's participation in, as well as the products resulting from, the daily composing time.

William was drawing on language from unofficial worlds—the language of popular media and of folk traditions—but he also was entering into the official activities of composing, including planning, drafting, reflecting, and, in William's case particularly, performing. Moreover, his stories became part of the official culture of the classroom, even as they drew on unofficial sources; the stories were talked about by other children, requested as stories to hear again, and even imitated by his classmate Paul.

William's increased investment in the official world and his reflectiveness about his texts and their social meaning were in fact displayed at the very publishing party whose guests William had seemingly disregarded. At the party, William read his cussing bird piece to the invited guests with enormous pleasure. However, he made a key adjustment for the audience, as he explained to Louise and his classmates as they chatted after the party guests had left:

> *William:* I had, like, to put something different in the cussing bird story. When I had the F word, I had to say something different. I was gonna say, "He said the F word." But I said, "never mind." [William had read that "He said a bad word."]
>
> *Louise:* That was smart. You have to consider your audience.

For his classmates, of course, he emphasized the tough talk and slapstick; indeed he deliberately planned to do just that. When William finished his first story about the cussing bird, he immediately commented on the next tale:

> *William:* That's gonna be the next one I'm writing about—a fish. This is a true story . . . A true story about a fish. It's gonna be re::al rad. A lot of cussing and a lot of biting.

And it was, real rad that is.

This cussing and biting highlights the role of William's stories as kinds of crossroads—as texts that were supported by, and supporting, William's action in multiple social worlds. Such crossroads are themselves built by crossing textual, social, and cultural boundaries, as I explain in the closing section of this chapter.

Stories: Artful Tools for Crossing Boundaries

William, like all story composers, crafted everyday voices; he emboldened, exaggerated, and intermingled them to make his points, to "express" his feelings about the world. But he did not use "neutral words" in that composing (Bakhtin 1981, 293), but words voiced by someone in some social situation. Child authors like William, or grown-up ones, craft voices that in theme, style, or structure are linked for them, and for their readers, to specific situations and to the values and authority structures of those situations.

Thus authors not only play with the boundary between the real and the imagined, they also play with social and cultural lines influenced by age, status, sex, class, race, ethnicity, and on and on. Artful stories do not smooth out or hide tensions, nor do they directly manipulate them—they craft them for display. And they do so by intermingling voices drenched in cultural meaning. Curses and pleas, television come-ons and playground put-downs, literary allusions and rap song rhythms—all can coexist in the story.

Moreover, these social and cultural boundaries may be crossed not only within children's stories, but also in the very fact that those stories exist within the official classroom world. Contrary to the oft-assumed opposition of vernacular or peer ways with words to school ways (e.g., Labov 1982; Ogbu 1987), stories are vehicles for bringing diverse voices into the classroom itself. Thus William brought into the official classroom world "true stories" that captured part of his identity outside the classroom. Indeed, the importance of a composing link to families and, in some cases, to cultural or racial identity, was clearly evident in other children's successful interactions, both in official and unofficial worlds. (For a discussion of the theoretical link between composing and cultural identity, see Ferdman 1990.) For example, Ayesha regularly wrote rhythmic verse and story poems about African American heroes; her texts earned her classroom appreciation—and also her mother's.

In the class pleasure in William's stories, the children themselves came together, which is the last and most important social and cultural boundary I note. That is, social and cultural boundaries were crossed not only within William's tales, but in the very coming together of William and his classmates to enjoy his stories. Those stories may have been classroom favorites, in part at least, because their sharing in a classroom forum touched common chords in the children. For the diverse details of the children's lives, when crafted, can reveal their connections.

They were all, at the very least, children in an adult-governed world. And in that world, where politeness and kindness are the ostensible values, William pushed hushed emotions beyond the point of embarrassing self-revelation ("personal business," in Rashanda's terms); his bold voices were crafted, in fact, with language tools valued in the official school world. This delight in tough talk in polite places (this legitimate way to "express myself") is common in childhood. Teasing the adult world through language is a cross-cultural if not universal pleasure of childhood (Opie and Opie 1959).

Further, the children all enjoyed the music of language itself—its rhythm and rhyme, an enjoyment that is also a near universal in childhood. Many children took pleasure in rhyming their talk as much as possible, an interest that may have been strengthened by the popularity of rap. In fact, William's and Ayesha's own pleasure in a story poem that April presented was particularly poignant because both children had expressed explicitly to Louise a desire not to sit by that child. And yet when April shared the text that follows, William and Ayesha were the most vocal of all in their calls for her to "read it again." (The piece is not only carefully crafted, it is also rather slapstick in its humor and, perhaps, a child's version of a Robert Louis Stevenson classic.)

My Shadow

I saw my shadow sneaking
over to my bedroom door
I spied on him, then quickly
I walked over with my sore.

I wrestled with my shadow.
I kicked him half to death.
I called him names like "Pinocchio,"
and "Little Beth de Seth."

I gave him all my socks
they say
Well maybe one or two.

But when my shadow walked out the
door with me,
I hit him with my shoe.

In short, in a classroom like Louise's, classrooms which contain a diversity of children and a diversity of stories, both professional and child made, and a classroom stage upon which to perform, children themselves may discover both their differences and, in those very differences, their similarities. While not discounting the importance of all the kinds of genres children do and must learn to compose, it is in crafted texts and especially in stories that children may bring in the complexity of their lives. And in the sharing of those texts, they may find that they are all children, governed at times by unreasonable adults; they are all—or so we hope—dreamers who want to grow up to be powerful, respected people; and they are all susceptible to being wound up in the music of language, if just for a moment.

Such discoveries of commonality are not automatic—and they inevitably come mixed with the classroom tensions (for teacher and children) suggested by the description herein of curricular coexistence, takeovers, and resistance. But still, I believe, as I know Louise does too, that those moments of being all wrapped up together inside a crafted tale are important for children's sense of themselves as interconnected people, "fellow planeteers" (to use a child phrase I love) who, soon enough—as Darren suggested—will have their own children needing teaching, guiding, and of course a healthy dose of stories.

References

Bakhtin, M. (1981). Discourse in the novel. In M. Holquist (Ed.), C. Emerson and M. Holquist (Trans.), *The dialogic imagination: Four essays by M. M. Bakhtin* (259–422). Austin: University of Texas Press. (Original work published 1934–1935)

Bauman, R. (1986). *Story, performance, and event.* Rowley, MA: Newbury House.

Bruner, J. (1986). *Actual minds, possible worlds.* Cambridge, MA: Harvard University Press.

D'Amato, J. D. (1987). The belly of the beast: On cultural differences, castelike status, and the politics of schools. *Anthropology and Education Quarterly, 18,* 357–360.

Dyson, A. Haas. (1993). *Social w rlds of children learning to write in an urban primary school.* New York: Teachers College Press.

Ferdman, B. (1990s). Literacy and cultural identity. *Harvard Educational Review, 60,* 181–204.

Goss, L., and Barnes, M. (1989). *Talk that talk: An anthology of African-American storytelling.* New York: Simon & Schuster.

Heath, S. B. (1983). *Ways with words: Language, life and work in communities and classrooms.* Cambridge: Cambridge University Press.

Labov, W. (1982). Competing value systems in inner-city schools. In P. Gilmore and A. A. Glatthorn (Eds.), *Children in and out of school* (148–171). Washington, DC: Center for Applied Linguistics.

Ogbu, J. (1987). Variability in minority school performance: A problem in search of an explanation. *Anthropology and Education Quarterly, 18,* 312–334.

Opie, I., and Opie, P. (1959). *The lore and language of school children.* Oxford: Oxford University Press.

Roberts, J. (1970). *Scene of the battle: Group behavior in urban classrooms.* Garden City, NY: Doubleday.

Smitherman, G. (1986). *Talkin and testifyin: The language of black America.* Detroit: Wayne State University Press.

Tannen, D. (1989). *Talking voices: Repetition, dialogue and imagery in conversational discourse.* Cambridge: Cambridge University Press.

12 "All the Things That Mattered": Stories Written by Teachers for Children

Sal Vascellaro
Bank Street College of Education

Celia Genishi
Teachers College, Columbia University

*Sal Vascellaro and Celia Genishi explore the links between teachers'
lives, stories, and teaching. The setting is a children's literature course
that Vascellaro teaches, and literature and talk about it are the vehicles
that help form a community of writers whose audience is the children in
their classrooms.*

In Lionni's story for children, *Frederick* (1967), the mice prepare for
winter by laboring through the golden sunny days, gathering corn,
nuts, and wheat, working day and night—except for Frederick, who
spends these days storing the rays of sunlight, gathering the colors and
words of summer. As the trials of winter emerge, the stored food,
obtained through sweat and sacrifice, gives out, and it is then
Frederick who sustains them. He does this by telling stories, stories
themselves nourished by the sun's warm and powerful rays, the colors
of things alive and growing, and by the longed-for words of other
seasons.

In this section of our chapter, the first author describes the
course he teaches, for which the final assignment is to write stories for
children. (Thus he writes about the course in the first person.) The
course is part of a master's degree program at Bank Street College for
students already teaching or preparing to teach young children, three-
year-olds through third grade. Given this age focus, the study of picture books with their poetic, concentrated text is central to the course,
and most frequently students write their own stories as picture books.
This assignment is given as a way to synthesize what they have gained

from listening to, reading, reflecting on, discussing, and writing about stories for children. It is also seen as a different way for students to connect deeply with the child's voice within themselves. When the students first hear the assignment, many cringe but take some comfort in that it comes late in the course, during the last nights of class.

On these last nights, when the stories are to be read aloud, the class of twenty-five students seems unusually quiet. They are obviously nervous. Even seemingly light-hearted, poised students appear tense. Some students want to read first—or last. I draw up a list. The moment is very intense. And as they read, we notice and feel a change in the class, in ourselves and with each other. Students describe the experience of the last night, each saying something special: "It was a special part of me that I was sharing with others, hoping that it might touch them as well. . . . I felt like you could probably see the gleam in my eyes as I read my story. . . . I don't think I realized how personal the experience of sharing one's writing can be." "Everyone offered comments that gave me even more insights into my own childhood and my writing process. Their responses really brought my story to life in a way that reading it to non-teachers never would have." "We learned a lot about each other those two nights, about our interests, what and who we care about, and about our lives, our childhood and families, our past and present." "I felt my experience as a child was transformed into something alive in the moment. I also felt the story allowed the child in me to have a public voice connecting to others. . . . It was a liberating experience." "The interplay with classmates I came to know during the course on the days we told our stories to each other was a golden moment for me, the feeling of unity with a group of colleagues, fellow teachers."

At the end of one "last night," one student, overwhelmed by the experience of everyone's story, asked if this was unusual, if they in fact were exceptional writers and thinkers. It did seem unusual, and they did seem exceptional; yet this event had happened each of the eight times I had taught the course. Each time the group felt that same powerful sense of the moment as these private worlds became public through their stories, most of which were about their own childhoods.

At a certain point, it became clear that the objectives for this assignment had been realized in unanticipated ways. In hearing these stories, I had seen experiences from my own life flash before me, some lived through, others dreamed of and yearned for. What were the possible meanings of this assignment for all of us? In this chapter we will explore these meanings by discussing two questions in particular:

> What about the course had led the students to the unique ways in which they formulated and shaped their stories?
>
> What had these windows into each other's realities, these personal meanings, molded by the conventions of children's stories and directed outward to children and adults, to do with teaching or becoming a teacher?

The Course: Personal Meanings in a Public Forum

Writing for children as part of the teacher education program dates to the very beginnings of Bank Street College when its founder, Lucy Sprague Mitchell, gave writing exercises as a way for her students to understand and hear the qualities of a young child's language. It was an attempt to open their eyes to what children enjoy and, typical of Mitchell's experimental approach, it was firmly grounded in observing children and systematically recording their behavior and their language. Marcus (1992) describes this process in his biography of Margaret Wise Brown, who was a student of Mitchell: "It was one thing to strive for an intellectually complex understanding of children's behavior and development; it was quite another to reconstitute within oneself even a semblance of the actual framework of childhood—to see the world, as it were, through a 3-year-old's eyes" (60). Although her course was on a child's language, the sheer number and variety of "exercises" amounted to an in-depth experience in writing for children. Mitchell's own student, Claudia Lewis, continued Mitchell's course and expanded the experimental study of children's language into a study of children's literature. Lewis also asked students to write for children, and, like Mitchell, she presented exercises that focused on understanding children and their language.

> We felt that if the students opened their eyes to what children enjoy, if they try it themselves, they would be in a better position to create meaningful stories for children about their everyday experiences, as well as to stimulate children's use of language in discussions and in the telling of their own "stories."[1]

In planning the course, I included topics that had historically been a major aspect, such as the relationship between a child's language and children's literature. Also included were topics one would find in many children's literature courses, such as criteria for selecting books, major trends, poetry, folklore, storytelling, nonfiction, and the relationship between children's literature and literacy.

The course was also influenced by a presentation given by Vera Williams, a prominent writer for children, during a May 1989 children's literature institute at Teachers College, where she discussed the relationship between her own life and the stories she writes.[2] Williams spoke specifically about her book, *A Chair for My Mother* (1982), a story of a child who lives with her mother and grandmother, a family without a father. Together they struggle, persevere, and save to buy the most beautiful chair in the world, even after fire destroys their apartment. The story evokes Williams's childhood in the 1930s, a period of widespread poverty, when it was common to see families' possessions on the street. Although daily existence was a financial struggle, Williams's mother bought a chair, not the plush, beautiful one in the book. Unlike the family in the written story, even with scrimping they lived in fear of its being repossessed. With resentment, Williams as a child demanded to know "Why did you buy it?" *A Chair for My Mother*, a story of memory and desire, is a gift for the author's mother, a gift she could not give her in life—"the path she took and the path she wished she could have taken." As Williams spoke about her life and story, it became clear how important it would be to convey how the powerful wellsprings of fiction rise from one's lived experience.

Because literature presents a semblance of our shared human experience and our unique experiences as peoples and individuals, students were asked to dig deeply into their own memories of themselves as children. I wanted the course to evoke strong feelings that are so much a part of life experience—loneliness, pain, sorrow, loss, and also excitement, fun, wonder, and serenity.

Lewis became the model for the way literature was presented to the students: putting the story in the forefront and, when possible, reading it entirely, not intruding critically on the presentation, and eliciting an open-ended response. As a result, students were offered opportunities to have powerful encounters with these books, opportunities to experience the stories aesthetically. Rosenblatt (1978) views this type of response as an event in time, a dynamic transaction between the reader (the listener) and the text—both essential agents in making the literary work come alive:

> The reader brings to the text his past experience and present personality. Under the magnetism of the ordered symbols of the text, he marshals his resources and crystallizes out the stuff of

> memory, thought, and feeling a new order, a new experience,
> which he sees as the poem [the literary work]. This becomes
> part of the ongoing stream of his life experience, to be reflected
> on from any angle important to him as a human being. (12)

Through this aesthetic response to a literary work as opposed to a
more analytic response which Rosenblatt calls an "efferent" stance,
readers are more alive to the experience of the moment of encounter
with the text. They are sensitive to all that is evoked by the sounds and
nuances of words, the flow of language, while actively moving from
detail to totality and, at the same time, integrating feelings, ideas,
attitudes, and life meanings and experiences—"a fuller arc of his responses" (43).

To offer these opportunities for aesthetic response, to evoke a
powerful response, I selected many stories that grew from and expressed a significant emotion, stories like *A Chair for My Mother* that
the writer "needed" to tell, and read these aloud throughout the fourteen weeks of the class. Since many picture books offer minimal text
with sensorial images, with the rhythmic flow of language that
Mitchell had found to be so satisfying for children, they are poetic if
not strictly poetry. From these evocative texts, students were constantly "constructing" the worlds of stories written for children, being
forced to confront the child within them, their own childhood. By
being offered these opportunities for an aesthetic response, students
would in turn, I hoped, through the insight and conviction gained
from their lived experience in the course, also offer these same opportunities to their own students. Schools so frequently seem to demand
the efferent response, even to poetry.

It later became apparent that the students' childhood experience
was also alive through being read to, since the authenticity of one's
early experience of literature is frequently evoked through the intimacy of the human voice. Students frequently describe how reading
aloud to their own students is one of the most intimate and pleasurable
experiences they have as teachers, perhaps because they sense the
same feelings in their children. The graduate students were frequently
surprised that being read to, either by me or their fellow students,
was such a central component of the course, and many felt it the
experience through which they gained the most insight into language,
style, meanings, and source of appeal for children. As one student said,
"I just couldn't believe we were supposed to listen and not expected
to do something except take it all in, think about it, discuss our responses, and then do our own research." They were also surprised

how, during the final sessions, their own stories seemed different, somehow transformed, through the hearing of their own voice reading them publicly.

As I read more and more to the students and we discussed our responses, it became clear how, by putting the aesthetic and evocative aspect of the literature in the forefront, the students' own life stories were inextricably a part of the process. It also grew clear that, as one children's writer (Wells 1990) says so well, "Other people's books are the best teachers of writers" (139).

The process of reaching the final assignment begins on the first night of class, when the students are asked to introduce themselves and tell about their favorite book as a young child and describe why it was so meaningful to them. Carla Poole, a course assistant, felt that students see right away that their personal experiences have a prominent place in the course, and when I refer to their selections and comments in future sessions on the meanings of stories for children, the "students are surprised and realize that they have been put in the position of having something important to say." Simply asking for the students' response to a story or asking what they see as the appeal helps them begin to get the message that their ways of perceiving are integral to making the literary work come alive.

When the students shared their own book selections in small groups, instead of beginning with a didactic discussion of why they selected the book, they frequently told the story they had selected and just as frequently told their personal story, such as "when I was a child my family also moved a lot and. . . ." In these small groups, students articulate their thoughts as active, responding readers. Poole felt that this merging of personal and professional knowledge in discussing a story was similar to the adult writer expressing experience through a child's eye and that such experiences enable one to evolve as a teacher. Because I told many stories about the author's lived and felt story and its relationship to the written story, like that of Williams's *A Chair for My Mother,* students understood these written stories differently, from an author's perspective. (At least two students trace the birth of their own story to hearing this one.) And finally, Poole noted, as students repeatedly expressed concerns over what was for many the frightening prospect of writing a story, I would respond with a conviction that students grew to accept, "You have a story that must be told"—and I was available for further discussion. Over time, many students came to realize that they had stories worth telling and, most significantly, felt safe enough to share these personal worlds and make them public. As one student described this safety: "We had what we needed, a setting where we felt safe and supported as we tap into deeply personal themes in our own lives."

Uniting the Personal and Professional:
Three Teachers and Their Stories

Although students were not asked to write autobiographically, most chose to do so, drawing from a full range of lived experience. The autobiographical stories were windows into family and cultural differences, subtle differences in ways of being, yet were surprisingly similar in theme and situation. Students wrote of loved ones, family, friends, and pets. They told of "little" adventures, stories of the child's world when the adults are not around; stories of struggles, loss, and separation; stories of growing up and coming of age, initiation stories, stories of one's struggle to achieve identity. A few students also wrote stories from experiences in their own classrooms. Because the form of the telling was left open, many skillfully drew from the many models they had experienced throughout the course, most frequently using evocative, tight text with a definite rhythm and in some cases verse. Most stories were conceived as picture books, with a dynamic interplay between text and visual image. Some students sketched the illustrations or verbally described them. For some, the illustrations were as evocative as the text.

Although some of the stories were not precisely autobiographical, much of the writer's self took form in the story. Students told these stories in the manner of tales taken from their own cultural backgrounds. Some chose to rewrite stories passed down through their families, stories they had grown up with and were to them as real as their lived experience. Others wrote works of fantasy, such as animal stories, grounded in their own life passions, while others created concept books, such as alphabet books, filled with humor and ingenuity.

From among the many evolved and powerful stories, the texts of the following three were selected to present here: *Sometimes in the Bathtub,* by Heather Smith-Willis; *One Plus One,* by Monique Marshall; and *When Night Comes,* by Veronica Najjar. These were selected because of their obviously different style, age focus, and situation, but surprisingly similar themes. In diverse ways the authors address questions of human difference, of safety and security, and of vulnerability as children move beyond the home. Each was shared in classrooms with children, as well as in the graduate class. Because the illustrations are inherent to the experience of these stories, their full power can only be hinted at here.

Sometimes in the Bathtub

Written and Illustrated by Heather Smith-Willis
DEDICATED TO:
My husband Stephen
My parents and
My sisters Kathleen
and Krista

Every evening at 7 o'clock we get ready for our bath. Sometimes we all take our bath together.

Sometimes in the bathtub, Daddy runs our bath water. He gives us plastic cups and scoopers to play with and puts red food coloring in the water.

Sometimes in the bathtub, as a special treat Mommy gives us special soaps shaped like Mother Goose characters. Sometimes she reads us the stories that go with our soaps while we're in the tub.

Sometimes in the bathtub, Mommy puts in scented bath oil that makes the water silky and the whole bathroom seems to smell like flowers.

Sometimes in the bathtub, we get to have bubble bath from a box. That was before the doctor said we were allergic to it.

Sometimes in the bathtub, I pretend to swim instead of washing with the soap that doesn't sink.

Sometimes in the bathtub, we take turns sliding down the back of the tub to see who can make the biggest splash.

Sometimes in the bathtub, Kathy makes a really big splash and our hair gets wet all over. Krista doesn't like this game and she always gets out.

Sometimes in the bathtub, we get so noisy that our dog Bear comes in to see what's happening. Then Mommy comes and makes him get out.

Sometimes in the bathtub, Mommy says we have to wear a shower cap if we're going to play the sliding game. Mine is yellow with white lace.

Sometimes in the bathtub, we make such big waves that the water goes over the top and gets on the floor.

Sometimes in the bathtub, I drop the big towel in by accident and we laugh so loud that mommy says it's time to get out.

Sometimes in the bathtub, I watch all the water and bubbles go down the drain until the last bubble is gone.

Sometimes in the bathtub, my hair gets wet even with the shower cap on and Mommy has to blow it dry before I go to bed.

Next time in the bathtub, I'll try to make the biggest splash of all without getting my hair wet.

The End

"All the Things That Mattered"

Smith-Willis evokes the universal childhood ritual of taking a bath. It is a story of three sisters and a great moment they share together, told through the eyes of the middle child, Heather. It is also a story of their parents, how they set the stage, offer the props, then leave as the children invent this world together. The adults are never intrusive or overly controlling. Yet the security and comfort of their presence are never far away. The world they offer their children is safe and predictable.

The story moves from one special moment of fun to another as each evening the bathtub seems to grow to Olympic size, as Figure 1 shows. Though the sisters are of different ages, the bath offers a moment of fun among equals. The greatest fun is seeing who can make the biggest splash. With irreducible simplicity, the story captures the young child's intense pleasure and awe in little things. "Sometimes in the bathtub, I watch all the water and bubbles go down the drain until the last bubble is gone." It is as though the regularity, safety, and fun of these days would last forever. The ending evokes the consummate bedtime story, *Goodnight Moon*, in that it too "is a ritual preparation for a journey beyond the world" (Marcus, 187).

Figure 1. From *Sometimes in the Bathtub,* by Heather Smith-Willis. The story is formatted horizontally and is 20 x 15 inches. On each double-page opening, text is presented on the left page and a full-page illustration on the right. (Photo courtesy Joyce Culver.)

As in *A Chair for My Mother*, this story too grew from memory and desire. It was sparked for Smith-Willis by seeing a photograph of herself and her two sisters as children in a bath together, and she realized how their adult lives had led them in different directions and just how much she missed the closeness. "That was a time when we were very close. It was a special time when I was allowed to be Kathy's buddy—without her friends around. It was a time we always had so much fun. I wanted to re-create that fun and preserve it."

In re-creating this time through the eyes of a six-year-old, Smith-Willis also preserved *how* she saw and felt as a child. This story is told in what Lewis (1981) calls "the language of sensory perception" (18), a language children know and use themselves, a language as physically alive as they are, "close to the living source." In showing "all the things that mattered," Smith-Willis also shows how they mattered—felt through the child's senses and imagination. The sense of place is described as the child experiences it, powerful and rich in evocative detail.

The story is at once universal and specific, with the illustrations especially showing the specific. It was important for Smith-Willis to show the family as African American. "I think all children should be able to pick up a book and see faces that look like their own. It's unfortunate that my sisters and I didn't have a book like mine to enjoy."

The illustrations are bold, brightly colored cut paper collage, without extraneous elements. Yet they are filled with critical details, such as the bath caps, "each a different color," the slippers, "those big round fluffs," and of course the bathtub. At times filled with red or blue coloring, at times filled with pink and white bubbles, at times actually filled with flowers from the scented bath oil, the bathtub seems to grow as we move from one little adventure to the next, subtly merging fantasy with reality in ways that children do all the time.

In writing this story, Smith-Willis also wanted to create a material for the second graders she teaches. "I wanted it to be easy to read: simple, repetitive, and also fun. I wanted the language to be accessible, even for the kids I teach who struggle with reading." Perhaps she wants for her students the competence and independence her parents allowed her to experience in the bath, while also structuring their environment for "safety." When she read the book to her class, she was surprised how everyone liked it and, just as important to her, how they were able to read it later. The students obviously experienced the fun she wanted to capture and preserve.

They were filled with questions revealing surprise and a new perception of their teacher, such as "How could you do this when you're here all the time?" "How did you learn to draw?" "How long did it take you to illustrate one page?" "When can we buy it in the store?" They were very interested in how she put together her Matisse-like cut paper illustrations. To give them insight into the mechanics of the illustrations, she had them experiment with the stencils she created for each of her characters.

In reflecting on the meanings of this process of writing her story for children, Smith-Willis concludes:

> This was hard, really hard, a lot harder than it looks, that is, to capture something that has so much meaning for you. I look at this book and I remember all the fun and it makes me feel close to my sisters again. Perhaps that's why people describe the book as warm. I guess, because my book means so much to me personally, I look at books differently. I try to focus on books that will have meaning for the kids in my class and hope they too will know this meaning. I also think more about where my children are coming from, their perspective. Doing this has made me see a lot more from their eyes. I am now better able to do this because in writing this book I remembered how a child sees—and it has been fun.

One Plus One
Written and Illustrated by Monique Marshall

For my mother,
who taught me
the peace sign
and in loving
memory of Bill.

THE SONG

Mommy sings me lullabies
in German.
Stroking the top of my
chestnut brown head,
braiding the thick,
down my back
mass of hair,
She purrs softness
"Arme, schwarze Kate,"
she hums.

THE BEACH

My dad swings me easily
up   uP   UP to his broad, black, deep
brown
    ever so high shoulders

    "O.K. Baby," he breathes and
rumbles
down inside his lovely self.
  . . . and I hang tight beneath his chin,

And I curl up inside
and smile.
Her sweet black cat.

squeeze my legs 'round the strong
neck.
My cheek rests on his shiny brown suntanned
head,

Knowing,
He'd never let His Baby
Fall

[1]

[2]

THE SWING

We are *flying*
Together
to the tops
of the trees—
My legs wrapped around her
strong waist.
I can only swing this high
with Her—
Laughing aloud, the Butterflies
inside us Both
help steer our swing
through the Autumn air—
Only the leaves
F
a
l
l
down.

THE TRUCK

His sunburnt Blackbrown
Hand
gently grips the Big Rig's
Wheel. Just one
Hand
Drives the Truck across
the country—
(ME, snug in the passenger
seat)
HE, keeping time,
Full-finger snapping
with his other.
Deep baritone,
Humming soul song's
with the radio.
His Body
keeps the Truck
D   N
  A   C   N
        I
            G
across the road
towards some far away
destination . . .
I hope we
NEVER
get there.

[3]

[4]

THE MAGIC

Once I woke up
alone
and my mother
was not there—

THE ROAD

Driving the truck
with his high knees—
Both hands are
FREE
tapping softly,

Not anywhere in the apartment.
i threw my smallness
against the old, worn,
embracing couch,
and cried
        from emptiness.
I tore myself to smaller
        pieces, until . . .

She Magically appeared
and dried my tears
with her love li ness.
Making
me
whole
again.

[5]

THE SUNTAN?

Walking down German streets—
Even mother's voice
sounds unfamiliar.
My Oma speaks only
her own language—
Strangers stare,
but do they
really see
me?
"Yes,
   it's
    a
     suntan."
when they ask?

[7]

THE COLOR

I am coloring
with a brown crayon.
But the face that I
color
is lonely . . .

For, looking around
I am surprised to see,

keeping rhythm on
ME
as we race through the night.
The rich, soft Blackness
slides by my window.
I sleep
always Knowing . . .
He would NEVER
let His Baby Fall.

[6]

THE KISS

"Gimme some sugar,"
he begs in his husky, deep
low, familiar growl.
and when we kiss our lips go
        SMACK!
in only the way they do with
        DADDY.
Mommy's Kiss is different.
        The quiet kind
                are
                        Hers.

[8]

THE QUESTION

        Although I live with Her
and not with Him,
I am part of Both
of Them.
and sometimes I wonder

        if
        I'm
        Black

no one	or
has done	White
this	or
but	When
me.	They are gone
	Where I'll fit
	in.
[9]	[10]

"The Pieces of a Puzzle"

One Plus One is a story of a child growing up and eventually imagining her world apart from her parents (see Figure 2). Marshall tells this story through a series of ten poems, the first six of the child's experience of her white German mother and her African American father, who are separated. Each of these is told as "one plus one," the child and parent alone, and is connected by the child's sense of security through being a part of one, then the other.

In very different ways each parent is a powerful presence, at times larger than life. They are strong, protective, and steady and also playful, warm, and gentle. The young child exists as though physically a part of each of them. Even when her father takes her across country in his truck, she lives in the pleasure and safety of their world together. In "The Magic," the fifth poem, foreshadowing the end of the story, her world of security is dramatically disrupted when she wakes up from a nap on the couch and finds herself alone. With a child's intense fear of abandonment, she is shattered until her mother "magically" appeared, making her feel "whole again."

In the last four poems, she moves out into worlds, such as the street or school, not encircled by him or her and becomes aware of being different, alone, estranged from the people around her, even her mother, grandmother, and classmates. As she walks down a German street with her mother and grandmother, to the strangers' question she answers, "Yes, / it's / a / suntan." In her school she realizes, "I am coloring / with a brown crayon. / . . . / no one / has done / this / but / me." Marshall ends her story with the child alone asking a question that did not have to be asked earlier, wondering, "When / They are gone / Where I'll fit / in."

In ending with this question instead of happy resolution, Marshall forces the reader to move beyond the present, beyond immediate impressions, and to share the child's insecurity. This child can never go back to the younger self, comfortably rooted in mother and father.

Figure 2. From *One Plus One,* by Monique Marshall. The story is formatted horizontally and is 11 x 7 inches. One poem is placed on each page and is framed in illustration or visual design. The poems placed to the left and right of each other convey the story's tension. (Photo courtesy Joyce Culver.)

It is a story for young adolescents—or children and adults of any age—questioning their place in the world. She has also written a story for children like herself, neither black nor white, not knowing which world they belong in—so different from the clear, predictable world conveyed by Smith-Willis. Yet her story also speaks to children of immigrants, children of new family structures, all children whose worlds are unclear.

The book grows from the totality of her lived experience, but most especially from recent experiences. Before writing the story, she attended a wedding on her father's side of her family. At one point in the wedding party, everybody danced together as a group, from the youngest child to the oldest relative, and because she did not know the dance, she could not join them. "I didn't grow up with that dance, and I felt left out. Yet I also felt this bond with my family. There were things like that that were really powerful that were happening to me."

When Marshall read *All the Colors of the Race* (Adoff 1982), a book of poetry about a little girl who is also biracial, she knew she wanted to do something similar. Like Smith-Willis, who wished she had experienced books that reflected her own life situation as an African American child, Marshall says, "If I had read a book like it when I was a child, it would have changed my life. I never really knew another person who was in my position and I felt that little girl in the book was." Yet there were striking differences. Adoff's little girl, unlike Marshall, had grown up white and black and was completely comfortable with both aspects of herself. Marshall had a different story to tell: "I felt that I had a lot of really complex feelings that I wanted to deal with in writing and share with people."

She began her process of conceiving the story on the very first night of the course, when the assignment was given. She developed her ideas in her work with the children for whom she was assistant teacher. During certain writing times, students and teachers alike wrote ideas for possible stories, and she used these times to focus on what was becoming for her a life agenda, the black-white side of herself.

Marshall chose poetry to convey the intensity of her inner struggle and the "one plus one" format to graphically represent the ever-present tension. Her illustrations (see Figure 2), so different from Smith-Willis's clear, simple, evocative statement, are like the "pieces of a puzzle" and reflect the child's experience of her different worlds. Each illustration frames and extends the text in technically and stylistically different ways, incorporating close-up photographs of mother, of father, and herself. At times she uses soft watercolors to evoke "her loveliness" and "the magic" and blocks of color to reinforce the dramatic contrasts of her story.

As the story evolved, in the experimental style of Lucy Sprague Mitchell and in the more recent process writing approaches, Marshall read it to her class of third and fourth graders and asked for their input. In certain instances they found the wording awkward, which helped her "find the right words." Mostly, they were struck with the power of her story. One child commented, "It was like the pieces of a puzzle, yet they all fit together." Even though she had openly spoken to the children of her interracial background, it was through this story of herself as a child that it became real. They found it unbelievable that, as a child, she was the only one in her class who was brown.

After her sharing the story, children spoke of aspects of their own lives in their families. One child told for the first time in school that he was adopted. Another spoke of how his extended family was biracial. Through the reading of her own story for children, Marshall created a setting in which it was safe for the children's stories to surface, where children could feel less alone. In the actual reading to her children, she says, "I felt like I was baring myself. I was giving something of myself to these kids, and even though it was a little scary, I liked the feeling." She felt closer to the children—as she did to her peers in the course when she read it aloud.

In reflecting on the process of writing her story and its connection to what she wants to offer children, Marshall describes how sharing was so significant: "Sharing with peers and the children makes a difference—we usually don't do this. Theoretically, I knew sharing was important, but it was eye opening sharing myself and seeing how much I and the children got out of it. When I have a class of my own, I'll have them share." She also saw this kind of writing as significant and powerful, "coming from a personal place, not like the writing that's usually done"—which may certainly account for the closeness she describes. By helping her "see what a person has to go through to come up with a piece of writing," Marshall views the entire process of writing differently. Perhaps she will do many of the things she would have done anyway, like sharing, but will now do them with subtle differences, with greater insight and sensitivity. She knows she wants to continue writing with the children, even with the many demands on a teacher's time.

Marshall feels that modeling is the critical aspect. Throughout her own process she has modeled what she most values. In allowing herself to be vulnerable, in trusting freely, she has made it safe for others too to be vulnerable. She has shown that there are many kinds of families and that being different is a part of the human story. She has made it acceptable to express loss and fear as well as pleasure. She has let the children know that their questions, their important questions, have a place in their school life. Throughout her process she has given the powerful message that through writing one can express what is deeply significant, with style and beauty. On the day she read her story to her children, she received a letter from five of them telling her that they thought the story was so good it should be published, and if she should take it to a publisher to tell him they say so. Each child signed the letter.

When Night Comes
Written and Illustrated by Veronica Najjar

When Night Comes it Happens . . .
When all is still and
they're alone.

They've been waiting.
Waiting for a chance to come
alive.
Waiting patiently to leave
    their high perch
    their safe nest
    their quilted world.

It begins slowly . . .
    the twitch of a small head
    the ruffle of red feathers
    the beating of delicate wings

Songs fill the air.
  A Rat A Tat A Tat
  Jay, Jay
  Kee, Kee
  Whoo, Whoo

They lift themselves up.
   They flutter
   They flap
   They glide
   They swoop

They enter a world where a
cardinal can feel safe flying with
an eagle.
A hawk can swoop down and meet
a fluttering hummingbird.
Where a woodpecker can leave its
lofty perch and share a worm with
a sandpiper.

When day breaks
the night's adventures are over.
They slowly return to their quilted
world and wait.
Wait silently and still
through the noise and activity
surrounded by people who will
never know
what really happens When Night
Comes.

But if you look closely
you may just find
a forgotten berry
a half-eaten nut
a stray feather
or hear the echo of a song
left behind in the night.

a rat a tat a tat
jay, jay
kee, kee
whoo, whoo

The Quilted Harmony

Unlike Smith-Willis and Marshall, who tell stories of lived experience,
stories about people, Najjar brings to life her children's own creation,

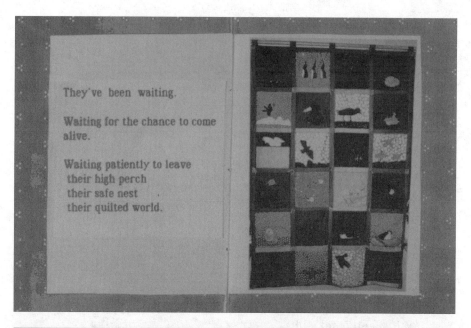

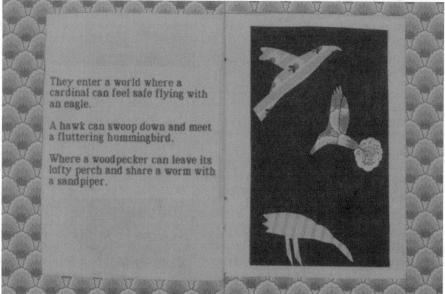

Figure 3. From *When Night Comes,* by Veronica Najjar. The story is formatted vertically and is $5\frac{1}{2}$ x $8\frac{1}{2}$. On each double page, text is placed on the left page and illustrations on the right; both are framed in quiltlike patterned borders. (Photo courtesy Joyce Culver.)

a quilt of birds which they had made together. In doing so she conveys a magic moment when a child's reality and fantasy merge, as in the many stories in which children's toys come to life. Out of the artistic harmony of the many patterns and fabrics of the quilt emerges a generous, safe, and nonviolent world. And like *The Wizard of Oz*, the story ends with a hint of reality. The world has changed in small ways and has become a better place.

Najjar has created a work at once alive with movement and sound and serene in ways reminiscent of literature to lull the child to sleep. In nine short pages she has done what Margaret Wise Brown has said books should accomplish for a child, "to jog him with the unexpected and comfort him with the familiar" (Marcus 1992, 250). The pages themselves seem to come alive through the quiltlike patterned borders and patterned silhouettes of the children's birds, with each figure emerging in flight from a stark black background (see Figure 3).

For Najjar, the book was one way to keep alive what the class of second and third graders she taught the year before meant to her and also what their study of birds meant to them. The study spanned most of that school year, and the quilt itself took five months to complete. Each child fashioned a square for the bird he or she had researched. Tremendous time and energy went into depicting the reality of each bird in the context of its environment. Najjar saw how deeply each child connected with his or her own square and how the children came together as a group through this shared effort—symbolized in the quilt.

The actual idea for the story was sparked by the memory of the day they culminated their study with a celebration. As the assistant principal left their class party, she looked up at the quilt hanging on the wall and said, "You know, it's really amazing how they always go back to the right square when daylight comes." Najjar was surprised at her children's reaction. They seemed suspended in time, silently living in the imagined possibilities of the statement. She saw how the idea excited them and wanted to create for them what she had not had as a child: "I was not touched much by literature as a child. I wanted it to be different for the children I teach. I wanted their excitement to live in my story. I wanted the ending to give them a lasting feeling." The story she went on to write, then, is an attempt to offer to children the possibility and pleasure of literature that she had experienced as an adult by bringing to life magically through language what they had created through their hard work—thereby moving their work to a new level of experience.

Although the story is not autobiographical in the sense of telling a lived story from her childhood, it too grows from the wellsprings of Najjar's experience and embodies her life as a teacher. The safe, harmonious world so perfectly captured in the quilt is something she works on each day with her children:

> I spend an enormous amount of time as a teacher working on tone, working with the children on community. If they learn nothing else, they learn how to live in harmony, how to hear each other, how to work out conflicts. This is an endless struggle. Like the birds in the quilt, all my children are very different. When we studied predators and prey, we learned how so many are prey. Like in the very different kind of world that comes alive at night, in this classroom it's all right to be next to a hawk. I try to create a safe environment where each child is listened to and accepted, where differences are accepted.

Like Marshall's, her story is also about being different, perhaps different in family structure, different racially, ethnically, different in language, in temperament, different as individuals. Yet there is greater possibility of resolution for Najjar's theme, achieved through a teacher's dream and her children's work. Perhaps her story is also a metaphor of her hopes for the children.

When she shared the story with her current class (because the school has mixed-age groupings, half of the children who had made the quilt were still in her class), she lowered the shades "to create the appropriate mood." The children seemed to glow, especially when a child heard his or her "own bird" mentioned. In Najjar's class the bird did indeed evoke the child. The children applauded, and giving the true testament to a child's pleasure, asked her to read it again. Since they had seen their teacher creating the quiltlike cut paper illustrations during free times in the class, they were especially excited to see the result.

In reflecting on the process of writing the book, like Marshall, Najjar felt close to what children must feel when they create stories. She would think, "Here I am stuck for an idea, dry. Now I know what the kids experience." Like Smith-Willis, she felt that in thinking hard about what they would enjoy, what would have an impact, she connected more intimately with who her children are and with herself as a child. Najjar concludes her thoughts on the book by saying, "I felt good that I had done something that maybe is lasting."

A Path One Would Like to Take

The process of writing a story for children seemed inextricably bound to the teachers' evolving professional selves. Thus the paths they took as teachers were transformed in a number of important ways as a result of taking the course. Like Marshall and Najjar, many spoke of how their views of writing changed: they would teach in the future with a greater understanding and appreciation of the child's writing process. Writing in their programs was now seen as more than learning to read and write; it became a powerful means of self-expression for children as it was for the teachers, who had struggled to express themselves through their own stories. Not surprisingly, many teachers said that for the first time in their lives they saw themselves as *writers*. This confidence grew from their writing "coming from a personal place," as Marshall said. The creator's understanding of the source of the story led her and her colleagues to see new meaning in their children's life stories. They could see why the stories and books their children write mean so much to them, why it is so important to see one's self in a book.

In addition, the teachers' views of literature changed. For example, most of the teachers said they select and use children's literature very differently now. Like Smith-Willis and Najjar, many wrote their story with specific children in mind and, in doing so, felt they were teaching these children in particular rather than children in general—an approach they carry over to their book selection decisions. One student says, "I balance my own interests and inclinations with the abilities, scope, and inclinations of my children." Another student comments,

> It is one thing to examine the writings and illustrations of others, it is quite another to attempt it yourself. . . . It made me question and scrutinize my choices. As I wrote my book, I asked myself questions like: How can I phrase this so the population I write for understands it? Why am I writing this? What understandings do I want for the children (and adults) who read this? These are the same questions I now ask myself as I select books each week for my children.

Like Najjar, many students, in working to create a story within the conventions of children's picture books, found they understood the literature differently.

And this greater understanding of literature seemed to lead to a deeper understanding of children. Many, through growing close to the power of their own story, felt closer to their children in ways that changed their role as teacher. Some became aware of how the children's written stories were windows to worlds a teacher might otherwise never know or understand, how these worlds contained complex layers of experience, and how teachers only know part of a larger story. Because as adults they had felt safe to share their stories, to be vulnerable, many wanted to offer in their classrooms the support, sensitivity, and acceptance of a community where children felt safe to express what was important to them.

To construct their stories, the teacher-authors had reconstituted within themselves "a semblance of the actual framework of childhood" (Marcus 1992, 60). They relived the child's heightened sense of experience by reading and discussing many books in open and personal ways. Paley (1991) writes that "we cannot speak of the child's self without looking at our own" (156), and without considering their experience from a child's-eye view. To tell a "good story" from that viewpoint, the teachers evoked the people, places, and times of their childhoods. Yet gradually the authors shifted and altered one or more of these elements so that within their stories, like Williams (1982), they created fictions and often took "the path one wished one could have taken." They needed their stories not just to understand and come to terms with the past, but also to help them transform the present and construct the future. In crafting a literary and visual work at once satisfying to themselves, their peers, and their children, many saw themselves enabled to create what is important for the children they teach. The teachers' stories reflected a passion to create living spaces that are more accommodating than many they had known.

In this desire for transformation, the teachers were like other writers. In her autobiography, *One Writer's Beginnings* (1983), Welty (see also Paterson 1991) described aspects of her process of transformation from memory of lived event to story:

> The events in our lives happen in a sequence of time, in their significance to ourselves they find their own order, a timetable not necessarily—perhaps not possibly—chronological. The time as we know it subjectively is often the chronology that stories and novels follow: it is the continuous thread of revelation. (68)

What the teachers' stories revealed and continue to reveal was striking portraits of lived experience—relived, reinterpreted, distilled, and often transformed. Some stories revealed the cultural histories that made each writer's path unique, as the characters in two stories highlighted here showed: Smith-Willis depicted an African American family; Marshall focused on being biracial. And Najjar depicted birds that reflected the diversity of her children, who had studied these birds in depth. Whether or not they identified with these three writers' specific experiences, teachers in the course gained the sense that their own individual uniqueness—their memories of struggle, loneliness, communion, difference, and joy—linked them to others. Through the stories they created and shared, they became part of a human "quilted harmony." Their stories touched something universal, speaking so directly to their children and their peers about all the things that mattered.

Through the processes of speaking, remembering, and writing, many teachers found the stories to be healing. Like the sun-warmed stories of Lionni's Frederick, these stories sustain us. Through imagination, memory, and desire, they affirm who we are; they heal wounds not yet closed by time; they allow us to dream and to realize who we can be as people and teachers of children—one and the same. These stories offer a path one *would like* to take, filled with possibility.

Notes

1. The comments of Claudia Lewis, as well as those of Heather Smith-Willis, Monique Marshall, and Veronica Najjar about their stories, come from open-ended interviews with the first author. Comments from other teachers are excerpts from written responses to a questionnaire about the children's literature course.

2. Vera Williams was the featured speaker at the "Literature in the Classroom" conference, held in May 1989 at Teachers College, Columbia University.

References

Adoff, A. (1982). *All the colors of the race.* New York: Lothrop, Lee & Shepard.

Lewis, C. (1981). *Writing for young children.* Garden City, NY: Anchor Press/Doubleday.

Lionni, L. (1967). *Frederick.* New York: Pantheon Books.

Marcus, L. S. (1992). *Margaret Wise Brown: Awakened by the moon.* Boston: Beacon Press.

Paley, V. G. (1991). The heart and soul of the matter: Teaching as a moral act. *The Educational Forum, 55*(2), 155–166.

Paterson, K. (1991). *The spying heart: More thoughts on reading and writing books for children.* New York: Dutton.

Rosenblatt, L. M. (1978). *The reader, the text, the poem.* Carbondale and Edwardsville: Southern Illinois University Press.

Wells, R. (1990). The well-tempered children's book. In W. Zinsser (Ed.), *Worlds of childhood: The art and craft of writing for children* (121–143). Boston: Houghton Mifflin.

Welty, E. (1983). *One writer's beginnings.* Cambridge, MA: Harvard University Press.

Williams, V. (1982). *A chair for my mother.* New York: Greenwillow.

13 The Contribution of the Preschool to a Native American Community

Susan J. Britsch
Purdue University

In her chapter, Susan Britsch reveals how stories may serve as the life-blood of a community, sustaining it through difficult periods of change. The community of interest is a small Native American tribe, and stories provide a major tool for bringing together the learning and living of community elders and preschoolers.

During the nineteenth century, the Tachi Yokuts people lived on the north and west shores of Tulare Lake, in south central California. Their territory extended over the Kettleman Hills and across the plains to the western foothills of the Mount Diablo chain of the Coast Range of mountains (Latta 1977).

In winter, the people lived near the place where the western hills approached the lake. In summer, they crossed to the east and gathered seeds closer to the eight-hundred-square-mile lake that provided fish for eating and tule reeds for building homes, baskets, and boats. The swampy shores of the lake nourished berries and grasses, clover, fiddleneck, and watercress.

During the spring and summer, groups of grandmothers and children would spend their days fishing beside the slough that served as the inlet to the lake. Children would listen to the ladies chat and gossip in Tachi as they fished or washed the clothes, or gathered blackberries from nearby bushes. The land was green; the sun was warm and constant. The earth and sky, Grandmother and Grandfather, fed both the body and spirit. It was, as many say today, "like paradise."

The Yokuts linguistic family once comprised as many as sixty language-dialects spoken by thousands of people throughout California's Central Valley. At one time, the Tachi Yokuts language was probably spoken by as many as 1,500 people (Kroeber 1925) living in five villages close beside Tulare Lake. Tachi is now known and recurrently used by approximately thirty people who live in a small Native American community located on the nineteenth-century site of one of the old Tachi villages.

Most speakers of Tachi are no longer of child-bearing age, so the language is not learned in the homes of contemporary Tachi families. Small children have a sociolinguistic acquaintance with the language; that is, they may know several speakers (usually grandparents or great-grandparents), and they understand that certain kinds of social situations motivate the use of Tachi among adults. In general, however, the children's linguistic knowledge of Tachi extends to only a few words or phrases—isolated tokens from a linguistic game that is strangely foreign to them and for which they do not know the broader set of rules.

Parents in the community are now becoming increasingly concerned that their children have not had sufficient opportunity to hear about the times when their grandparents were young and lived in traditional homes, to learn stories that teach traditional values and beliefs, and to become acquainted with their ancestral language as a way of communicating among a people. To address this situation, a pilot language renewal program—Tachi as a Second Language (TSL)—was inaugurated in the community in the fall of 1987.

The TSL Program operated throughout most of the 1987–88 school year within the framework of the community's Head Start Program. The goal of the program was language exposure, not language mastery: its primary task was to make the Tachi language a more familiar and hospitable presence within the lives of the children, while acquainting them with basic vocabulary, sentence structure, and the use of simple conversational routines. The language sessions were conducted exclusively in Tachi. As an educator and linguist, I acted as curriculum designer and language specialist for the program. This gave me the chance to become involved in the very life of a language I had endeavored to learn for several years from elders in the community.

The Elders and the School

Within the context of the community's linguistic situation, the real "knowers" of Tachi—the elders who learned Tachi as a first language—represent a tremendous resource within the community. They are regarded as the true teachers of the language by parents who are not speakers or who may possess a comprehension-centered knowledge of Tachi. On the other hand, children are regarded as the community's most important learners, so it was felt that any ancestral language-learning effort should first concern both the oldest and the youngest people in the community. It is upon just this interaction that the Tachi as a Second Language Program was built and carried out within the preschool.

Two elder women worked with small groups of children in the classroom four times each week for approximately an hour per day (within a four-hour program). The elders were aided by the preschool's head teacher, a young woman whose command of Tachi is primarily receptive. Within the structure of community roles, the teacher did not view herself as one who should be responsible for the teaching of the language. Instead, she saw herself as a "coordinator," to use her word.

At the beginning of the school year, the teacher actually directed the classroom activity herself—initiating interactions, suggesting variations in practice, and modeling dialogues with the elders. But this would become awkward when, for example, the elders would spontaneously interject language with which she was unfamiliar. As the school year progressed, the elders became more and more comfortable with conducting the language sessions cooperatively on their own. This gave them the opportunity to use Tachi with each other when discussing clarifications or offering suggestions.

This approach, in turn, helped the children to feel more comfortable as they saw Tachi being used as a primary means of interaction. This was reflected in the children's social response to the language sessions: by the end of the school year, some children began to appropriate the teaching role themselves. They, in fact, initiated the language sessions by pointing to familiar objects to request identifications, for example, from other children. In the community, children began to greet one of the elders in Tachi, and they would proceed to verbally demonstrate their knowledge of various language items learned in school. The children had thus begun to appropriate the role of "knower" in the community's sense of the word, as well as in the school-oriented sense of the term.

Acting in the capacity of coordinator, the teacher also organized regular planning sessions during which she and the elders would discuss the language and activities to be used throughout the coming week. Originally planned as brief technical meetings, the planning sessions soon expanded to afternoon-long conversations during which the elders' recollections of elements of the Tachi language rang with images of their own life experiences. This infused the planning sessions with another, less overt, purpose; the elders began to create a "community of memory" (Bellah et al. 1985) as they began to retell the history of the community through the vehicles of the ancestral language and their own personal histories. Bellah describes the process as follows:

> In order not to forget that past, a community is involved in retelling its story, its constitutive narrative, and in so doing, it offers examples of the men and women who have embodied and exemplified the meaning of the community. These stories of collective history and exemplary individuals are an important part of the tradition that is so central to a community of memory. (153)

Thus, in one of the planning sessions, the elders recalled the seasonal experience of gathering plants, including fiddleneck, with their mothers and grandmothers. These memories incorporated long-forgotten language and life experience, prompted by the whole of the elders' more immediate experience of the language with the children.

As curriculum designer, I responded to this particular element of the retelling by preparing a unit that involved the elders and the children in picking fiddleneck and preparing it for eating. The design of the unit focused on a cooperative exploration between the elders and myself of the teaching process they had experienced when their grandmothers had taught them to gather and prepare fiddleneck. In this way, the retelling extended into the classroom, enlarging the presence of the elders beyond the role of "knowers of language," as they transmitted knowledge of self constituted by connections to others. This is the full sense of the word "community," as Bellah sees it—the sense that must underlie the use of the language in teaching if that teaching is to address the *processes* of learning that the traditional way of life has to offer children in the contemporary society. As Tafoya (n.d.) points out, it is through the interpersonal processes of learning— not through exposure to particular curriculum products—that children can begin to accept what they have been given from the traditional language. Thus, although the Tachi used by the children was not at all elaborate, it represented the renewed presence of the language in the preschool—itself a community of lives within the whole of the evolving history of the community.

The School and the Community

Throughout the school year, the teacher's aim was to enhance the voluntary participation of both children and adults in the very open and flexible conceptual entity of the language program. She wanted to make it clear that the program was not a closed, school-bound block of activity, but a resource from which anyone in the community could draw or to which anyone could contribute.

The teacher encouraged the children to participate in the language sessions, but she did not make it mandatory. This approach is consistent with the community learning style, which emphasizes the learner's independence throughout a self-determined period of observation followed by learner-initiated attempts at practice. In this way, the experience of the program was *offered* to the children so that they could both accept and contribute at their own discretion. As it happened, at the beginning of the school year, the language sessions occupied a small corner of the classroom that the teacher had blocked off with portable bulletin boards and had furnished attractively. By the end of the year, more than a third of the total classroom space was devoted to Tachi, as both large and small group activities were conducted to accommodate the participation of all the children.

In a similar way, the program was offered to the community itself through various presentations in Tachi by the preschool children. One presentation was held at the community center during the week in March when the Tachi people traditionally celebrate the new year. Coinciding as it did with the new year's ritual, the presentation enhanced the theme of renewal in the community and helped to further renew the Tachi language as a communal possession, now being acquired by the most important learners: the children.

In a community where the traditional language, as representative of a traditional way of life, is obsolescing, it is easy for tribal members to lose hope for the future of that language. It is easy to feel that the children do not listen because they do not care to, or that they do not listen because they truly *cannot* learn the old language. Further, it is a belief in the Tachi community that language is not something that can be *taught:* language is something that is "picked up" from the context of lived experience. Thus "knowing" a language means understanding it because one has understood the experience from which it came. When the home experience of the language is missing, people find it difficult to believe that the school can provide anything comparable—and, in fact, it cannot. But in the preschool, the Tachi language program provided an opening within which a retelling of the community's story could begin. And throughout the retelling, the elders have represented much more than just the presence of the language in the school: they have embodied the presence of the traditional culture in the school through the acting out of their roles as "knowers," and through the ways in which they scold, praise, prompt, and demonstrate life and language to the children.

At the end of the school year, the Tachi tribe's eldest male member (now in his nineties) paid a visit to the preschool to observe the children and to find out not what they were learning, but how they were learning. After conversing with the teacher, whose talk was interlaced with the Tachi she had learned from the elders, he concluded that the teaching was being done "the right way." He had not believed it, he said, until he saw it happen. This was the feeling of many community members, but as each person now encounters the children and their use of the language, Tachi becomes less removed from lived experience and more accessible to rediscovery within one's own life as a part of the lives of others. The language curriculum, then, becomes a vehicle of the retelling as the elders make it more and more an expression of their own interactions with the children. As these two processes—the curriculum and the retelling—begin to merge, the language program in the school will continue to draw upon the intimacy and wisdom of the home, echoing the beliefs of the community, nourishing the strength of all its members.

Acknowledgments

Some of the ideas presented in this chapter are discussed more fully in a paper entitled "The Collaborative Development of a Language Renewal Program for Preschoolers," published in the winter 1988 issue of *Human Organization.*

I wish to acknowledge the invaluable help of the tribal chairman and of the tribal members who have contributed to and supported the language program discussed in this chapter. In order to protect their privacy, I will not name these people here; however, I wish to extend to them my deepest appreciation.

References

Bellah, R. N., Madsen, R., Sullivan, W. M., Swidler, A., and Tipton, S. M. (1985). *Habits of the heart: Individualism and commitment in American life.* Berkeley: University of California Press.

Kroeber, A. L. (1976). *Handbook of the Indians of California.* New York: Dover Publications. (Original work published 1925)

Latta, F. F. (1977). *Handbook of the Yakuts Indians.* Santa Cruz, CA: Bear State Books.

Tafoya, T. (n.d.) *The directions of Indian and Native education: Culture, content, and container.* Unpublished manuscript, Seattle, WA. Photocopy.

14 Stories as Ways of Acting Together

Shirley Brice Heath
Stanford University

Shirley Brice Heath takes us into still another site for community and for story—a youth organization in an inner-city neighborhood. The storytellers here are adolescents who use stories as ways of testing theories about themselves and their relationships to each other and to the world around them.

I will tell you something about stories,
They aren't just entertainment.
Don't be fooled.
They are all we have, you see,
all we have to fight off
illness and death.

Leslie Silko, *Ceremony* (3)

Much has been written on the socializing or even the humanizing aspects of storytelling, on this or that story's lasting effects. Yet educators generally rely for their extolling of stories on those written or told for and by young children. In the years since the publication of Britton's *Language and Learning* (1970), many movements and trends in education have celebrated children's stories. Books and articles far too numerous to list have described, explained, and praised how children respond to the same "call of stories" that Coles (1989), a psychiatrist, has illustrated for adults.

It is curious, therefore, that relatively little glory has come to the stories of young people—defined here as adolescents, teenagers, or young adults. Admittedly, it is and has always been far more romantic to talk of children than of those in the awkward transition between childhood and adulthood. But what of the stories told by young people? How do they use narratives, and are there particular ways in which they view and construct their stories? In particular, how do young people who see their life experiences as marginal to those of the mainstream use stories? If their ways of creating and using stories differ from patterns we have come to expect for younger children, then how have they learned to create such stories? One psychologist has told us that "a life is created or constructed by the act of autobiography" (Bruner 1993). What then does it mean for young people to construct themselves by the telling of their experiences, beliefs, and feelings? Do their tales create some sort of cultural stability when society offers little such steadiness for them?

The data on which this chapter is based come from transcripts of audiorecordings made during the activities of young people from ages fourteen to eighteen in inner-city youth organizations over five years of participant-observer research.[1] These recordings were made during the everyday activities—practices, planning sessions, games, and performances—at community centers and gathering places for members of youth organizations in a study designed to learn how the lives of inner-city youth are spent outside their home and school hours. These young walk daily on the edge of what mainstream Americans would consider disaster and life threats; most have very little, if any, stable family support, and most have found school a place that offers them little in the way of positive identity. The young of this study, however, have found their ways to neighborhood youth organizations—national organizations such as the YMCA, Boys and Girls Clubs, and scouts, or local church-affiliated or grass-roots groups such as dance or drama troupes, sports teams, or social clubs. There they have found places to belong and to count on as sources of support and optimism for their futures.

Teen Drama

In an inner-city Boys and Girls Club each day of the summer, teens who auditioned early in June for the coveted twenty or so spots on the teen drama team prepare for their grueling performance schedule of the year. They choose themes which they will want to use for the dramas they script. Later they hear experts on these topics (such as AIDS, teenage drunk driving, runaways, date rape, and drug usage) and use information from these talks and films to develop performances for schools, juvenile detention centers, and youth groups throughout their city. Their performances consist of three parts. The first is a brief play on one of the themes they have chosen; the second is a dialogue between the audience and the actors, with each actor remaining in the character he or she has just played in the performance. The third part is a follow-up session in which each performer speaks in his or her own voice about matters treated in the play and what it felt like to take the particular role of this performance. During the academic year, and often during the summer, the group performs three or four times a week.

During the late summer, while hard at work perfecting their lines and practicing in character to be able to answer the questions their future audiences may put to them, the youth tell many stories. They do so to lighten their workload, cut the tension of the "heavy" scenes they often play, and, most often, to support their arguments for particular points they want to make about how the lines should go, where and how actors should move, and what audience responses may be.

The story below emerges out of a teasing session between a boy and girl about to perform.[2] Each is "highsiding" (belittling or cutting down) the other, and the adult leader, who has been part of the jesting spirit, reminds David (African American) that he had gotten a ride to the Boys and Girls Center from Amy (European American), the girl he is now giving such a hard time.

1. *Leader:* She gave you a ride.

2. *Amy:* Yes, I think I did.

3. *David:* It was a uh, it was uh, it was uh ride of my life.

4. First, we almost

5. *Amy:*   David, you know/

6. *David:*   /First, first, we almost had a
   wreck coming off my street. "Get ready to die!"/

7. *Amy:*   /I'm a good driver, I knew

8. she was gonna wait=

9. *David:*   =This car was comin [3-second pause] down

10. the street and was turnin on my street. She had to pull

11. out—and stop three or four times before you could, and

12. laughing the whole time. And then, the window [4-second

13. pause] on the passenger side [2-second pause] goes down by

14. itself you know. Now, it did this three or four times.

15. And then, you know, you cannot take off in her car when

16. the air conditioning is on. Once you, you come to a stop sign,

17. have to turn the air conditioning off, take off, and then

18. turn it back on. So, I'm sittin/

19. *Amy:*   /It had [laughing]

20. *Leader:* It's possessed.
21. *Amy:* cause I'll have it all the way down to the floor like—
22. [imitates a struggling car against background of group laughter]
23. *David:* So, I'm sittin at this stop light, burnin up,
24. sweatin. I see the devil sittin next to me, it was so hot
25. [stands up and uses wide-sweeping hand gestures]. She's
26. sittin up there [imitating Amy's laugh] he, he, hee. And
27. then, we're comin on our way to Teen Drama, by Eddy's
28. Chicken, she almost runs the light right into this other
29. car. Her, her friend tells her "STOP!" She wouldn't have
30. stopped=
31. *Amy:*   =I was about to stop=
32. *David:*   =Then=
33. *Amy:*   =she always just tells me—
34. *David:* We got to Hemphill [street]. I don't know where she
35. was at, she was gonna get in the turn lane and try to go
36. like that [acts like he is in a car and makes a super wide
37. turn using all the lanes]
38. *Amy:* [laughter]
39. *David:* She's lying and says she wasn't, but she had her
40. signal on=
41. *Amy:*   =I was not, I was changing lanes to the middle
42. lane, thank you.
43. *David:* When you drive, Amy, you do not take a big turn
44. like this [again imitating her turn] to get to the next lane,
45. OK? It was the ride of my life. We got to the, we got to the
46. stop sign up here at Lipscombe, little kid walk out, and
47. she about run over him.
48. *Amy:* [laughing] I was not. Man, you lying.
49. *David:* I'm lying? Did you or did you not [pause] almost
50. hit those little kids?
51. *Amy:* I did not [with careful articulation on the final *t*]
52. *David:* It was a ride of a lifetime [shaking his head in
53. disbelief]. Believe me.
54. *Amy:* We'll see if I ever give you a ride again.

This story carries many features that mark the stories of teens. They usually tell such narratives in the presence of friends who shared the experience and also before one or more third parties not present at the actual shared event. Individuals announce their own stories, usually with the goal of "doggin" or teasing other co-participants in the event. These listeners provide backup—the laughter and other sound effects that reinforce the drama of the telling. They often add their own dialogue, details, or rebuttals. The storyteller who initiates the story remains, however, in control of the group and summarizes the tale, often with a reminder to the audience that they should believe the teller and not those who were simply there at the event but did not initiate this telling.

Such tellings often create a string of stories, with individual participants adding their own version of the event, with the opener, "Now, let me tell you what REALLY happened!" The stories embody description, persuasion, exposition, with argument implicit; but they must also include humor—achieved through character development, word play, and satire. Punctuating the stories are gestures, often highly animated, and looks at members of the audience to see if they acknowledge understanding slang or references to local places, and register appropriate amusement or horror at the events recounted.

Stories that achieve any status among teen associates such as those described here must have some actual basis, but they must also achieve humor through exaggeration and hyperbole in abundance. Tellers include much internal dialogue thought, though not expressed, at the time of the actual event. In addition, during the story's telling, they create on-the-spot dialogues between teller and other participants to increase the liveliness and participatory nature of the story.

Unspoken in any direct way in such stories are the tensions, fears, competitions, and marginalized areas of knowledge from which they draw. These stories' background themes, like those of any interpersonal verbal teasing, stand as serious matters within the community, matters so serious they can only rarely be directly articulated.

In the case of Amy and David, their early jesting in the initial portions of practice had led Amy to call David "a monkey." He responded, "So was that a racial, a racial remark, uh?" Amy replies: "I didn't say you were a *black* monkey. I just said you were a monkey." Later in the conversation, the two tease about the fact that David lives in a less desirable part of town than Amy does, and her taking him home after practice might not be a g od idea. Throughout the story, listeners are left to believe that only Amy and David were in the car;

thus the tension between the two of them is highlighted. However, at line 29, David mentions "her" friend and clearly separates himself from Amy *and* her friend, as well as from any part of the causes of the entire event. He leaves, therefore, the strong suggestion that Amy was "out of control" on this early morning ride for reasons that are left for listeners to guess.

This story and others of the youth carry subtle messages about these young people's sense of the extent to which any one of them can take on the outsider's authoritative voice. In the excerpt above (lines 49 and 50), David assumes the role of prosecuting attorney, and Amy responds as witness secure in her self-denial. In this exchange, the laughter of both dries up; they take on serious facial expressions and upright postures and speak in their assumed dramatic roles for this brief on-the-spot dialogue. Stories of young people often include some public authority, who is played with appropriate dramatic gestures and shifts of voice quality, along with rhetorical questions and expressions of emotional evaluation. Many of their stories carry a curious combination of didacticism and daredeviltry; at the same time that celebrations of foolhardiness or ventures into danger events are heard, so are internal lessons (for example, lines 43 and 44 regarding the way to turn a corner).

From Gangbanging to Youth Service

Although most of the stories told by the inner-city youth are of their own experiences, they also often use these familiar experiences to reshape stories that tell of events and people quite distant from them. A common way of doing this occurs when youngsters in a group hear of something that has taken place outside their environment. They begin to reshape that event, often with the lead-in "It's like. . . ." They construct the world "out there" into their own by reshaping the narratives of others to fit their own worlds. But a clear *we-they* undertone pervades these stories to indicate that, though *we* know what *they* are like, *we* cannot be *they*.

During the events in the former Soviet Union in August of 1991, young men in a gang intervention group connected with a YMCA in an inner-city area told of the attempted coup by reshaping it as gang battle. They similarly reshaped the conflict in the Middle East that led to Desert Storm: "It was like their gang [that of the forces of the United States] was against the Iraqi gang . . . it was like a big old war, big old war. Like a gang fight."

Summary statements regarding these metaphoric reshapings link what is "out there" with what the young people know; unstated explanation is assumed to follow. In other words, "If you know the way it is here, and you can pick out points of comparison between here and there, then you can handle both." Young people from inner-city gangs described the U.S. involvement in the Kuwait-Iraq conflict as "that's their thing to take care of." The distance between *them* and *their thing* and *us* and *our thing* rarely escapes underlining in their stories.

Their retellings in response to something outside their direct experience usually then take a direct comparative frame, in which the base of what is known is taken as something to move from to knowledge that is not verifiable by direct experience. In a conversation in which a new kind of drug just coming to the West Coast was mentioned by an outsider, one of the local young men (Latino) responded:

55. *Isador:* I think nowadays everybody just has their own/

56. *Roberto:*   /yeah/

57. *Isador:*   /their

58. own way of experience, you know. Like I experienced—I

59. experienced a lot of drugs before in my life, but I mean,

60. I've never been [inaudible] to, you know, any kind of

61. other phase or nothing like that. But I think pretty much

62. nowadays kids these days are, in these days and age, are

63. going to drugs so fast and experiencing so many drugs,

64. that I mean, they're liable to do anything, you know. Not so

65. long ago there was this lady who was smoking wickets, and

66. I don't know if you know what that is, but it's like

67. embalming fluid, it's PCP. They smoke reefer and they dip it

68. into embalming fluid and they smoke it, and like it gets them

69. some kind of high that they really don't know what they're

70. doing.

71. *Roberto:* Hallucination.

72. *Isador:* Yeah, hallucination. So she was taking her baby a

73. bath, and I don't know, she forgot about it, and when she

74. realized it, oh, the bathtub is running over, and when she

75. went to the bathtub, her baby was in the bathtub drowned.

76. Her husband came in, he was on the same thing, wicket

77. [inaudible], and he says "What'd you do to my son?" And,

78. and, boom, killed her. So his baby and his wife is dead, and
79. he's in jail now today.

This story establishes a comparative frame between the speaker and the young group of "these days." The story is punctuated with evaluative comments (lines 61 and 64), explanations (lines 66 to 70), details of dialogue, and uses of the present tense (lines 74 and 77) to highlight the impending critical action that will give the turning point of the tale. The effect of the actions of the tale stands unmistakenly in the present (lines 78 and 79).

How Tales Are Structured

Among youth familiar with street life, direct contact with violence is an everyday event. They need not spend their time simply chronicling events. Instead, they leave an unspoken sense of meditation or thinking about action and knowledge. Grammatical structuring plays an important role in developing this theme: shifts between past and present tense, uses of modals or conditionals, and expressions of the speaker's own comparative experiences (lines 58 and 59), and mental state (of disbelief, horror, sadness, puzzlement, and so forth—lines 61 to 64).

In both the stories illustrated here, as well as in any sample of story that exceeded ten lines in our corpus, tellers shifted between present and past tense to foreground certain events so as to move the story forward. David shifts back and forth between present and past, using the present to highlight the central focus of each of the critical incidents of "bad driving" on Amy's part. He offers his commentary to listeners through the use of a conditional perfect (for example, "wouldn't") as well as present tense (lines 23 to 29), and when he uses the present tense to involve the audience, he shifts to past tense to describe Amy's actions. Isador similarly shifts to present tense to describe the turning event of his story, as well as to lay out his own evaluation of background causes and resulting consequences. He uses the past tense to offer background information on events that supported or led to the critical actions.

Young people begin their stories by suggesting a narrative through their use of prototypical openings: "It was," "There was," and so forth. With their shift of time focus, especially in narratives of comparison such as that of Isador, they hold the present and themselves in opposition with the past and others—either in action or in emotional response to the event. David moves back and forth between his story and its dialogue, and the here and now of a staging of dialogue with the present audience. In addition (in line 14), he uses "now" to bring the listener back to the scene of events and to narrow the framing of the story. Isador, in his several repetitions that establish the "then and now" aspect of his story, establishes its basic two-part comparative frame. The final "he's in jail now today" once again repeats the presentness of repercussions of the events and suggests the ongoing nature of events carried out under the influence of drugs. The narrative sets up a tension with many of its non-narrative features, especially the generalizations (for example, line 64) of Isador's story and the dialogue exchange (lines 43 and 44, 48, 49 to 51) of David's.

Through these stories and those of other teens, the listener watches the teller go through thought processes and emotional responses almost as though in real time while within the frame of a past narrative. Listeners, including Amy in David's story, are invoked, sometimes literally, to *think* about events, to take them out of the story's frame of *just* being something that did happen. Instead, the telling brings them to the action of the events and to interactions in the moment to persuade them to reflect and to incorporate ideas related to the story into their own perceptions (for example, the way to turn a corner or the repercussions of "weird" or of mixing drugs). Young people tell stories not then so much to invoke common memories as to project perceptions or reflections they want listeners to store. But such a didactic purpose cannot go unveiled. Hence, stories must be on the surface clear entertainment, joking around, or just comparing what is going on out there with what the youth themselves do. When Isador talks to adult outsiders about his storytelling with younger street kids, he says:

> I think I—I think I'll be good for kids because of the simple fact is I've been through it, and I can sit down with a kid and tell him "I've been through what you've been through, or maybe even more," you know, "and I could tell you things that you would never believe but I bet you one day will come true in your life, and you're going to say 'Oh no, I shoulda listened to Isador.'"

Common expressions such as "I don't know" or "I'm not sure" suggest possibilities beyond events of the telling and establish a distance between the teller and any apparent authoritative position as knower. When the young step into such positions, they do so by assuming the voice of the outsider and not that of their own personal character. Being serious, thoughtful, or prescriptive within the inner city or about topics such as racial tensions, drug use, or family violence marks one as vulnerable and sensitive—qualities that do not make for survival in the transition between childhood and adult life in urban areas.

Stories as Theories

The tellers of these stories are young people whose narratives in both content and form find little place within classrooms or other main-stream institutional settings. These stories do, however, coincide in numerous ways with those that are described in many highly accept-able and mainstream settings for adults. Scholars in several disciplines have repeatedly noted that, for adults, stories are theories; they need not be replaced by abstractions or explanations. Coles (1989) wrote of his own revelation of his need to learn in his early days of medical practice to set aside the abstractions he had learned "in one school setting after another." His mentor told him:

> The people who come to see us bring us their stories. They hope they tell them well enough so that we understand the truth of their lives. They hope we know how to interpret their stories correctly. We have to remember that what we hear is *their story.* (1989, 7; italics in the original)

Coles reflected on how he was to use these stories in his own thinking and perception that would lead presumedly to informed and re-formed actions: "[N]ow a difference obtained: I was learning new abstractions [the stories of his patients] and using them . . . to help understand the palpable pain and suffering of another human being" (8). Mink, a philosopher and literary critic, echoes this view of sto-ries—especially those created by fiction writers—as theory: "[N]arra-tive form as it is exhibited in both history and fiction is particularly important as a rival to theoretical explanation or understanding" (1987, 185). This role of story as a way of explaining and of prompting others to new perceptions makes special sense for those who see their experiences as somehow marginal, as lying outside the mainstream of their associates.

If we can risk giving a generalization to the stories of youth, then it is possible to say that the message of their stories is not "Here is the world; take it or leave it," but instead, "Here is something to think about." Einstein and other scientists have similarly noted the power of stories and the observations that both spawn them and are spurred on by them: "The theory determines what we can observe."

As one literary critic (Hanson 1989) has noted, the story in the United States may well have been dominated by "losers and loners, exiles, women, blacks—writers who for one reason or another have not been part of the ruling 'narrative' or epistemological/experiential framework of their society" (2). Stories align themselves with hidden or mysterious dimensions of subjective experience—particularly appropriate for those who see their vision as alienated and set apart.

Ironically, as gangs have turned more and more to the use of weapons that bring such brutal harm, and as the streets of inner cities have become more like war zones, it is no longer the case as it was in earlier years that the words of stories are the dangerous or provocative weapons in youth encounters and confrontations. Simply being in the wrong place, wearing the wrong sign, or making an inappropriate gesture provokes violence and harm now. Direct communication between the warring parties rarely takes place.

The same is true, more often than not, for confrontations within the homes of these young people. They report that when trouble begins they do not enter the fray, but find ways to retreat—outside, to the street, to a friend's house, or to their youth organization. The stories the young tell each other have become the least lethal weapons they have; indeed, in Leslie Silko's words, they have become the only thing they have to fight against "illness and death." They use their stories to bond with each other, coating their stories often in humor, testing their relationships within the storytelling and listening group, and comparing themselves and their situations with those of others. Stories, when they can be told in safe places, are their theories, ways of testing what others feel and think and how they and their friends stand in contrast with others. These uses of story are, ironically, just those that psychiatrists, literary critics, attorneys, and others have extolled for adult stories.

Connections to Classrooms

But adults rarely get to hear stories of the type described here. The occasions and relationships of intimacy and common knowledge and trust rarely present themselves for youth and adults to come together through story, as adults and younger children do. But what if the marginalized youth of these stories were to want to find ways to bring their stories to link with those of literature and theory in academic settings? What difference might it make to know more about how inner-city young people tell and receive stories and attribute meanings to them in their everyday lives?

First and foremost, classrooms must be safe places. Adults must not offer their summative comments or elaborate on the moral implications of the stories of young people. In addition, it almost goes without saying that adults must realize that if they ask for stories to be told directly to them, rather than to young peers, the stories will not be those of the daily interactions of youth. With care, sensitivity, and flexibility, however, teachers who want to integrate the range of competencies of students' everyday stories into the classroom can do so with comparative and analytical perspectives on classroom textual materials. The following types of situations created in the classroom can help in these efforts:

1. Learners work in small groups to record, transcribe, and study stories collected from family members and friends. They use these stories in class to develop questions to ask storytellers and listeners about the functions and evaluations of stories and to compare the kinds of background knowledge expected for each story to be comprehensible.

2. Following such small-group work, the class creates a composite picture of the regions, cultures, and languages reflected in the stories of the class. Some whole-class discussion enables students to prepare for more small-group work in which they consider themes, structural features, and uses of particular techniques of style of the stories they have collected.

3. Further small-group work centers on talking about differences and similarities of themes, uses of particular structural characteristics (such as setting and character descriptions, dialogue, and references to folklore, myths, and proverbs), and occasions and purposes of telling stories. Each group works out a comparative chart of such features, identifying stories also by their region, language, and culture of origin.

4. Beyond and within these group exchanges around stories, learners can write their own stories to contradict, expand, or parallel those they have collected. For example, elders interviewed may tell stories of family reunions and occasions of celebration of cultural membership; the young may write counter-stories that reflect their views (perhaps unfavorable, ambivalent, or openly resistant) of such occasions.

This interplay of class discussion, small-group work, and individual writing and reading of stories prepares learners to move to the study of different types and uses of printed stories: news stories, fictional tales, traditional stories, or accounts of daily events. Ways in which these differ in structure, background knowledge assumed, and expectations of uses can provide the frame for preparing a composite picture for comparison with the stories collected in the class. For example, the individual stories from Amy Tan's *Joy Luck Club* may parallel some of those written by students in class who question or challenge traditional cultural celebrations or myths pertaining to women, men, children, outsiders, or animals. From their comparative analyses of their own collected and written stories, learners can begin to approach published stories with a sense of expertise and familiarity. But they must do so in *a safe place* and from a solid grounding of appreciation of the intricate features of style and substance of their own stories.

This type of work with stories—collecting, comparing, analyzing, and cataloguing—as well as reading and interpreting builds from two central themes: stories occur in every society, but cultures shape their forms and uses in multiple ways that vary across ages and situations of listeners, as well as the sociohistorical circumstances of the group. Some stories, such as those told by agricultural and nomadic groups, appear to depend on inside knowledge regarding seasons and metaphors of development. Other stories, such as those of groups that see themselves as marginalized and exploited within their own society, appear to move from description to dialogue without precise steps that lead to a clear plot as customarily defined in classroom instruction. Still other stories rest on expectations of shared background knowledge regarding animals, places, or root literary works (such as the *Bible* or the *Qur'an*) or oral sayings or myths (especially those regarding taboos or societal "secrets").

Learning to expect the unexpected in stories told by the young becomes necessary across cultures, times, and regions and thus enables students to consider the important narratives that frame their own lives. These narratives fit no plot structure studied in classrooms, but they may often mesh with stories of older members of the out-of-school group.

Such framing and reframing do not simply refer to group histories or distant figures, but perhaps even more importantly to young people, their everyday planning, personal relations, and veiled theories, perceptions, and reflections on themselves, others around them, and the conditions of their lives. These latter stories rarely receive attention in classrooms, and yet these do more of the work to shape everyday learning than do tales of faraway events, ancestors, and places. Through the stories they tell, young people persuade, argue, describe, and entertain. The two stories analyzed here illustrate also the ways in which they use shifts of dialect, perspectives, and roles to indicate both their sense of relationship with each other *and* their theories about actions and possibilities within their cultural worlds. Moreover, they use stories to suggest what taking risks might mean, their strong interdependence with their peers, and the restraints that outside authorities and the inevitable outcomes of some actions can hold over them. When David takes on the voice of the law and when Isador tells of loss and death from drugs, their stories give them ways of influencing peers without risking loss of face. Through their tellings, they are both within and outside events and conditions recounted, and their own reflections and considerations of causes and consequences create one of several subtexts their stories hold.

Notes

1. This research project, "Language, Socialization, and Neighborhood-based Organizations: Moving Youth beyond Dependency on School and Family," was funded by the Spencer Foundation. Senior associates who worked with the project's co-principal investigators, Heath and Milbrey W. McLaughlin, were Merita A. Irby and Juliet Langman, who collected data and worked closely with teams of twenty junior ethnographers in the youth organizations studied. Language data are drawn from a million-word corpus of language transcripts made from audiotape recordings within the youth organizations. This chapter is an abbreviated version of a chapter in *Suitable Company* (forthcoming). Findings from the project are further detailed in Heath and McLaughlin (1993).

2. The slash marks [/] indicate interruption of one speaker by another. The equal sign [=] indicates a latching of talk where the second speaker picks up from the first speaker and continues talking.

References

Britton, J. (1970). *Language and learning.* Harmondsworth, England: Penguin Books.

Bruner, J. (1993). The autobiographical process. In R. Folkenflik (Ed.), *The culture of autobiography: Constructions of self-representation* (38–56). Stanford, CA: Stanford University Press.

Coles, R. (1989). *The call of stories: Teaching and the moral imagination.* Boston: Houghton Mifflin.

Hanson, C. (Ed.). (1989). *Re-reading the short story.* New York: St. Martin's Press.

Heath, S. B., and McLaughlin, M. W. (1993). *Identity and inner-city youth: Beyond ethnicity and gender.* New York: Teachers College Press.

Mink, L. (1987). Narrative form as a cognitive instrument. In B. Fay, E. Golob, and R. Vann (Eds.), *Historical understanding* (182–203). Ithaca, NY: Cornell University Press.

Silko, L. (1977). *Ceremony.* New York: Viking Press.

15 Writing as a Foundation for Transformative Community in the Tenderloin

Carol E. Heller
University of Illinois at Chicago

Carol Heller allows us access to the inner workings of a women's writing group in "the Tenderloin," a San Francisco neighborhood. She shows us how, amidst the urban problems that surrounded them, the women formed a supportive community. Within this community, they transformed their daily lives into powerful stories and imagined for themselves and their neighbors alternative possibilities.

Every big city in America has a neighborhood, often many, where people from the "better parts of town" would just as soon not find themselves after dark—neighborhoods where, through quirks of history or geography, poverty and despair have become unmistakable, as has the restlessness and violence to which these conditions are so closely related. In San Francisco, this neighborhood, called the Tenderloin, is forty square blocks located just south of the opulent downtown shopping area. Within its tightly packed population of 25,000 exists the largest concentration of intravenous drug users, welfare recipients, mental health patients, and homeless people in San Francisco. For many years, the Tenderloin's crime rate has been the highest in the city.

While other cities have used the name "Tenderloin" to signify the city's "underbelly," San Francisco's Tenderloin received its name, as the story goes, by special circumstances many years ago when a not-too-ethical city policeman who "earned" a side income via drug traffic declared, "No more hamburger for me. From now on, it's tenderloin." In the lore of this city, the name has come to be a symbol of

drugs, crime, food lines, homelessness, and in the eyes of many outsiders an inarticulate hopelessness. But little by little the worlds within
this neighborhood have been rearranging themselves, shifting. This
shifting has occurred less as a visible change to outsiders, more as a
transformation within the consciousness of the community itself. As
Rob Waters, former editor of the twelve-year-old *Tenderloin Times*,
states of this San Francisco neighborhood:

> Today's Tenderloin is redeveloping itself from the inside out. . . .
> It is a change that fails some statistics tests. The Tenderloin's
> real transformation is one that you would have to have been
> here a good while to fully sense. A change in direction, in
> momentum, felt at ground level. . . . A transformation best un-
> derstood by meeting some of the people who are making it
> happen without making headlines. (Waters 1987)

In the coming pages, I will introduce some of the people who I
believe are contributing to this transformation. They are poets and
writers living or working in the Tenderloin. With the support of
community-based writing groups and public readings, these writers
are not only telling their stories, but in so doing they are bringing their
community together in gatherings which foster critical reflection of the
writers' varied histories and imaginations, as well as the social conditions which surround daily life in their neighborhood and in the wider
world.

Writing in the Tenderloin

Writing is a profoundly difficult undertaking under the best of conditions. In the last twenty years, literacy researchers like Emig (1971) and
Dyson (1989), among many others, have explored the circumstances
which support the growth of written expression. Leo Tolstoy, Charles
Dickens, Tillie Olsen, Alice Walker, and George Orwell are among
many novelists who have addressed the particular struggles that poor
people face in order to write—in order to maintain, in Olsen's words,
"creation's needs for full functioning" (1978, 6). As Orwell says of his
hero Gordon Comstock, in *Keep the Aspidistra Flying,* "He couldn't cope
with rhymes and adjectives. You can't, with only two pence and a
halfpenny in your pocket" (1936, 6). Through his hero, Orwell reminds
us that writing is an activity that is nourished by security, by quiet, by
a sense of safety and order in one's daily rhythms. The creative spirit
is offered little of this in the Tenderloin. Yet here, creative spirits are
providing each other nourishment in groups and gatherings.

Women Writers Workshop

The Tenderloin Reflection and Education Center, an independent learning and resource center, sponsors a storytelling and culture group, an artists' and activists' group, and a workshop particularly for women writers, all of which meet regularly in the Tenderloin. In the writing workshops, those just beginning to express their thoughts on paper to those more experienced convene with facilitators from the Reflection Center to find an audience of peers, to express content, experiment with language, and hone form. In the writing workshops, too, participants discuss social issues and plan ways for their creativity to intersect with grass-roots politics as enabling forces for the wider community.

Ben Clarke, director of the Tenderloin Reflection and Education Center, was one of the driving forces behind the establishment of the adult writing program. He explains the philosophy:

> We focus on content, on issues. We base the writing groups on a liberation model in which the experience of participants acts as the core of the learning process. We want to involve members in articulating and reflecting back on their own experience. . . . We want to create a record of this world. Many people here have fallen through the cracks . . . and in spite of that, through that, have so much to say. They're only beginning to recognize that they do. It happens through being heard.

Seventy-six-year-old Leona Walker, a member of the Tenderloin Women Writers Workshop, is one participant who became involved with community action projects partly as a result of support from her writing workshop cohorts. Encouraged by the group's members, Leona, a widow who long ago in her native Oklahoma wrote poems of daily life, began to write poems about her new neighborhood. The group encouraged her to send these as well as letters about housing and street conditions to local papers or to San Francisco's mayor. For the last several years she has headed a nationwide group of elderly citizens in protest against the sale of subsidized housing and, functioning as a writer-advocate for her elderly neighbors, has successfully blocked a federal sale of several buildings in the Tenderloin.

Like Leona, thirty-four-year-old Cleo Meeks, also a member of the workshop, began to use her new belief in the power of the written word on her community's behalf. Once homeless, she began the "Homeless Link," a newsletter of poems, stories, and articles by homeless people. Like Leona's efforts, Cleo's are being met with some success, winning her meetings with the mayor's commission on homelessness. Leona Walker and Cleo Meeks are but two of dozens of Tenderloin residents of varying ages, ethnicities, and backgrounds who have participated in the Reflection Center workshops. Not all of them have become activists. Indeed, participants use the writing groups to fulfill varying functions in their lives. While each participant has unique characteristics, living as poor people in a rough urban neighborhood unites them. So does the intense desire to connect with each other and tell their stories.

In October of 1987 I began to visit the Tenderloin Women Writers Workshop, then the newest writing workshop in the Tenderloin. As a graduate student in education, I had become increasingly interested in the growing body of literacy research which explores the roles that reading and writing assume in different groups and communities (Heath 1983; Dyson 1989, among many others). By exploring and documenting the growth of the Tenderloin Women Writers Workshop and its individual members, I hoped to contribute to a fuller understanding of the varied social contexts that support writers and the craft of writing. What became increasingly clear during my three years of participating in the workshop was that, through reading their own and examining each other's stories, poems, novels, and plays and through participating in discussions that emerged both from these texts and from less text-bound interactions, workshop members were in fact participating in a multilayered educational undertaking. In the groups and in the public readings and pamphlets which emerged from them, the members' histories and experiences became vehicles for social analysis and often, as for Cleo and Leona, for personal and social action.

Tenderloin writers, often in the company of writers from other neighborhoods—who ironically seemed to seek in this marginal setting a certain hope and moral guidance—listened to and analyzed poems and stories that encouraged renewed meaning and vitality in their own lives and in their own stories. The experience, knowledge, and insight stemming from members' widely different histories and reference points and offered so generously in these gatherings constituted the emerging strength of this workshop. At the same time, this endeavor revealed how many levels of support and education can occur simultaneously in settings that one might initially view as accomplishing a more narrowly defined literacy function.

It also became clear that to look at the workshop through a lens narrowly focused on the obvious literacy activity occurring would leave out far too much. The functions the workshop served, functions I came to think of as levels of support for participants, were highly interwoven and built upon the workshop's philosophical foundation that writing is not looked upon as separate from real life, but is used to form meaningful connections to that life. The levels of support included (1) building skills as writers through the writing critique itself, including forming definitions of oneself as a writer and engaging in complex examinations of language; (2) sharing life histories and experiences; (3) telling "mirror stories" (similar stories inspired by others), which often leads to the breaking of silences; (4) boosting identity and self-esteem, as people, as writers, and as public presences; (5) raising consciousness and political awareness; (6) sharing information and resources; (7) bonding and building an internal community; (8) pure and simple teaching and learning; (9) supporting each other to take action in the world.

Community Writing as Cultural Forum

Communities like the Tenderloin are rarely included in the academic discussions surrounding the meaning of literacy. People who live in such settings are seldom seen as strong spokespeople for literacy's capacities. Historically, the trajectory of educational research has typically extended from mainstream settings to marginal settings, the latter all too often being viewed as the "deficit-like" terminus for mainstream research. Yet, as Holzman suggests, there may be "truth at the periphery that might not be as evident in the center" (1986, 157). For indeed it is in such settings that relationships among people living in community, struggling in community, and writing in community may likely reveal the foundations of such humane, civil—yes, transformative—sites of learning as those for which we all search.

Bruner (1986) might call such settings "cultural forums" where storytelling is encouraged and granted validity as a mode of knowing. Greene (1990) has described such settings as "social harbors" where people come together "to enact a process of moving persons into the kind of relationship that may enable each of them to become, to desire, to reach beyond themselves" (332).

The following section introduces the Tenderloin Women Writers Workshop during one of its first meetings in 1987. Already in those early weeks, and then growing with almost synergistic power as the participants became closer through time, these powerful functions were being enacted.

The Stories Unfold

Beatrice, an Anglo in her forties, has just finished reading a journal entry describing an evening of life in the hotel where she lives. It's a stream-of-consciousness piece, an entry that both describes some of the characters living in her building and suggests the chronic noise and disruptions that form the background of her life there. Her writing contrasts with the more focused poems that Mickey, an African American in her fifties, and Jan, an Anglo in her forties, had read just before her. "It's not a finished product," Beatrice says somewhat apologetically as she finishes. Mary TallMountain, a sixty-nine-year-old Athabaskan Native American and the only published writer in the group, reassures her that her writing is at a very early stage and that she might pick one part of her journal and try to turn it into a story, even a made-up one. "I see a story in there. It's all there. It has time and action and conflict." Martha Nichols, an Anglo in her thirties and the group's facilitator, and Maria Rand, a sixty-three-year-old Anglo, agree. After telling the group that she has almost no quiet time to attend to the writing she wants to do, Beatrice offers that she'll give it a try.

Maria's Ruby Brooklyn Arrives

It's Maria Rand's turn to read. Wearing an oversized denim coat and clutching a manila folder thick with typing paper, Maria, who's been chomping at the bit to read ever since she arrived today, lets out a jubilant chuckle, "This is my story of life as a young chick, life on the road!" She chuckles again, seeming to delight in the secrets she's about to disclose. Maria had read the beginning of her novel last week, but offers background now for the women who weren't there.

> This is from my novel, my life history. It's going to be called *The Life and Times of Ruby Brooklyn.* I must explain that when I was eighteen years old I went on the road by myself. I was curious and wanted to see the world, so this is me at eighteen in Chicago . . . I'm real tough!

Another delighted laugh and she launches into a saga whose chapters will take her much of the first three years of her time in the workshop to complete.

> Have you ever been to Chicago when the wind is whistling down Wabash? Well, let me tell you, one winter some forty years ago, I landed there, tired and dirty and very hungry. Oh just to be alive and young and free. To hear people's voices, look

at their faces. Just to be where the action was. That's what I wanted. And the neon lights didn't disappoint me. The band was playing "Night Train" and the stripper was giving it all she had. I stumbled around in the dark trying to find a seat. The place was full of servicemen in tight fitting pants. . . .

Maria reads on, looking up above her bifocals to check on the responses of the group; she laughs, apparently delighted to discover her rapt audience. As her story continues, she describes the beginning of young Ruby Brooklyn's life on the road. In this passage, she had wandered into a strip joint where soon a group of young marines, mistaking her for a prostitute, would eagerly solicit her services. Ruby, at once shocked, angered, and terrified, slams one of the soldiers over the head with a bottle and runs out of the nightclub in tears.

> I walked the streets alone until I found a serene little bar called the College of Complexes, what is known to squares as a way out beat hangout.

"This was the beat era," she explains to workshop members, many of them younger than she. "And I'm an old beatnik!" Another huge, Maria Rand laugh springs forth as she reads of her heroine, Ruby Brooklyn, dancing the night away at the College of Complexes, only to return to her hotel room in the wee hours of the morning to find she'd been locked out, her suitcase deposited in another room, the money she had saved and carefully hidden in its secret pocket stolen. Salima, a fifty-year-old African American, utterly attentive to Maria's reading, nods and laughs at the images the scene evokes; it's almost as though the picture might be a familiar one to her. Before she concedes the floor, Maria, who's gone a bit over time, asks to finish just this passage, which ends with Ruby's attempt the next day, with no money to her name, to find a much needed meal. As she finishes reading, voices of Tenderloin kids playing on Leavenworth Street are heard in the background.

> After wiping my mouth with a red Irish linen napkin, I tipped the waitress my last quarter, and asked to see the manager . . . he was wringing his hands, his face wrapped in the phony practiced smile of head waiters. As soon as I mentioned I had no money, he turned into an old man with colorless eyes and saliva spewing from his mouth. He was flinging his arms and poking his finger into the air. "What do you mean coming into a respectable place and not having money?!" Poor man. I was starting to feel sorry for him. Evidently life hadn't prepared him for this kind of emergency. He demanded to know why oh why had I picked on his place. "Cause I was hungry," I said. This

seemed to throw him into another frenzy. . . . "OUT! OUT! OUT!" He threw me out. "And if you come back, I'll kill you!"

Maria ends her reading with another bellowing laugh. "OK I'll give somebody else a chance to read. But this is my childhood!"

Salima, her gray fisherman's cap angled over her forehead, is the first to respond. "Yea I can relate to that too. I can relate to those streets too."

> *Maria:* Really?
>
> *Salima:* Yea!
>
> *Maria:* The mean streets! Of course this is when I was eighteen, when covered wagons were circling the Indians!

Mary TallMountain, Salima, and Maria let out a great laugh.

> *Salima:* [still laughing] Yea, I can relate to that too. That's all right!
>
> *Maria:* Oh, I got a good education, baby.

A discussion begins, prompted by Martha's question of whether the marines in the nightclub might have said a few too many "fuck you's" to Ruby to be believable.

> *Maria:* That's the way they talk!
>
> *Salima:* You don't know servicemen!
>
> *Beatrice:* I'm from Minnesota, but I know that's the way they talk!
>
> *Maria:* I'm not using those words to shock anyone. That's just the way they talk.

Others enter the conversation. Several agree that she should keep the "fuck you's" in, but remove some of the qualifiers. Martha talks up the power of simple language. She cautions Maria on her wordiness, but praises her story too. "It's ten times better than a lot of stuff that's out there." Maria brings up her past efforts to publish other stories she's written.

> *Maria:* I keep sending it out and they send me back rejection slips. One agent told me I wrote like Charles Bukowski. . . . So I said, "well, if I write like Charles Bukowski and you like Charles Bukowski, why don't you publish me?"
>
> *Salima:* Good question!
>
> *Maria:* But she didn't answer my question.
>
> *Martha:* Your stuff, it's got more of a narrative. It's the same kind of material.

> *Maria:* I thought, "Oh to Hell with it," but I'll get back to it
>   now.

Others offer Maria tips. Beatrice would like to see her send it to a
friend of hers in Minnesota. "It's so midwest; the character of the west
coast is different." Taking up the suggestion, Martha offers to bring
Maria names of smaller publishing houses in Chicago and encourages
others to keep thinking of good advice for her. She reminds people of
Saturday's Tenderloin reading, hopes that Maria will read *Ruby Brooklyn* for that event, and asks Salima, who had volunteered earlier, if
she's ready to take the floor.

Salima's Message to the Tenderloin

Salima takes off her cap and moves to a spot near the door where she
can stand. Reading from a piece of notebook paper, she laughs with a
hint of stage fright as she imitates the ring of a phone and mimes the
action of picking up the receiver to answer a call:

> Hello? Who? No, you not back again. Every time I try to get my
> life straight, you pop your tail up. Yes, I was lonely and we were
> friends. That was then. What? Don't make me puke. Listen,
> Satan, having you for a friend almost caused my life to end.
> Each morning I woke up you kept poking me with your devil's
> stick. You what? Sorry? That's a lie. The devil ain't never sorry.
> There you go, trying to trick me again, but it won't work this
> time. No, you listen! You caused me nothin' but shame and
> pain. Shame because I lost my self-respect, pride and dignity.
> [pause] Shut the fuck up! Let me tell you about fear and pain.
> The sickness of being your friend. Fear of going to sleep. Afraid
> to wake up. Not knowing what I had to do to stop my nose and
> ears from running. My nerves from crawling. My head from
> hurting. Hot and cold chills. Fever. Throwing my insides up.
> Diarrhea. Stomach's in knots. And every joint in my body was
> aching. I couldn't sleep, eat, nor think without your poison. Oh,
> no, Satan, I will not fall for your trap this time. [pause] What?
> You gotta go? No, you keep your tail right there and listen. You
> tricked me once. You tricked me twice. Now I kick you *out* and
> I'm in charge of my life! [pause] Say what? You'll take care of
> me? Don't make me sick! You took care of me all right. [pause]
> No, no, you listen! I was powerless and possessed by you. Yes,
> you took care of me all right. You sent me to prison. Time and
> many times I went to jail. But never again will I go through Hell.
> Oh, I almost forgot, you even put me in the hospital. Go to Hell,
> Satan, and get out of my life. Don't call me. Don't come around.
> And stay out of my fuckin' dreams. I don't have to live in fear
> and darkness no more. Our friendship is dead. I don't need that
> garbage. I have God in my life now. He told me to trust and

have faith, and He will save me from eternal Hell. [pause] You gonna . . . you gonna cry? [cracks up with laughter] Everybody know the Devil can't cry. [more laughter] Hello? Hello? . . . . He's gone.

As Salima looks up, the workshop members have broken into applause. Maria, Mary TallMountain, and Martha add loud theater whistles. The acknowledgment seems as much for Salima's fight for life as for the effectiveness of the dramatic performance itself.

> *Martha:* [still applauding] Well, I think you're ready to go! [referring to Saturday's reading]
>
> *Leona:* I'd say so!
>
> *Martha:* One thing, did you hang up the phone in the end?
>
> *Salima:* [laughing] Oh no, I forgot to hang up the phone!
>
> *Martha:* [laughing] That's the one thing. You gotta remember to hang up that phone!
>
> *Salima:* [laughing] OK! OK! I will! One thing . . . one thing, though [her voice getting serious], did I seem nervous?

Not one to let her guard down easily, Salima often gives the impression of a woman with an "attitude," a word she herself uses to describe the "don't mess with me" stance from which she characteristically meets the world. Now, three weeks into the workshop, that "attitude," which often seems invulnerable, makes way for something else. A number of workshop members assure her that in fact she didn't seem nervous. Martha, however, taking note of the seriousness of Salima's concern and the courage she may have summoned to ask, has a somewhat different take: "There's nothing wrong with being nervous, Salima! It gives you a lot of energy. It makes people take notice."

"It gives us an edge!" winks Maria. With a public bravado not unlike Salima's, Maria would discuss her own stage fright several sessions later and take pleasure in Martha's further confirmation that anxiety is often a necessary and positive ingredient that goes with reading one's work to others.

A Vision of Elegance from Mary TallMountain

Mary TallMountain moves to the spot near the front door that Salima has now inaugurated as the rehearsal stage for Saturday's reading. In an interview, Mary once described herself as "unbelievably various and interesting even to myself." Her face alone captures this. It is at once round and robust, frail and weary, her eyes filled with a quick, challenging intensity and a vast kindness toward and interest in whomever she's addressing. Favoring colorful gym shoes and whimsical, handpainted jewelry—striped goldfish earrings and a spider watch today—Mary does not look sixty-nine, though it's clear she takes great pleasure in the role of an "elder" in the tradition of her Koyukon Athabaskan Indian tribe.

"This is a story about one of our street brothers and it's called 'Them Kinda Dogs,'" Mary begins. "Butt's blue headband . . . uh, Butt's . . . uh, Butte's blue headband . . . oh my my my. Let me start again!" To the group's great amusement, Mary has opened with a sterling mispronunciation of her story hero's first name, and she's not about to live it down. No one, least of all Mary, can stop laughing. "Well you can only do that once!" says Leona. "You did it here for us so you won't call him 'Butt' on Saturday!" Several more minutes of laughter and Mary begins again. Her story is about an Indian man named Butte and his black Labrador, Thomas Mann, who live together in a vacated garage in San Francisco. It is one of several stories that Mary writes about transplanted Native Americans living in San Francisco, often in the Tenderloin.

> Butte's blue headband was the faded cotton of the City's regular street Indian. His hair, rippling heavily down off his bulwark-like shoulders, was the black that is unfathomable, hair which, when it fell forward of its own weight, he sometimes tossed back out of his way in a motion of indefinable grace. Faded Levi's further enunciated the symbol and statement of his city uniform. The jacket which served as armor against the chill morning smother of fog around Embarcadero Four was long since exfoliated of its fringes; the pristine red suede had been denuded of nap to its roots. Close inspection of his attire would have found it, though clean, worn nearly to its demise. His muscled legs pistoned along, followed by the clicking nails of the paws of Thomas Mann, who was the embodiment of elegance. Mann was a hunting Labrador, wearing a pelt and tail which surpassed Butte's Indian mane by several degrees of gloss. Mann's frank crystal eyes and his smooth head so roundly correct had won points from the American Kennel Association in his early years. His muzzle now sported a grizzle of silver, neat as any executive's above his morning moustache cup, and he emanated an aura of warm gentility. The union of man and dog was one of complete understanding; it often appeared that they spoke in an eccentric language not understood by any but themselves.

"Them Kinda Dogs," like a good number of Mary's other works that she would read in the workshop and for community performances, captures her sense of the elegance of poor people. To Mary,

Butte, a homeless man whose stature many would readily overlook, is a picture to behold. He is a man of "indefinable grace." His bond to Thomas Mann, "the embodiment of elegance," evokes Mary's regard for the deep and ancient affinity that exists between Native American people and animals. One doesn't know from her story what brought Butte and Mann to their present life. One does know that the two go forth with a great sense of honor and commitment to each other. Theirs is a life, too, that begins each day with a search for edible food in the city's dumpsters.

> On the cracked cement they slept in a well-matured twin mummy bag, warming each other through frosty nights when cold snaps brought icicles. . . . .Frisco weather scarcely fazed either because they had lived most of their life in Blackfeet country. Mann's dense mat of winter undercoat was enough for any outdoors working dog. In Montana, his work had consisted of hunting deer, birds, and small game. Here the hunting was different. He possessed an exquisite nose. It was of great value, informing himself and then Butte of the presence of tasty discards, their sort and quantity, reposing in any receptacle, open or closed. This talent narrowed the need for Butte to investigate. . . . Looking around, their manners almost identical, the proud lifted heads spoke of character and a certain finely honed style. "At Embark Four it ain't garbage, Mann," Butte was saying. "It's elegant gar-bazzhe." He accented the slow syllables in his best quasi-French manner. Mann nodded. His eyes glinted.

Not realizing that two watchful janitors have them under surveillance, Butte and Mann begin their search for food in a trash barrel outside a lavish downtown hotel.

> Casually, from his six-four, Butte looked down into it and thrust in a hand. Mann watched. With no haste, with utmost care, he received between his teeth the partly bitten hamburger Butte offered. He gave no sign of distaste. He did not allow his nose to quiver; each wet black pore was disciplined to stillness, lest he embarrass Butte.

"Hey, Chief, you can't dig in our disposal. . . . No bums allowed here." Their faces, as Mary describes them, delighting in the thought of an easy conquest, the janitors start to chase Butte when Mann, "like the first eruption of a far-off volcano," bares his teeth in protection of his companion and their food. The two escape, their breakfast intact. "I never did like them kinda dogs," scowls one of the janitors, his final assessment of the morning's incident evincing the toss-off attitude toward the poor that much of Mary's writing challenges.

Community Building in Education

In *Yearning: Race, Gender, and Cultural Politics* (1990), hooks writes a chapter called "Choosing the Margin." Her sense of "margin" and what can occur there is a powerful one. She is not, she states emphatically, "speaking of a marginality one wishes to lose" (149). "Not a sign marking . . . despair . . . [where] one's creativity, one's imagination is at risk" (150–151), but rather "a space that can tell stories and unfold histories" (152).

In the Tenderloin Women Writers Workshop, texts and dialogue grounded in authentic experience constituted not only a multifunctional form of community education, but also a powerful foundation of renewed community itself. Within their writing groups, members claimed new capacities to define and discover themselves both as knowers and as community members. Maxine Greene (Chapter 2 of this volume) reminds us that Dewey once said of democracy that it "is a name for a life of free and enriching communion." The functions which emerged in the life of the workshop touch, I believe, on the foundations of democratic sympathy that Dewey referred to, as group members and their facilitator tried to accommodate the needs of all participants, to understand the experiences of each other, and finally to support each other's need to publicly matter.

Perhaps the workshop's strength was its unwillingness to create false oppositions between the emotions and the intellect, the spirit and mind, the person and community. This kind of integration, what Britton calls "synthesis" (1989), is precisely what many in the forefront of educational thinking (Cazden 1979; Bruner 1986; Greene 1989; Dyson 1989) suggest we begin to see as a goal—even a requirement—for children's classrooms. Yet we rarely witness the enactment of such powerful "synthesis." Historically, as Britton reminds us, much of formal education has been guided by the assumption that learning in fact necessitates "screening out the affective" (1989). But he is convinced, as are Greene (1989), Dyson (1989), and others, that the exact opposite may likely be true. The affective, a fundamental ingredient of what Dyson describes as the deeply layered "embeddedness" of powerful learning settings, might be seen, as it so naturally was in the Tenderloin Women Writers Workshop, as a vital, welcomed part of the complex life of education.

Additionally, we are only beginning to understand the powerful role that community building has in effective learning and literacy settings. Cazden (1979), who returned to classroom teaching after years as a university researcher, discovered that, in spite of her rich store of knowledge about children's language and learning, teaching in fact became a futile enterprise in a classroom dominated by human distances, a classroom where a sense of community was missing. After months of struggling to infuse her students with a feeling of solidarity with one another and with her, Cazden tried to describe a model for her own growing classroom successes that might be useful to others seeking to bridge similar distances in their classrooms. She divided her approach into several categories: attempting to decrease psychological distances when social distances were facts of life (most of Cazden's students came from class backgrounds different from hers); finding ways for the lives she and her students led to connect outside the classroom; building a shared life through important events within the classroom; avoiding activities that increased, rather than diminished, distances. These strategies, worked out in various ways, were to serve her quest toward the classroom intimacy—the sense of solidarity—that she began to realize was vital for her students' emotional and intellectual well-being. And these same ingredients were among the qualities of group life that emerged so strongly in the Tenderloin Women Writers Workshop.

One of the cardinal features of the workshop was the significance its facilitators, ongoing members, and funding organizations placed on establishing a strong association between the workshop and the neighborhood of which it was part. The Tenderloin Reflection and Education Center planned an assortment of public events, focused on some feature of art, politics, and culture, to reinforce this link. Writing was not looked upon as separate from real life, but, through the workshops and public readings, as well as through a variety of community publications that featured Tenderloin writers' work, was used to form meaningful connections to that life. Increasingly, mainstream educators, too, are understanding the significance such vital connection can have for students to experience excitement and an authentic sense of accomplishment in classroom learning.

The facilitators of the Tenderloin Women Writers Workshop had a great deal to do, too, with the kind of community-in-the-making that the workshop became. Holzman (1989) once interviewed a group who had successfully worked in adult literacy and education projects in economically poor communities abroad. He wrote about his conversation with them:

> A nun who had gone out to the Philippines in 1947 told me stories that began as stories about literacy, but gradually became stories about community organizing. . . . They wish to

"accompany" members of local communities who are engaged in attempting to improve their own lives. (187)

Holzman's words might well describe how the group's facilitators, some of whom lived in fairly comfortable circumstances outside the Tenderloin, assumed their roles. With a light touch, commitment, humor, and friendship, they "accompanied" the members of the Tenderloin Women Writers Workshop. They became involved in the community; they gave support, information, writing tips, and criticism when needed; they held back and let the group do a lot of its own work together. Workshop participants felt that each facilitator had a genuineness, a trustworthiness, an abiding regard for and interest in them as people—traits Erickson (1984) might describe as "civility." Once again, more and more educators are recognizing the need for teachers to cultivate such traits—to talk less and listen more, to reconnect learners with their own communities, to guide and "accompany" them as students contribute more and more to the construction of their own learning based on their own lives and aspirations.

A Story of "Warriors"

Mary TallMountain owns a red tee shirt inscribed with the words, "A Warrior Is Geared to Struggle So Her People Will Continue." She enjoyed wearing it to the workshop, where it was greatly admired. In just the way that her tee shirt describes, Mary TallMountain and many members of the Tenderloin Women Writers Workshop were, in fact, warriors. Indeed many of the members of the workshop wrote so that their people would continue. Through a novel she focused on in her later workshop work, Mary saw to it that her Athabaskan ancestors would continue. She also saw to it that her "street brothers and sisters" like Butte would be offered stature and places of distinction in her stories. They, too, would continue. Maria's writing was driven by her desire to have Ruby Brooklyn continue, as well as her parents, grandparents, and those who represented her cultural past. And through her vibrant plays about her family in the pre-civil-rights South and through her stories about the Tenderloin, Salima saw to it that her mother and the many people she became committed to in the Tenderloin would continue as well.

While the Tenderloin Women Writers Workshop provided multiple levels of support—served multiple functions—for those who participated, perhaps the driving function that wove all the other levels of support together was that the workshop supported participants' right to be those kinds of warriors Mary's tee shirt describes. Here, participants were offered the requisite audience to have their own stories and those of the people they came from and cared about matter, were granted the right to have them continue. The workshop bore witness to all these powerful stories and, through time, became its own.

References

Britton, J. (1989). Writing-and-reading in the classroom. In A. H. Dyson (Ed.), *Collaboration through writing and reading: Exploring possibilities* (217–246). Urbana, IL: National Council of Teachers of English.

Bruner, J. (1986). *Actual minds, possible worlds.* Cambridge, MA: Harvard University Press.

Cazden, C. (1979). How knowledge about language helps the classroom teacher—or does it?: A personal account. *Urban Review, 9,* 74–91.

Dyson, A. H. (1989). *The multiple worlds of child writers: Friends learning to write.* New York: Teachers College Press.

Emig, J. (1971). *The composing processes of twelfth graders.* NCTE Research Report No. 13. Urbana, IL: National Council of Teachers of English.

Erickson, F. (1984). School literacy, reasoning, and civility: An anthropologist's perspective. *Review of Educational Research, 54*(4), 525–546.

Greene, M. (1989). *The literacy debate: Going beyond the functional.* Address to the American Educational Research Association, San Francisco.

———. (1990). Relationality in the humanities: A perspective on leadership. *Language Arts, 67*(4), 370–378.

Heath, S. B. (1983). *Ways with words.* Cambridge: Cambridge University Press.

Holzman, M. (1986). The social context of literacy education. *College English, 48*(1), 27–33.

———. (1989). Teaching is remembering. In M. Holzman and M. Cooper (Eds.), *Writing as social action* (221–232). Portsmouth, NH: Heinemann.

hooks, b. (1990). *Yearning: Race, gender, and cultural politics.* Boston: South End Press.

Olsen, T. (1978). *Silences.* New York: Delacorte Press.

Orwell, G. (1936). *Keep the aspidistra flying.* London: Harcourt, Brace, Jovanovich.

Waters, R. (1987, November 1). The Tenderloin transformed. *Image Magazine,* San Francisco *Chronicle,* 10–14, 31, 34.

16 Conclusion: Fulfilling the Need for Story

Celia Genishi
Teachers College, Columbia University

Anne Haas Dyson
University of California, Berkeley

In the end, why do we need our stories?

To produce food for the mind, for the senses, for the heart. To keep language alive. . . . What do we have from the past? Art and thought. That's what lasts. That's what continues to feed people and give them an idea of something better.

Susan Sontag (quoted in Garis 1992, 43)

We all need stories to nourish our selves, to feed mind and heart. In the three sections of this collection, the contributors have fulfilled the need in a range of ways through their art and thought, enriching our themes of "Connections between Story, Self, and Others," "Ways with Stories," and "Weaving Communities through Story." In this chapter we synthesize from our perspective— we hope without diminishing the richness of each teller's story—some ways in which authors have elaborated upon the original themes.

Connections between Story, Self, and Others: Why Do We Tell Stories?

A theme that links all sections of the book together is the role of story in fulfilling our need for a community in which each self both stands out and fits in. The challenge of increasing the number and quality of connections among our selves, within and across communities, is given a literary framework in Maxine Greene's chapter. Her own search for self took her first to the pages of a literary canon and the faces and figures created by long-dead painters. She later sought and found alternative selves, in the art of both men and women and those presenting nontraditional, often non-Western voices and images. She suggests that, as teachers, we seek the most spacious landscapes, the

most accepting communities, in which our stories reside next to contrasting ones and next to vacant places that wait for unexpected and
new storytellers.

Spacious landscapes provide sites for reconciliation of the traditional with the revolutionary, for the classical with the popular. Thus
next to Greene's chapter are two others that look less to published
stories and more to accounts of "ordinary" lives, the stories of selves
in families and varied sociocultural circumstances. The Goodhertz
family members structure their individual autobiographies, revealing
the tensions between family members who chafe to be independent,
while making sense of their lives only as they fit into the context of
their family history. Their individual ways of recounting experience
both shape and are shaped by the stories they remember. Jerome
Bruner points out that autobiography functions to uncover the tellers'
"recipes for experience," as they narrate and create their own definitions of the "examined life."

The origin of our storied selves, our ways of recounting personal
experience, is Peggy Miller and Robert Mehler's focus. Young children, as Anthony and his classmates demonstrated in Chapter 1, are
capable of telling their own stories, of expressing themselves in relation to particular social situations and people. Even in the preschool
years, children of all backgrounds are active participants in telling,
hearing, and being the topics of narratives of personal experience.
Thus stories serve to socialize, to construct selves in the frequent and
ordinary interactions through which children become members of
their communities. Embedded in these interactions are evaluative
statements and judgments formed by adults and children as they
decide how individual selves do or don't fit in.

Ways with Stories in the Classroom: Whose Stories Are Told? Whose Stories Are Heard?

Story as a means to constructing and seeing one's self in relation to
others, appreciating difference, and evaluating ourselves, others, and
experience are continued themes in the varied chapters of the second
section. "Difference" is reflected in a number of overlapping factors:
gender, age, class, race, and ethnic, linguistic, or sociocultural background. In contrast to many contributors who focus on small numbers
of classrooms or children, Geneva Smitherman considers some of these
factors on a large scale in the context of a well-known evaluation
project, the National Assessment of Educational Progress. Focusing on
African American high school students' writing, she and her collabo-

rators go beyond the usual measures of conventional writing and look for African American discourse features in the students' samples, such as rhythmic or evocative language, reference to race or color, or the rhetorical style of traditional black churches. When writers use these features, their scores tend to be better. So in this study, raters view as a strength the ability to incorporate the voices of students' own communities into imaginative or narrative essays. As noted in Chapter 1, musical and image-making features of language convey a distinctive sense of self that less culturally rich prose cannot capture.

Reflecting another difference, Ageliki Nicolopoulou, Barbara Scales, and Jeff Weintraub locate in preschool classrooms the missing female voices that Greene referred to in her chapter. These researchers seek to hear four-year-old middle-class children's imagined stories, which in this setting show strikingly clear gender differences. Despite their teachers' efforts to create a nonsexist environment, most of the time in their numerous tellings the girls' stories are "orderly," with conventional and peaceful endings, whereas the boys' stories are "disorderly," with violent events and endings. Where these differences in narrative style come from and whether they will endure are humbling questions that Nicolopoulou and her collaborators raise.

In her own consideration of gendered voices, Pam Gilbert suggests that a feminine style does endure, and its persistence may work against the construction of diverse selves. The elementary school girls in her study *continue* to tell orderly stories, similar in their orderliness to those in the data of Nicolopoulou, Scales, and Weintraub. These often have stock endings in which men save women so that all can live happily ever after. Romantic "fictions" (Walkerdine 1990), Gilbert and Nicolopoulou and her colleagues argue, are social constructions, fed in part by the cultural stories of the mass media. Gilbert suggests that, as we try to understand the origin and contexts of students' desires, we raise questions of the students themselves so that they encounter a multiplicity of voices and perspectives and the idea that less conventional, more divergent stories are possible—to write and to live.

Focusing on another type of sociolinguistic difference, Courtney Cazden raises the question of what adults are to do when children's voices are unfamiliar to the teacher's ear. During the common routine called Sharing Time, children's narratives may vary widely. And since adults' own social and linguistic background may differ from their children's, much of the teacher's work entails careful listening. In fact, whether children's narratives are heard and truly shared depends on allowing each child "equal access" to stand out as she or he takes a turn and then to fit into the classroom community as teacher and children work out mutual understandings of each story. As in Gilbert's study, making room for divergent ways of storying creates the potential for learner-responsive and changed curricula.

The themes of difference and transformation are developed further within the context of children's literature by Mingshui Cai and Rudine Sims Bishop. These authors build an argument for clear definitions of the varied types of *multicultural literature*. For them the mere inclusion in literature of characters of varied races and ethnicities is not sufficient because the goal of multicultural literature needs to coincide with that of multicultural education: to transform society so that it is more just and equitable. That transformation will depend on an understanding of experiences of *parallel cultures*, of people of color who tell stories of the heart about the cultures and communities from which they come.

Weaving Communities through Story: Who Are We?

Community as a contributor to the creation of self and story is maintained and highlighted as a unifying theme in the third section of this collection. Too, there are the repeated motifs of valuing difference and the common task of transforming the usually accepted—the canon. The authors all demonstrate that stories, like communities, are *social constructions* rooted in language (Berger and Luckmann 1967; Britton 1971; Vygotsky 1978). And as Anne Haas Dyson proposes in her chapter, stories are also a crossroads where these constructions take form, where people gather with their own interests and agendas and, like Bruner's Goodhertz family, with their unique histories. Those histories are replete with experiences both ordinary (Heather Smith-Willis's evening bath in Sal Vascellaro and Celia Genishi's chapter) and extraordinary (the homelessness of some participants of the writing group that Carol Heller describes). At the crossroads where the extraordinary and the everyday meet, stories "transmute the commonplace into an alternative reality," as Greene discusses in her chapter; they create the hope of better futures in which the tensions of the present might be eased or resolved.

The tension between different races, for example, has no simple resolution, but classrooms can become communities in which stories help diminish tensions. Vivian Paley, for example, addresses the question of whether one's skin color is of beauty and value in a particular society—and whether "who we are" is valued—as she weaves the memory of her own childhood disappointments into the experiences of fictitious princesses and the children in her classroom. Along with their classmates, three African American girls are carried into the world of Paley's story, where the heroes' skin color resembles the three girls'. The boundary between the story world and the classroom blurs as the girls' own imagined stories begin to feature heroes of color. Who the girls are begins to merge with who their heroes are.

This same blurring of boundaries appears in different ways in Dyson's chapter about a third-grade classroom and Susan Britsch's, about a Head Start program. The third graders of Dyson's chapter respond in complex ways to societal tensions, such as racism and war, which children talk about explicitly. The boundary they cross most often in their efforts to figure out how they fit in, though, is the one between the official and unofficial worlds, between the society of the classroom, with its expectations and school guidelines, and the world outside it. Children like William bring elements of the outside world into their stories; the pages on which they write become a forum for the handling of the personal tensions of complicated selves.

In an effort to preserve a "group self," the staff of a Head Start program create a unique curriculum, described in Britsch's chapter. The Tachi Yokuts people, of whom only about thirty speak Tachi, participate in a program that weaves Tachi as a second language together with activities typical of the Tachi Yokuts culture. It is the stories of the elders, though, that form the strongest threads, uniting the past with the present, through a dying language. The elders, families, and children at the Head Start Center construct a "community of memory" (Bellah et al., cited in Britsch's chapter), transforming their curriculum so that the traditional is preserved through a program for the very young, thus melding community treasures with school life.

The adults in Vascellaro's classroom experienced similar boundary crossings as they created stories for children. Although the college classroom is not traditionally a stage for narratives of personal experience, Vascellaro's course relies upon groups of student storytellers transforming themselves into communities of story writers and transforming their experiences into stories for children. Like storytellers in other chapters, these students use talk as a bridge between everyday life and story (see also Genishi 1992). Who they are—their lives as children, siblings, teachers, parents—all coalesce as their lived experience crosses over into the world of "literature."

The communities in which stories emerge, then, have much in common. And they often thrive in unofficial—non-school—settings such as Shirley Brice Heath and Carol Heller describe. Their respective chapters portray groups whose activities are typically seen not just as unofficial, but marginal. The lives of some of the young people in Heath's study and the writers in Heller's have involved such things as drug use, violence, and prison terms; many are poor, and some, homeless. Yet their capacity for telling stories makes them members of literary groups: Heath's young people are part of a teen drama team, whereas Heller's participants are members of a neighborhood writing group. Like the storytellers of other chapters, though, they attempt to cross boundaries, to bring their pasts into the imaginative worlds of literature. There, unconventional experiences are no longer "deviations," but the core of plots in which writers have room to enact their own stories. Thus stories help them shape a present where they no longer encounter the painful scene that Adrienne Rich (quoted in Rosaldo 1989, ix) has described:

> When someone with the authority of a teacher, say, describes the world and you are not in it, there is a moment of psychic disequilibrium, as if you looked into a mirror and saw nothing.

The stories in this volume help to widen the boundaries of life's curriculum to include the unexpected and ordinary experiences of diverse selves that developed in and out of classrooms. Thus stories represent ways of taking action to create the spacious landscapes where the "different" have audible voices and visible faces.

Conclusion

This book has been filled with crossroads, places where people meet, bringing their pasts, their differences, their hopes, their distinctive disciplines. What they bring has been woven into stories, grand and small ones: representatives of the traditional canon, next to stories of personal experience. At such a crossroads in such a community, the hero of a classic novel stands next to a child like kindergartner Mary who is learning her numbers. Her short story of personal experience notes that in the past, "I used to make my threes like that. Or like that. Now I make it like that" (in Miller and Mehler's chapter).

In short, then, why do we need our stories? Stories help us construct our *selves*, who used to be one way and are now another; stories help to make sense of, evaluate, and integrate the tensions inherent in experience: the past with the present, the fictional with the "real," the official with the unofficial, the personal with the professional, the canonical with the different or unexpected. Stories help us transform the present and shape the future for our students and ourselves so that it will be richer or better than the past.

There is a fable by James Thurber (1957) called *The Wonderful O,* which offers another way to view our need for story. The tale's villain, who runs the town, had the misfortune of losing his mother when she disappeared out of a porthole. So he has banned all words, objects, and people whose names contain the letter *O.* Life in the town becomes almost unbearable as people, things, ideas, feelings all vanish. But in the end, a horde of literary heroes, from Romeo to Goldilocks, comes riding into town. Following the return of the heroes, the people save themselves from the villain as they discover in stories words long banished—love, valor, memory, freedom. . . . The lives of the townspeople return to normal as those words again sustain them. But their return was enabled by a more important word: story, a community where words live, where, as they assemble in stories, they help us live freely and humanely.

Finally, stories are valuable because they give us a most important *O*-word: hope. Perhaps in the end, we need our stories to give us hope. They help us see possibilities, they give us what we need to envision a transformed future in which learners have satisfying social relationships, make sense of print, all see themselves in the world around them—in the dolls they favor, the books they choose, and the stories they tell, hear, read, write, perform.

References

Berger, P., and Luckmann, T. (1967). *The social construction of reality: A treatise in the sociology of knowledge.* New York: Anchor.

Britton, J. (1971). *Language and learning.* Hammondsworth, England: Penguin.

Garis, L. (1992, August 2). Susan Sontag finds romance. *New York Times Magazine,* 20–23, 31, 43.

Genishi, C. (Ed.). (1992). *Ways of assessing children and curriculum: Stories of early childhood practice.* New York: Teachers College Press.

Rosaldo, R. (1989). *Culture and truth: The remaking of social analysis.* Boston: Beacon.

Thurber, J. (1957). *The wonderful O.* New York: Simon & Schuster.

Vygotsky, L. S. (1978). *Mind in society.* Cambridge, MA: Harvard University Press.

Walkerdine, V. (1990). *Schoolgirl fictions.* New York: Verso.

Index

Editors

Anne Haas Dyson is a professor in the School of Education at the University of California, Berkeley. She is the author of *Multiple Worlds of Child Writers: Friends Learning to Write* and *Social Worlds of Children Learning to Write in an Urban Primary School.* Her research concentrates on children's oral and written language use in official and unofficial classroom worlds.

Celia Genishi is a professor of curriculum and teaching at Teachers College, Columbia University. She is the editor of *Ways of Assessing Children and Curriculum: Stories of Early Childhood Practice* and co-author, with Anne Haas Dyson, of *Language Assessment in the Early Years.* Her interests include children's language in the classroom and the role of stories in research and practice.

Contributors

Rudine Sims Bishop is a professor in the Department of Educational Theory and Practice at The Ohio State University. She is the author of the NCTE publication *Shadow and Substance: Afro-American Experience in Contemporary Children's Fiction* and has a particular interest in multicultural literature.

Susan J. Britsch is an assistant professor of literacy and language education in the Department of Curriculum and Instruction at Purdue University. Among her interests are child language socialization in families and communities, the interface between teaching style and issues of developmentally appropriate practice for children in specific communities, and children's stories, both told and written.

Jerome Bruner is a research professor of psychology and senior research fellow in law at New York University. He is the author of *Actual Minds, Possible Worlds* and *Acts of Meaning*. His research has included work in curriculum theory, cognitive development, child language acquisition, and literary theory.

Mingshui Cai is an assistant professor of education at the University of Northern Iowa. His major areas of research interest are reader response, multicultural literature, and children's literature. He is the recipient of the 1993 Virginia Hamilton Essay Award.

Courtney B. Cazden is a professor in the Harvard Graduate School of Education. She is the author of *Classroom Discourse: The Language of Teaching and Learning* and *Whole Language Plus: Essays on Literacy in the United States and New Zealand*. Her research has included work in child language development, educational anthropology, and applied linguistics.

Pam Gilbert is a senior lecturer in education at James Cook University of North Queensland, Australia. She is the author of *Writing, Schooling, and Deconstruction: From Voice to Text in the Classroom* and *Gender, Literacy, and the Classroom*. Her research has focused on the teaching of literature and on gender issues in English education.

Maxine Greene is William F. Russell Professor Emeritus in the Foundations of Education at Teachers College, Columbia University. She is the author of *Landscapes of Learning* and *The Dialectic of Freedom* and is particularly interested in connections among philosophy, education, and the arts.

Shirley Brice Heath is a professor of English and linguistics at Stanford University. She is the author of *Ways with Words: Language, Life, and Work in Communities and Classrooms*. Her research includes work in the ethnography of communication, child language socialization, the history and politics of language policies and attitudes, and educational practices for culturally diverse populations in school and community.

Carol E. Heller is an assistant professor of education at the University of Illinois at Chicago. She was formerly a research fellow with the Teaching Tolerance project of the Southern Poverty Law Center in Montgomery, Alabama.

Robert A. Mehler, after receiving a B.A. degree in tutorial studies at the University of Chicago, was research assistant to Dr. Peggy Miller from 1988 to 1991. He is currently in premedical training at the University of Illinois at Chicago.

Peggy J. Miller is an associate professor in the departments of Speech Communication and Psychology at the University of Illinois at Urbana-Champaign. The author of *Amy, Wendy, and Beth: Learning Language in South Baltimore,* she has a longstanding interest in language socialization in children from diverse cultures.

Ageliki Nicolopoulou is an assistant professor of education and child development at Smith College. She is co-editor, along with Barbara Scales, of *Play and the Social Context of Development in Early Care and Education.* Her interests include the role of play and fantasy in education and development.

Vivian Gussin Paley is a teacher at the University of Chicago Laboratory Schools. Among her books are *White Teacher, Wally's Stories, Boys and Girls, The Boy Who Would Be a Helicopter,* and *You Can't Say You Can't Play.* A classroom teacher for more than thirty-five years, she has created a continuing autobiographical study of young children in school.

Barbara Scales is the head teacher at the Harold E. Jones Child Study Center, University of California, Berkeley. Co-author of *Looking at Children's Play: A Bridge between Theory and Practice* and more recently *Play at the Center of the Curriculum,* she has a particular interest in the social ecology of the preschool and in children's storytelling and dramatic play.

Geneva Smitherman is University Distinguished Professor and director of the African American Language and Literacy Program in the Department of English at Michigan State University. She is the author of *Black Language and Culture: Sounds of Soul, Talkin and Testifyin: The Language of Black America,* and *Rap, Forty Acres, and the N-Word: A Dictionary of Black Talk.* Her interests include the oral and written language of African Americans in classroom and community settings and the politics of language in and out of school.

Sal Vascellaro is a member of the graduate faculty at the Bank Street College of Education, where he teaches courses in early childhood curriculum and children's literature. He is a doctoral student in the Department of Philosophy and the Social Sciences at Teachers College, Columbia University, and is especially interested in the "storywriting" of teachers.

Jeff Weintraub is a visiting associate professor of political science at Williams College. He is a social theorist and cultural sociologist who has also taught at Harvard and the University of California, San Diego. His publications include the forthcoming *Freedom and Community: The Republican Virtue Tradition and the Sociology of Liberty.* His central interests include the role of culture in formation of the self.